ProLogue

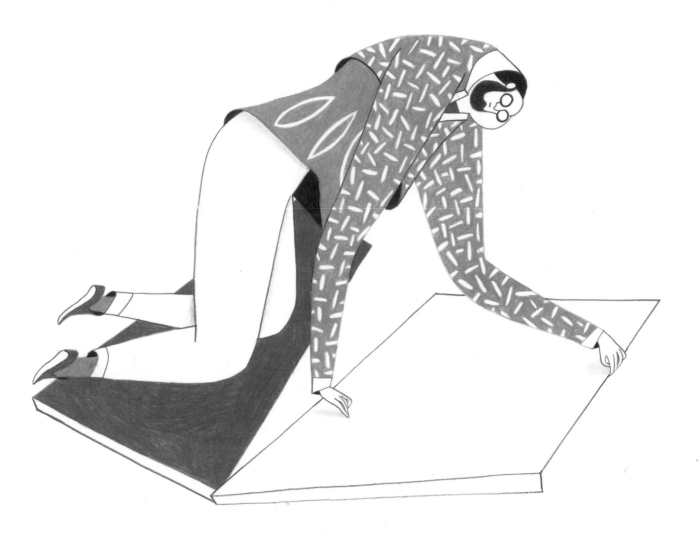

THERE IS A THEATRE WHERE ALL THE SETS OF ALL OF THE OPERAS SCHEDULED TO BE PERFORMED DURING THE SEASON EXIST SIDE BY SIDE ON A VAST ROTATING STAGE.

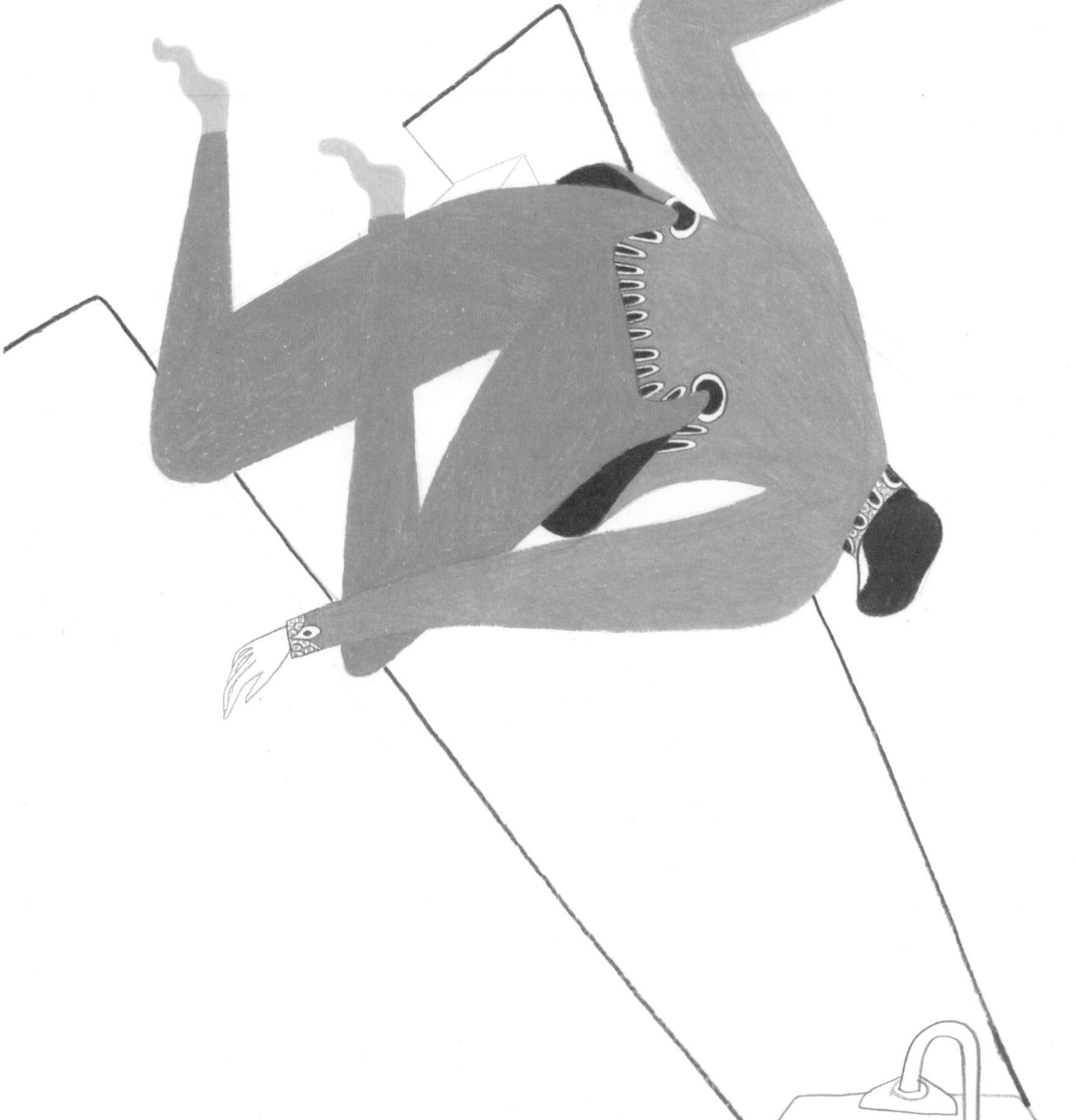

The Backstage

of a Dishwashing Webshow

The Backstage of a
Dishwashing Webshow

First edition.

Printed in China.

ISBN-13: 978-0-9991935-5-6
ISBN-10: 0-9991935-5-4

SA043
Library of Congress Control Number:
2019931009

Published by Secret Acres
200 Park Avenue South, 8th Fl.
New York, NY 10003

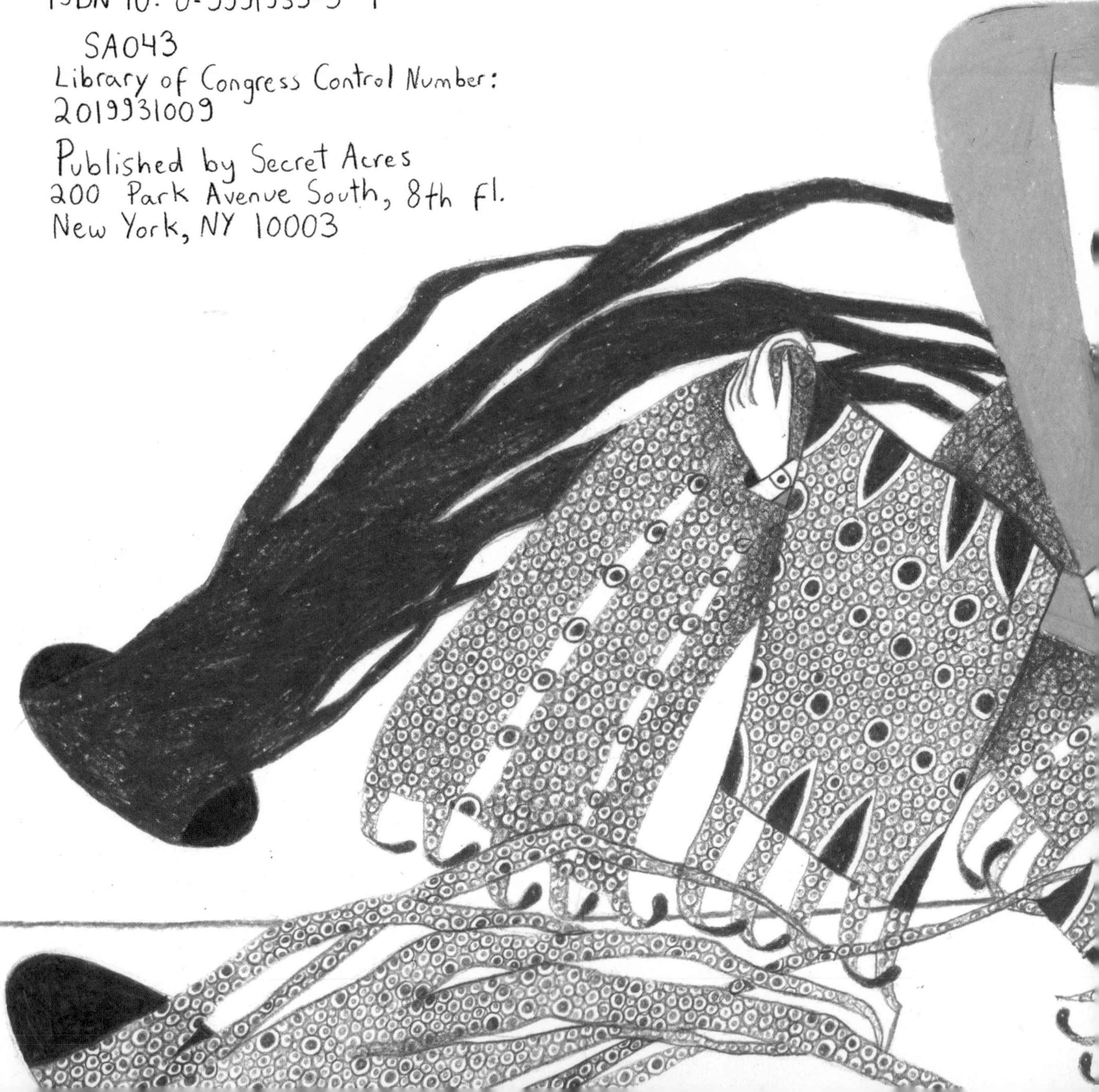

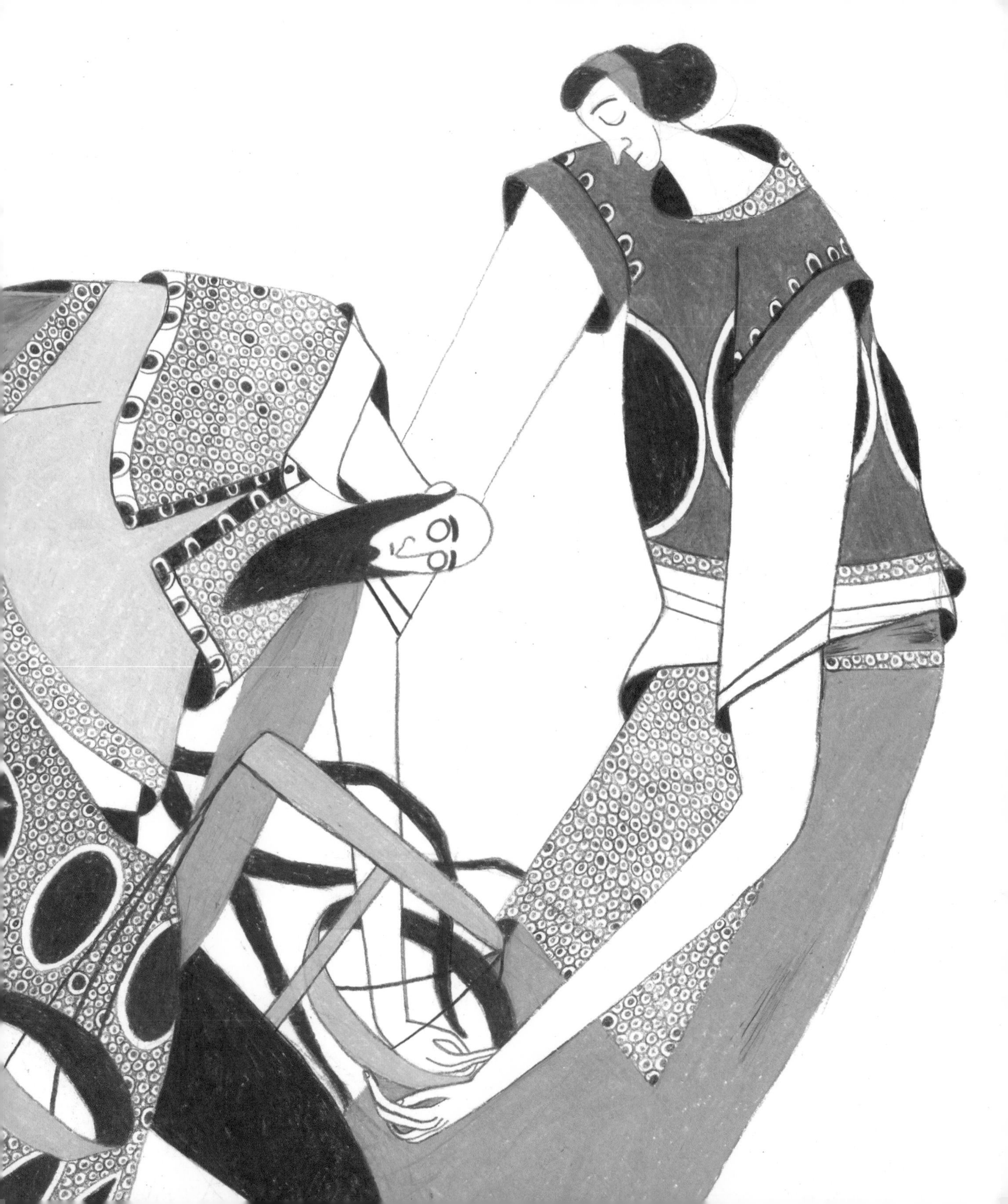

AN ACTOR MOVING FROM BACKSTAGE TO THEIR DESIGNATED MARK MUST TRAVEL THROUGH ALL THE WRONG BACKDROPS WHILE HOLDING THEIR LINES IN THEIR MOUTH.

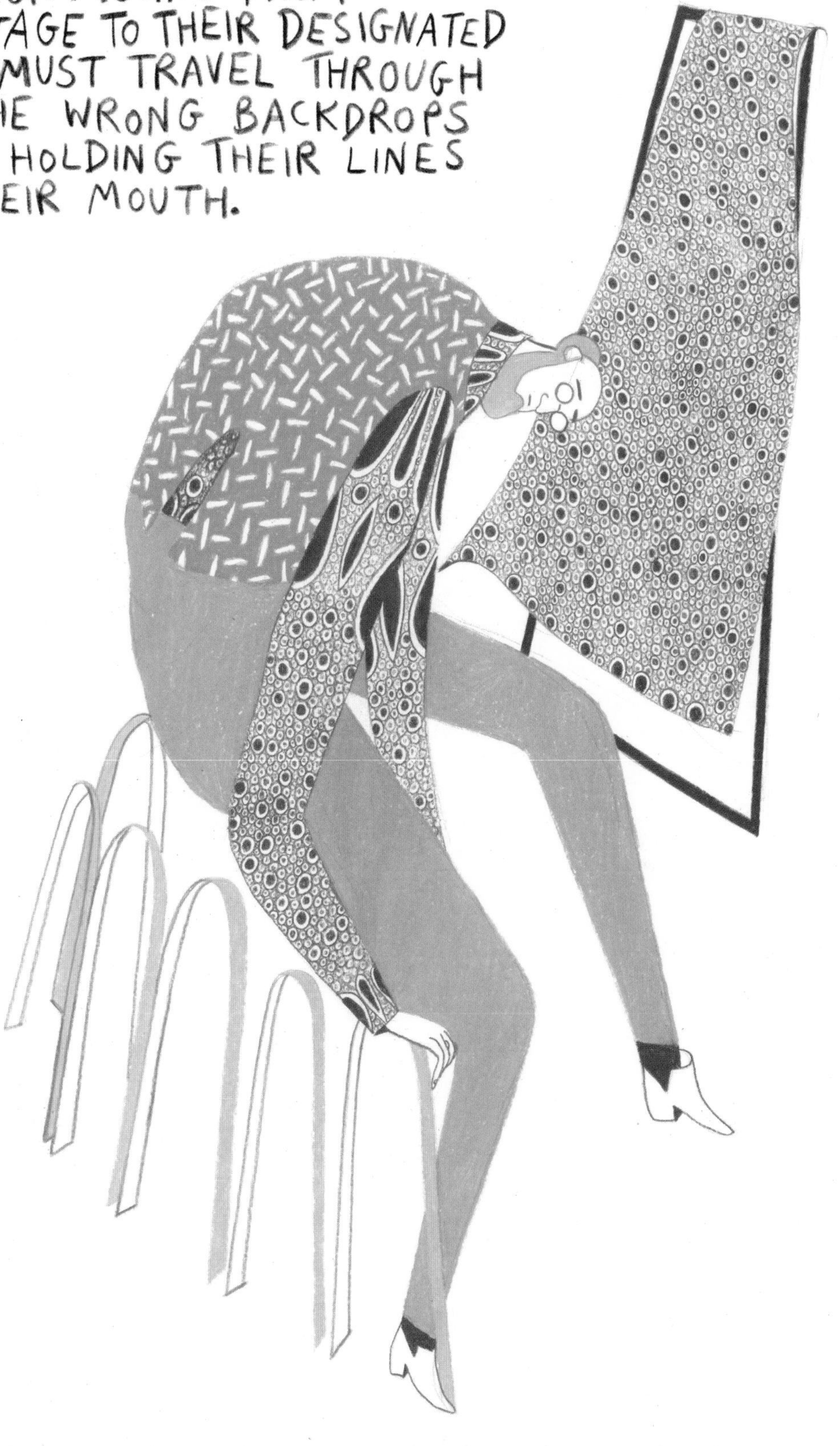

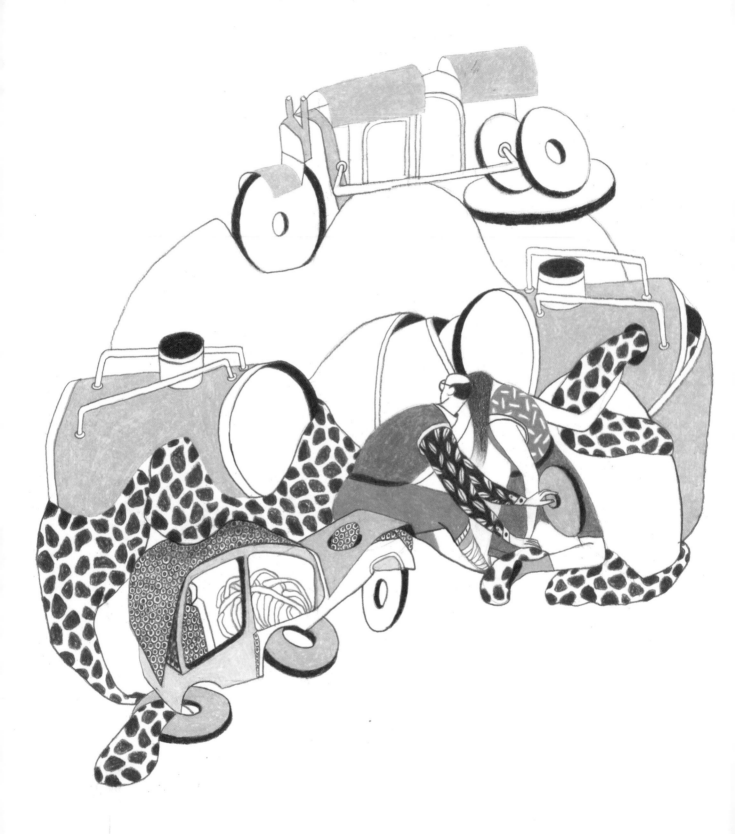

ON ANY GIVEN NIGHT, SET PIECES TO DIFFERENT PLAYS ARE CARRIED BACK AND FORTH ACROSS THE CURTAIN BY THE SAME PERFORMERS.

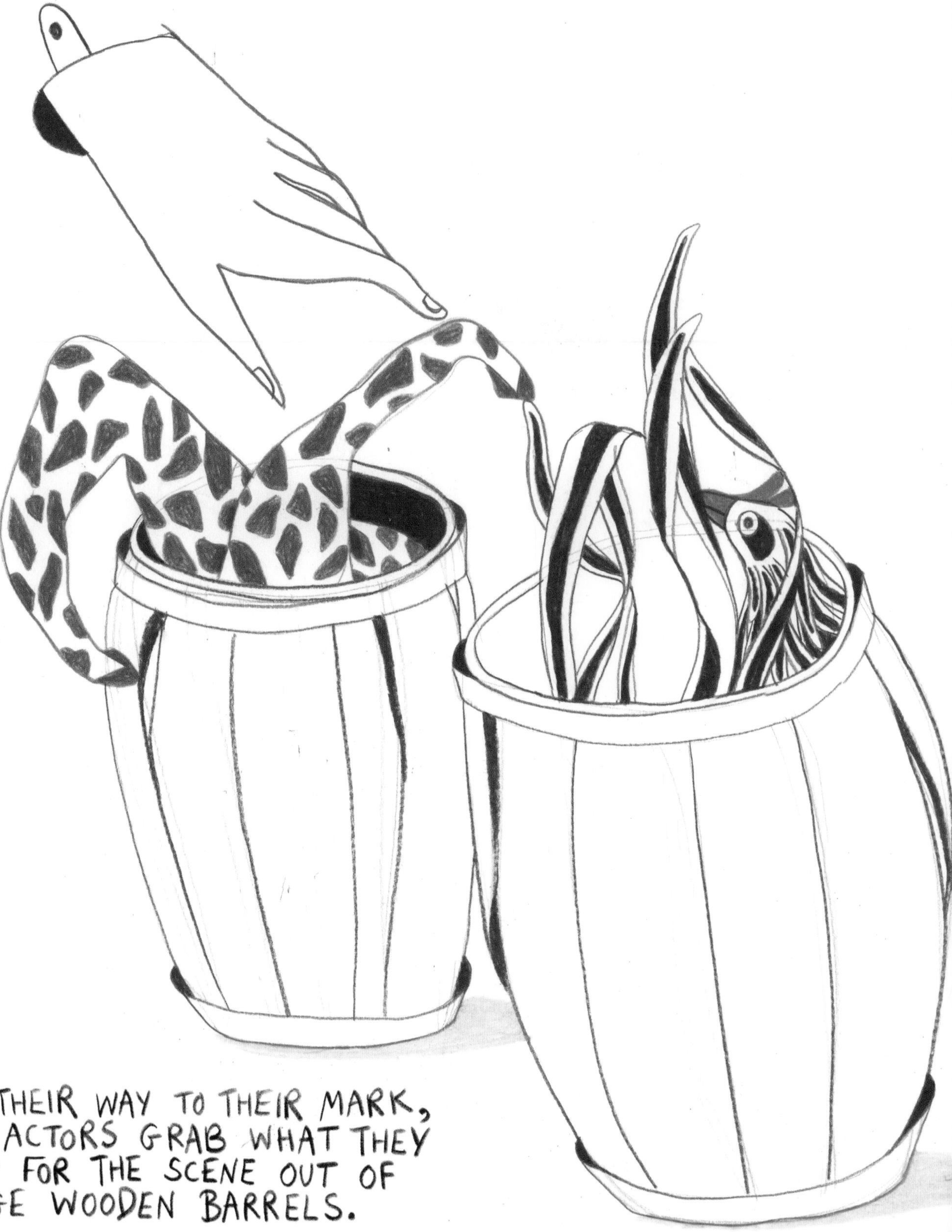

ON THEIR WAY TO THEIR MARK, THE ACTORS GRAB WHAT THEY NEED FOR THE SCENE OUT OF LARGE WOODEN BARRELS.

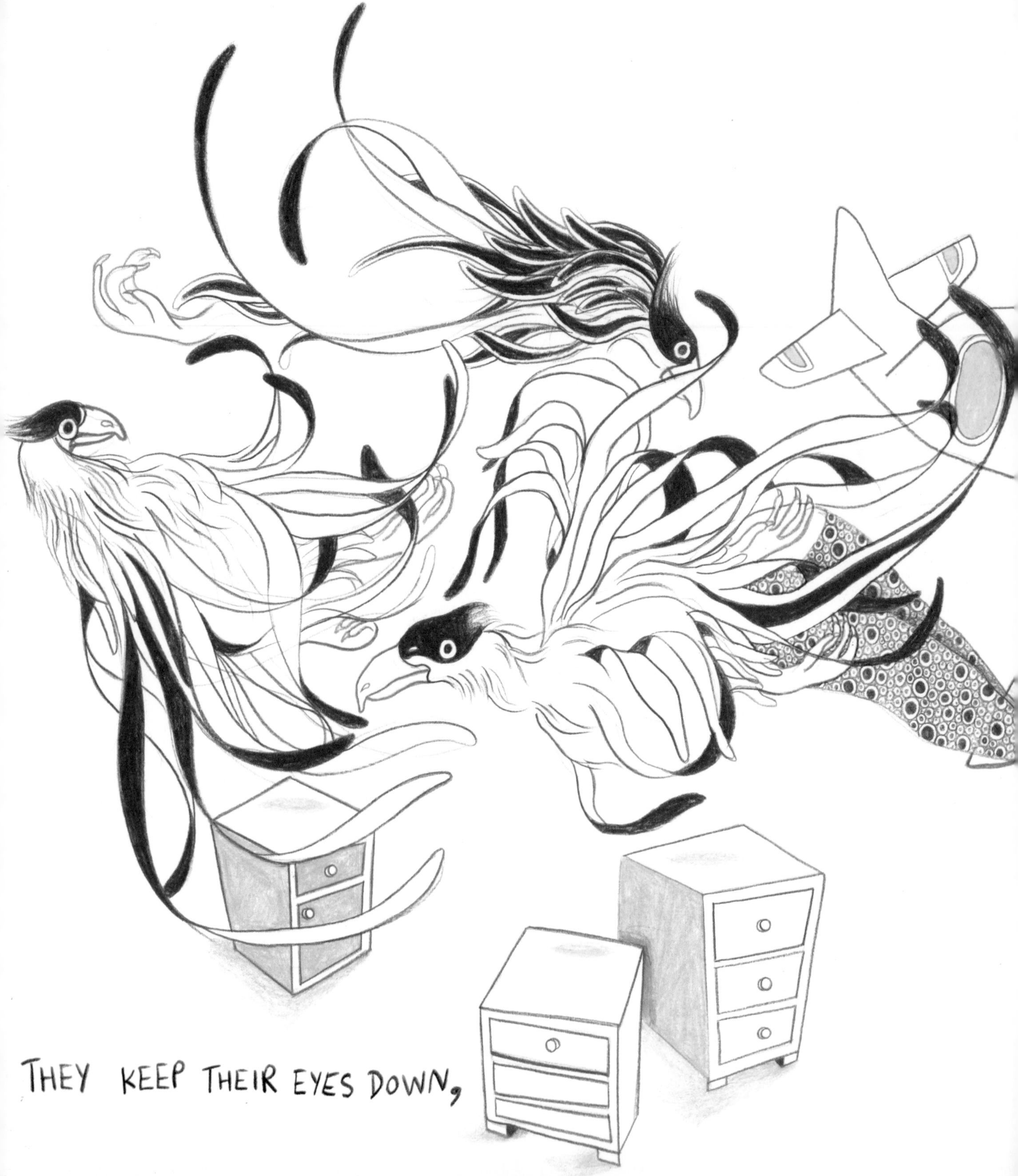

THEY KEEP THEIR EYES DOWN,

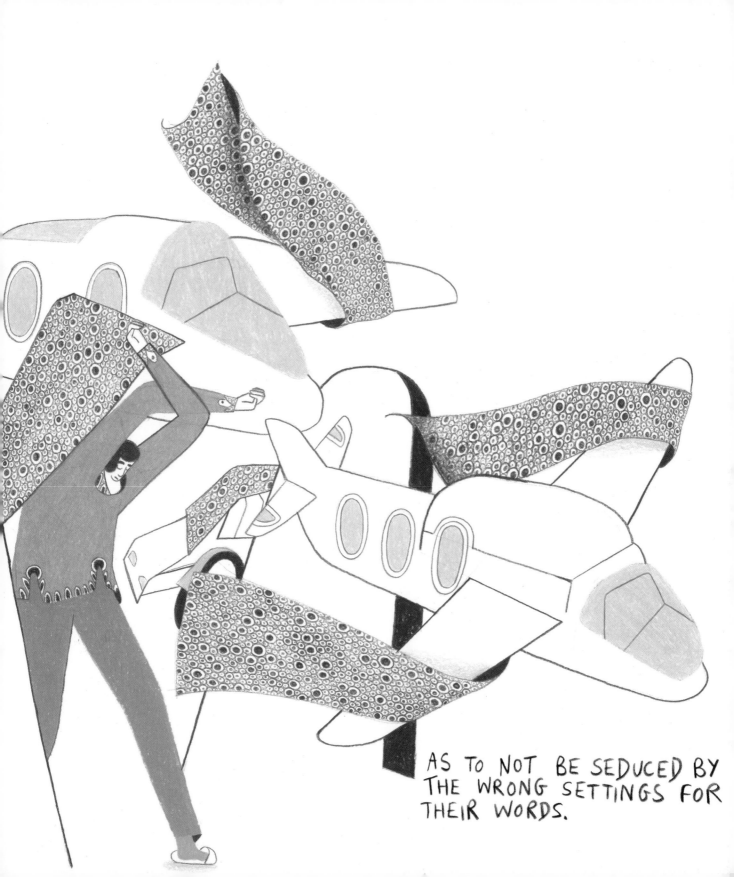

AS TO NOT BE SEDUCED BY THE WRONG SETTINGS FOR THEIR WORDS.

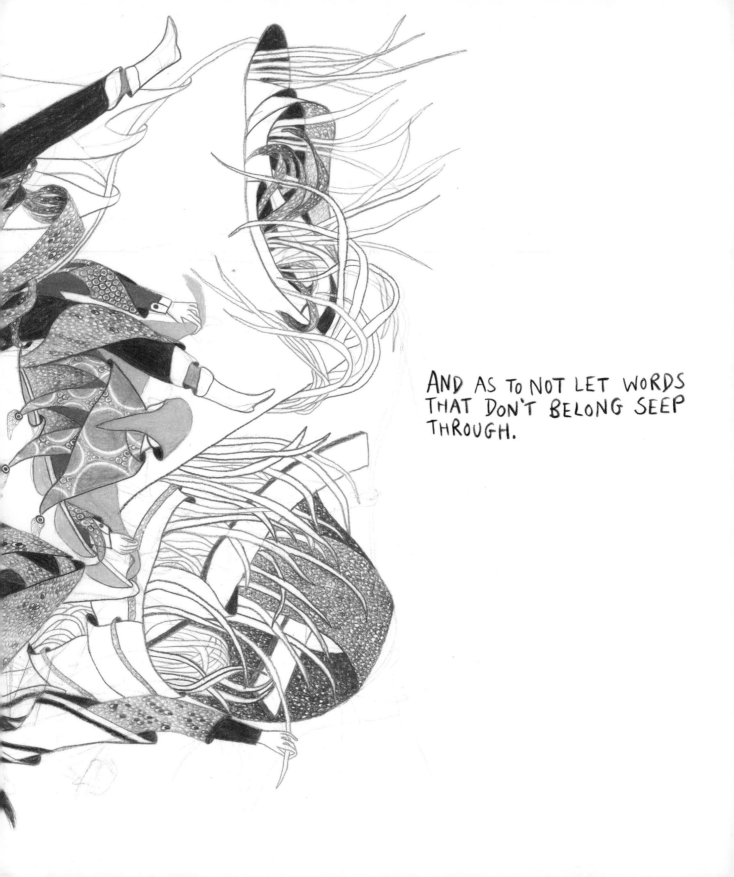

AND AS TO NOT LET WORDS
THAT DON'T BELONG SEEP
THROUGH.

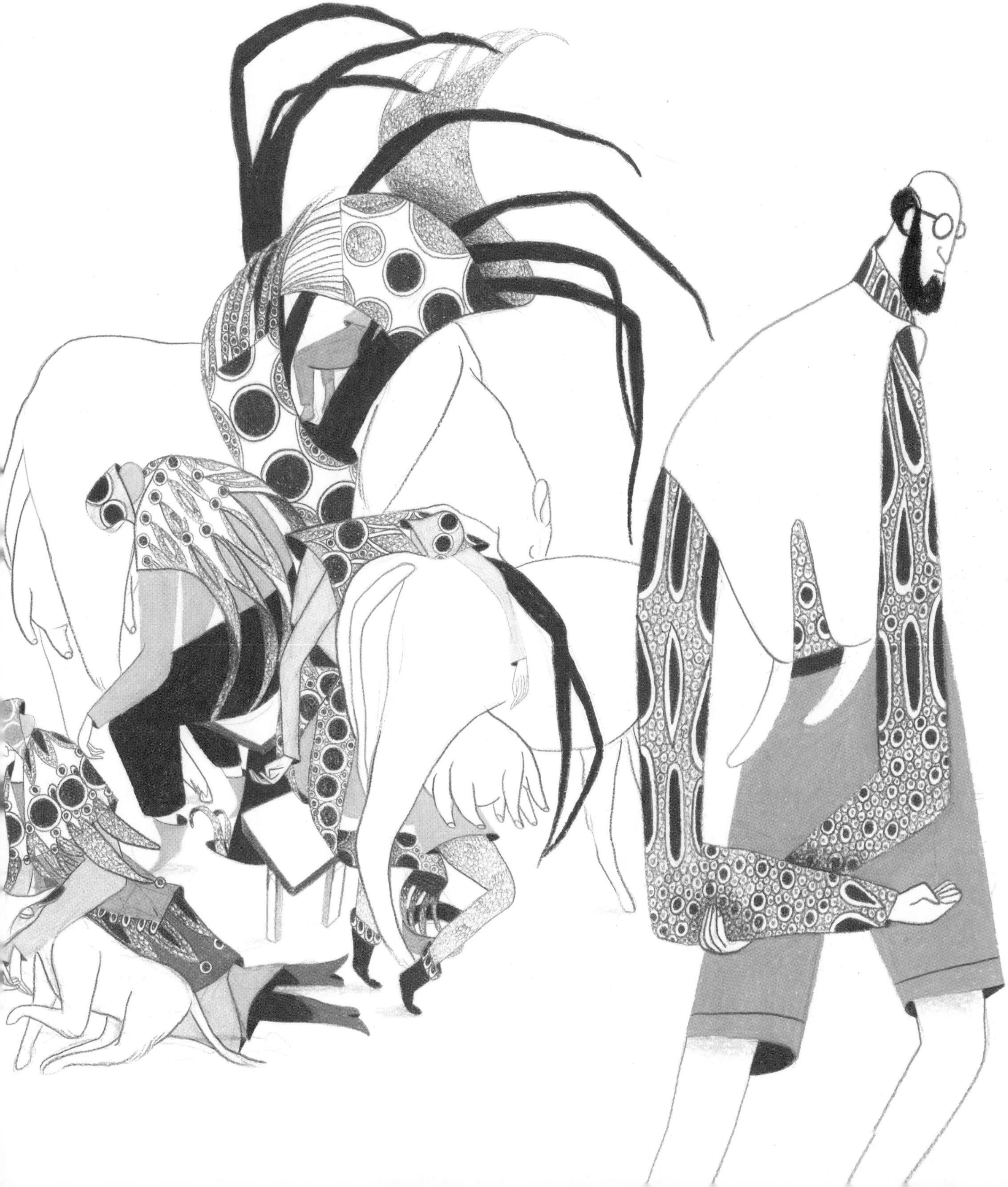

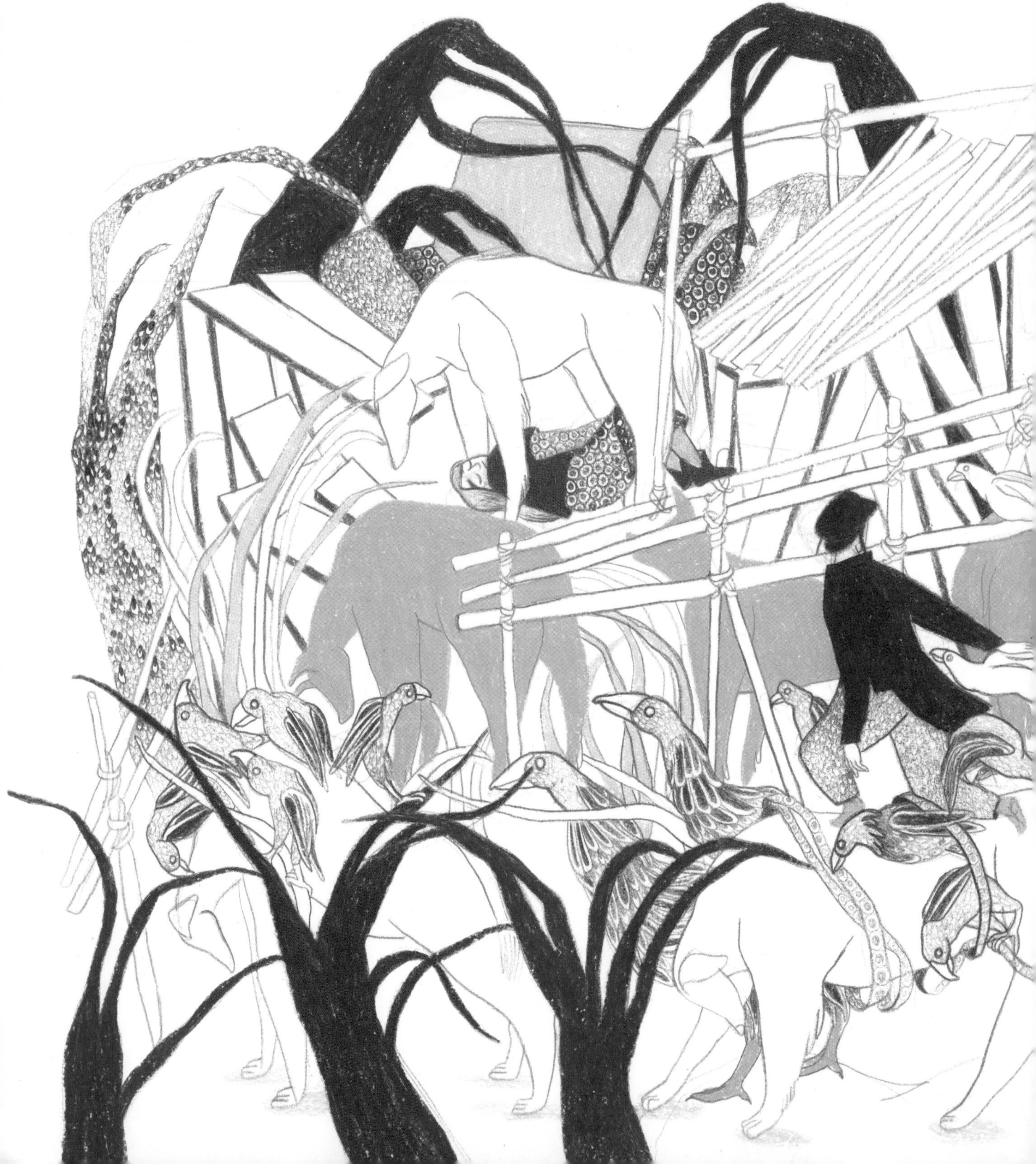

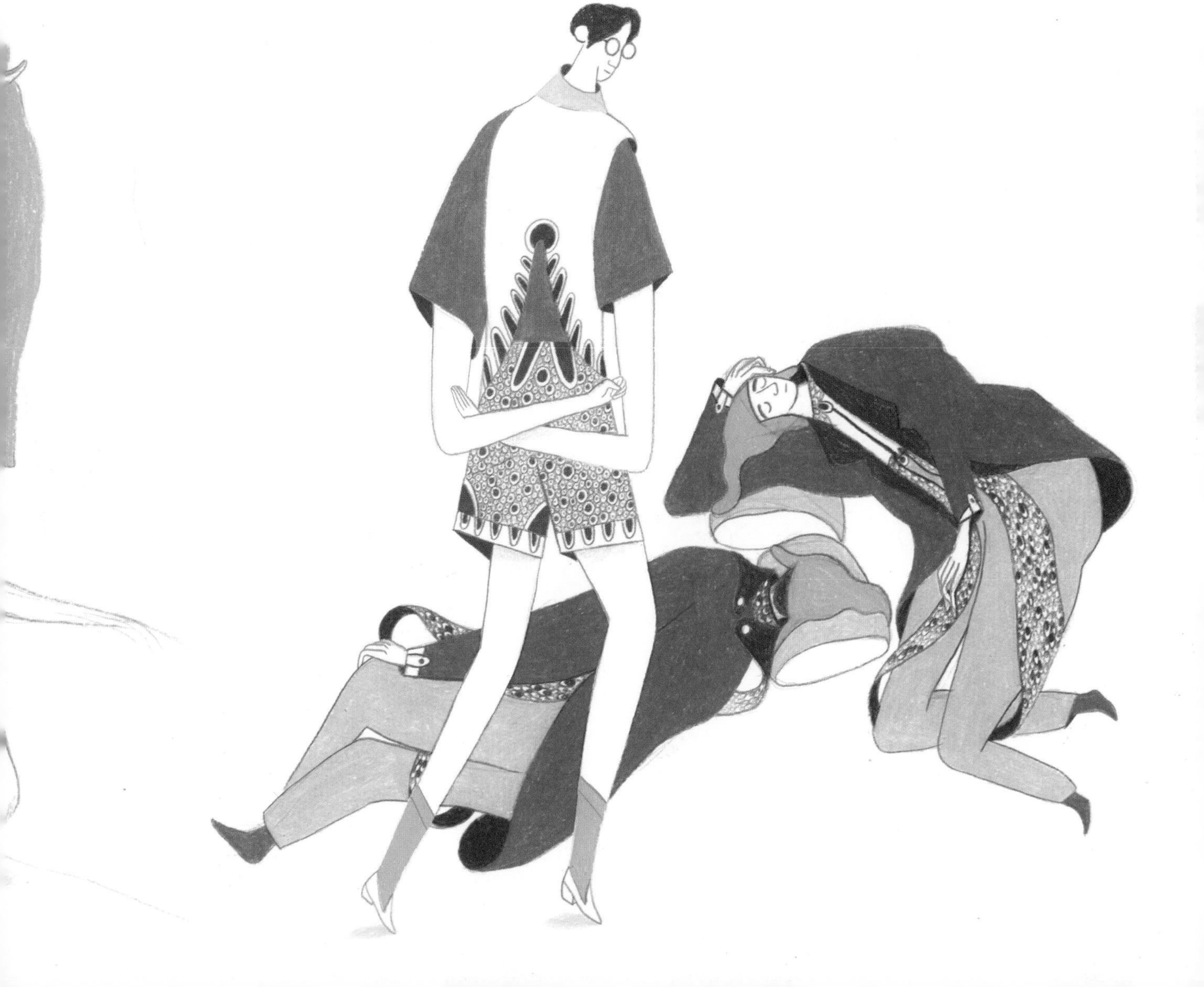

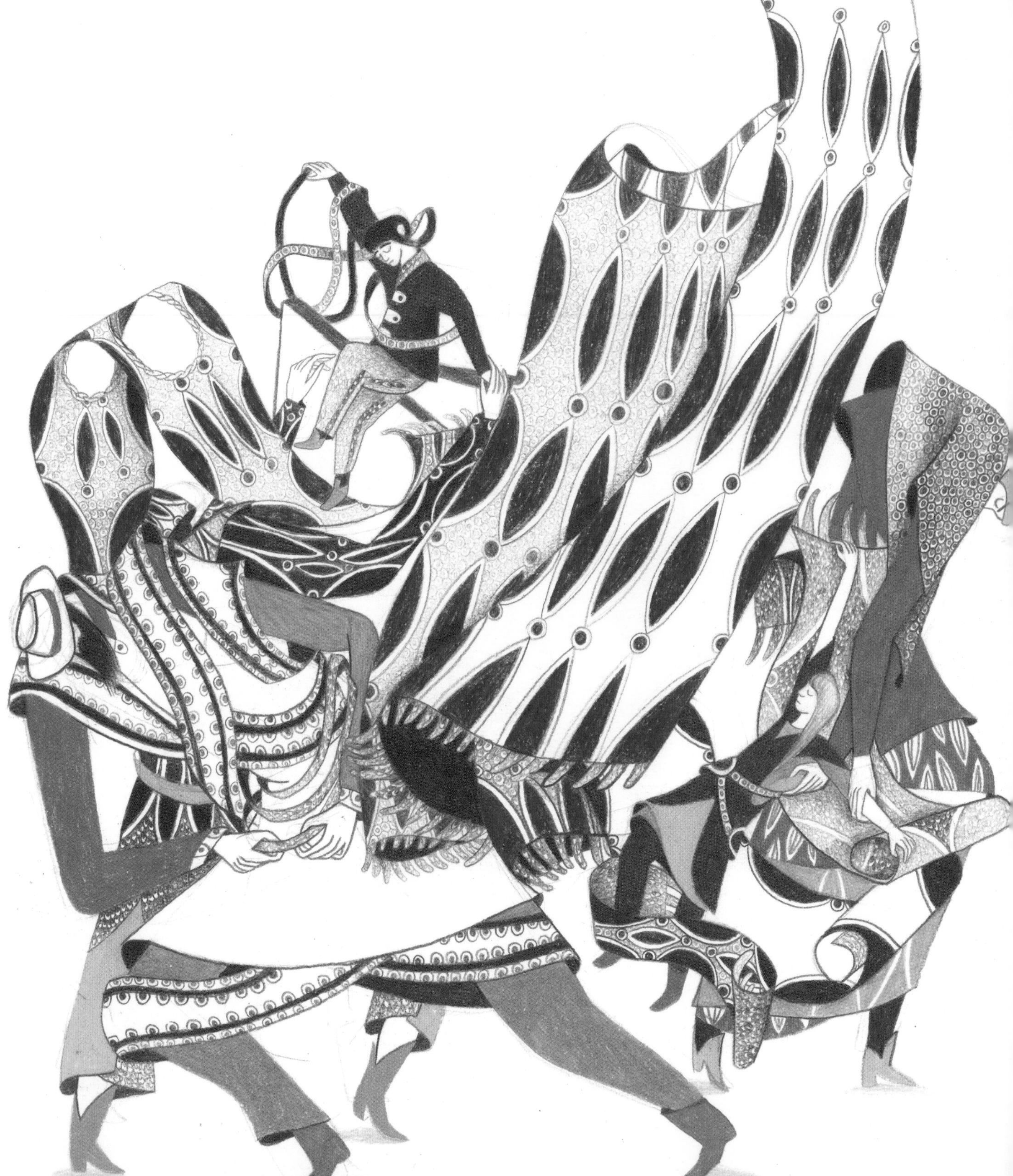

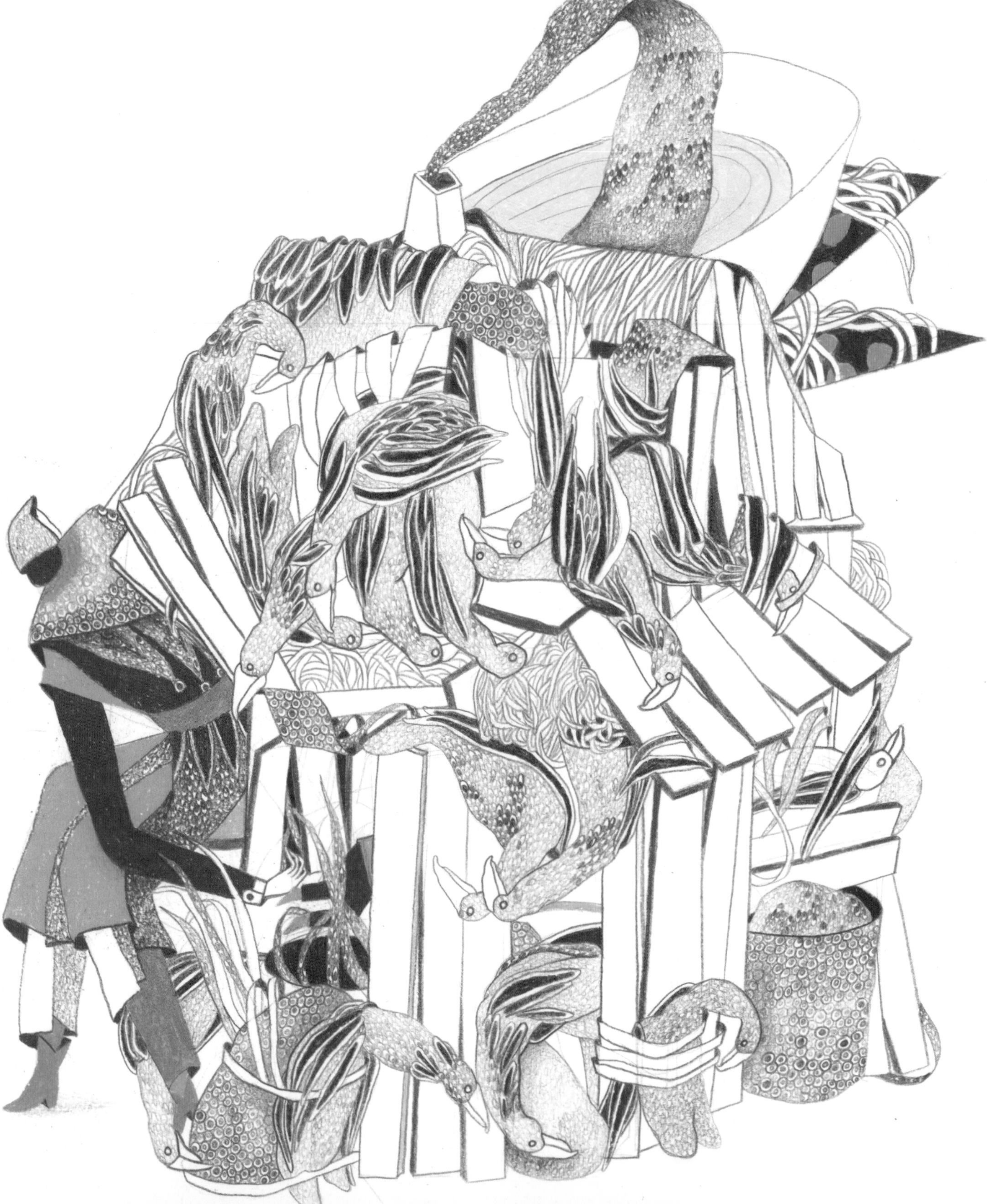

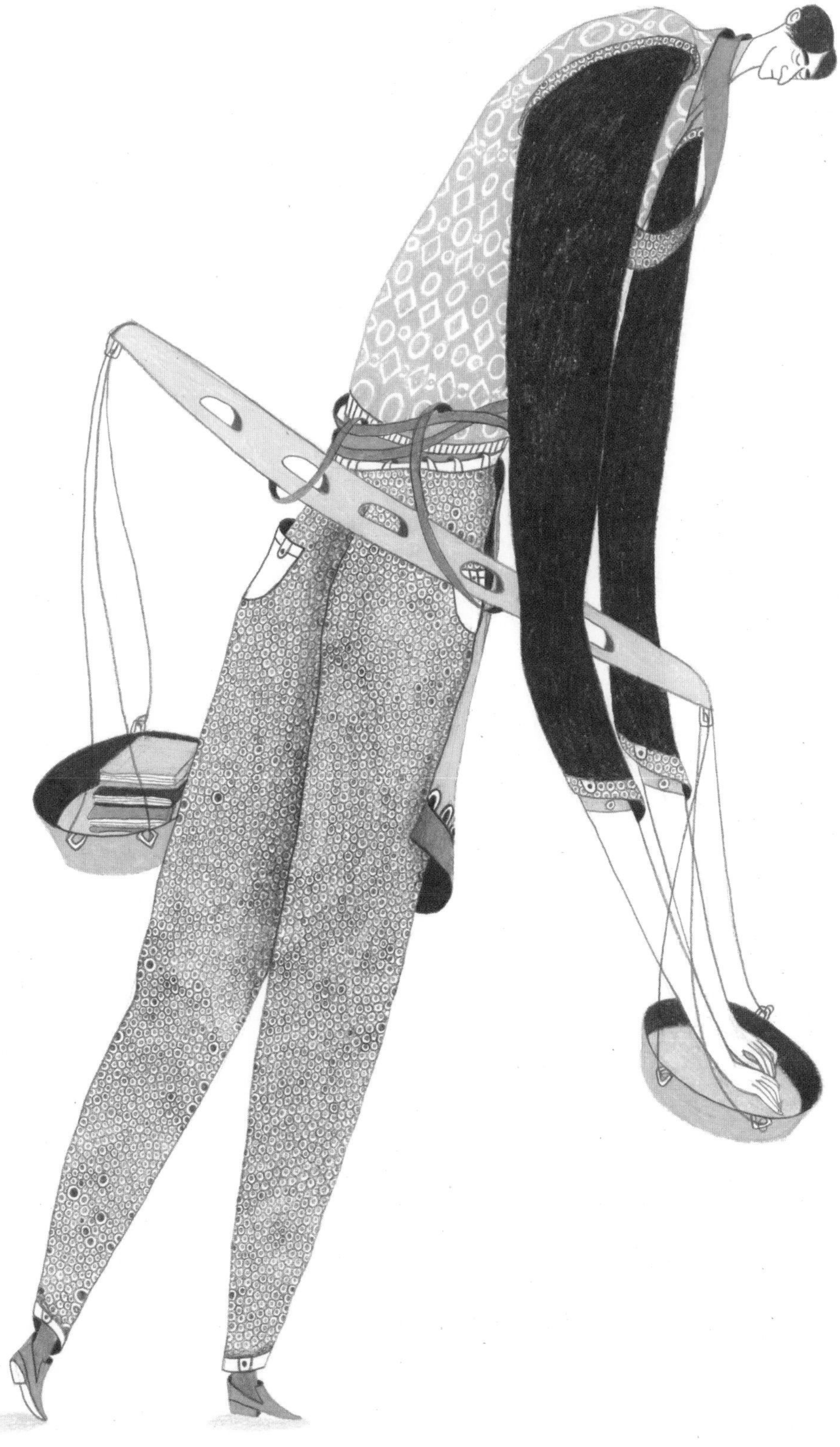

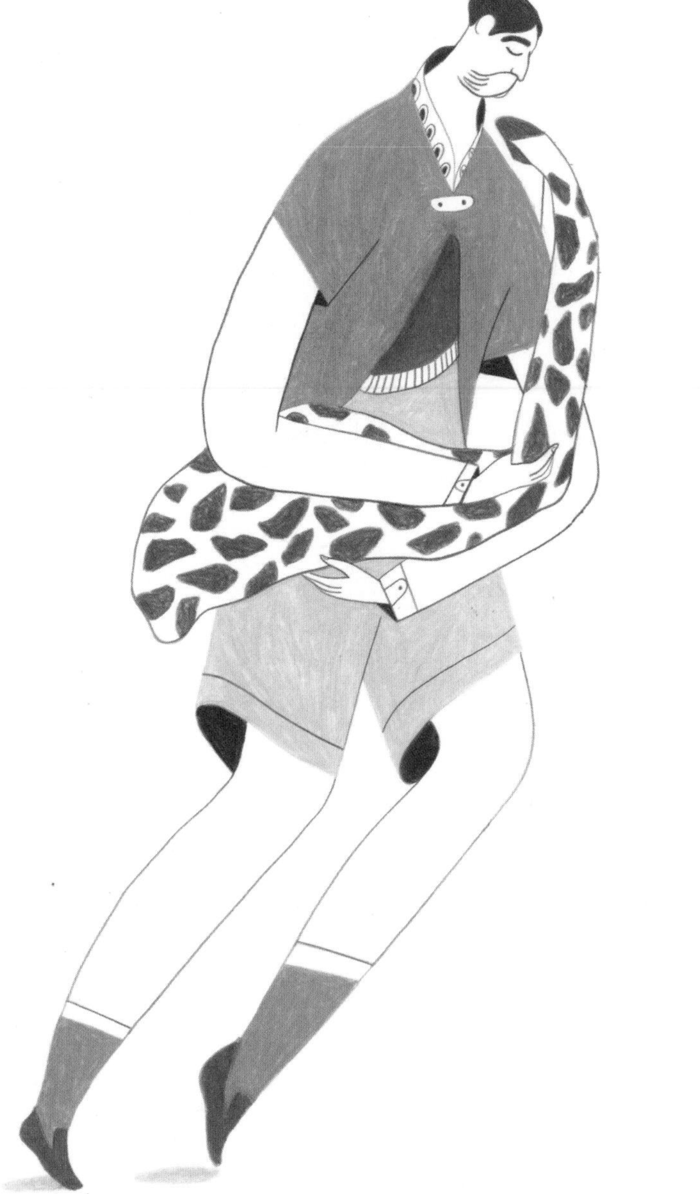

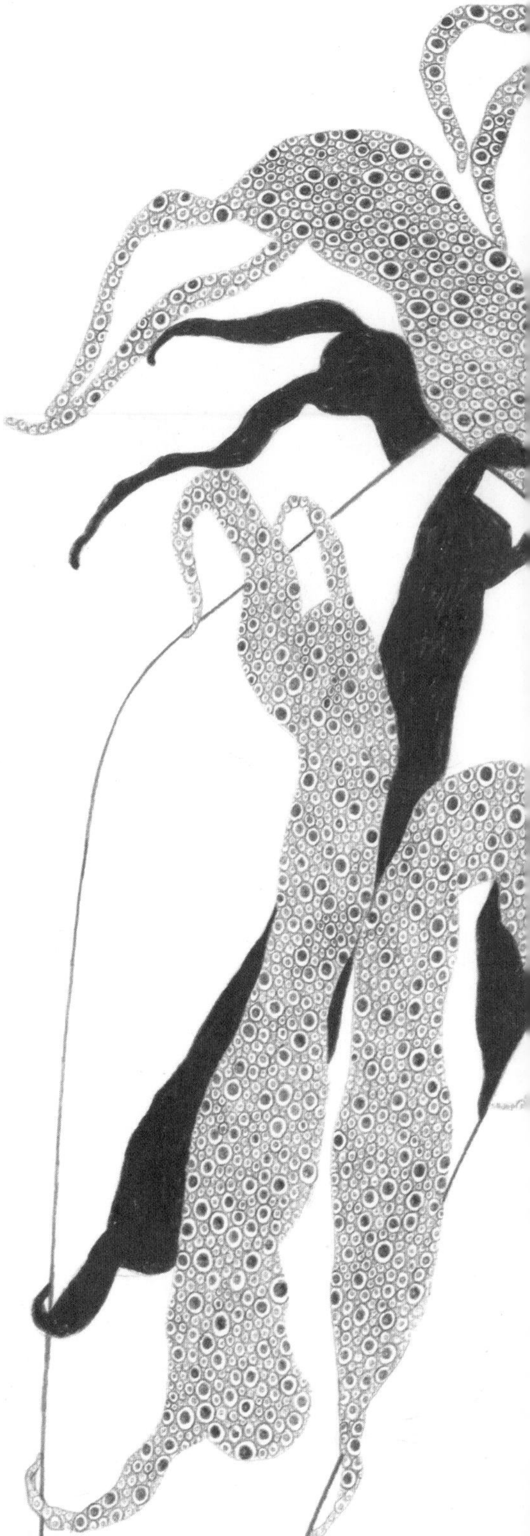

AFTER PASSING SEVERAL
OF THE WRONG CAVES,
FORESTS AND SWAMPS,

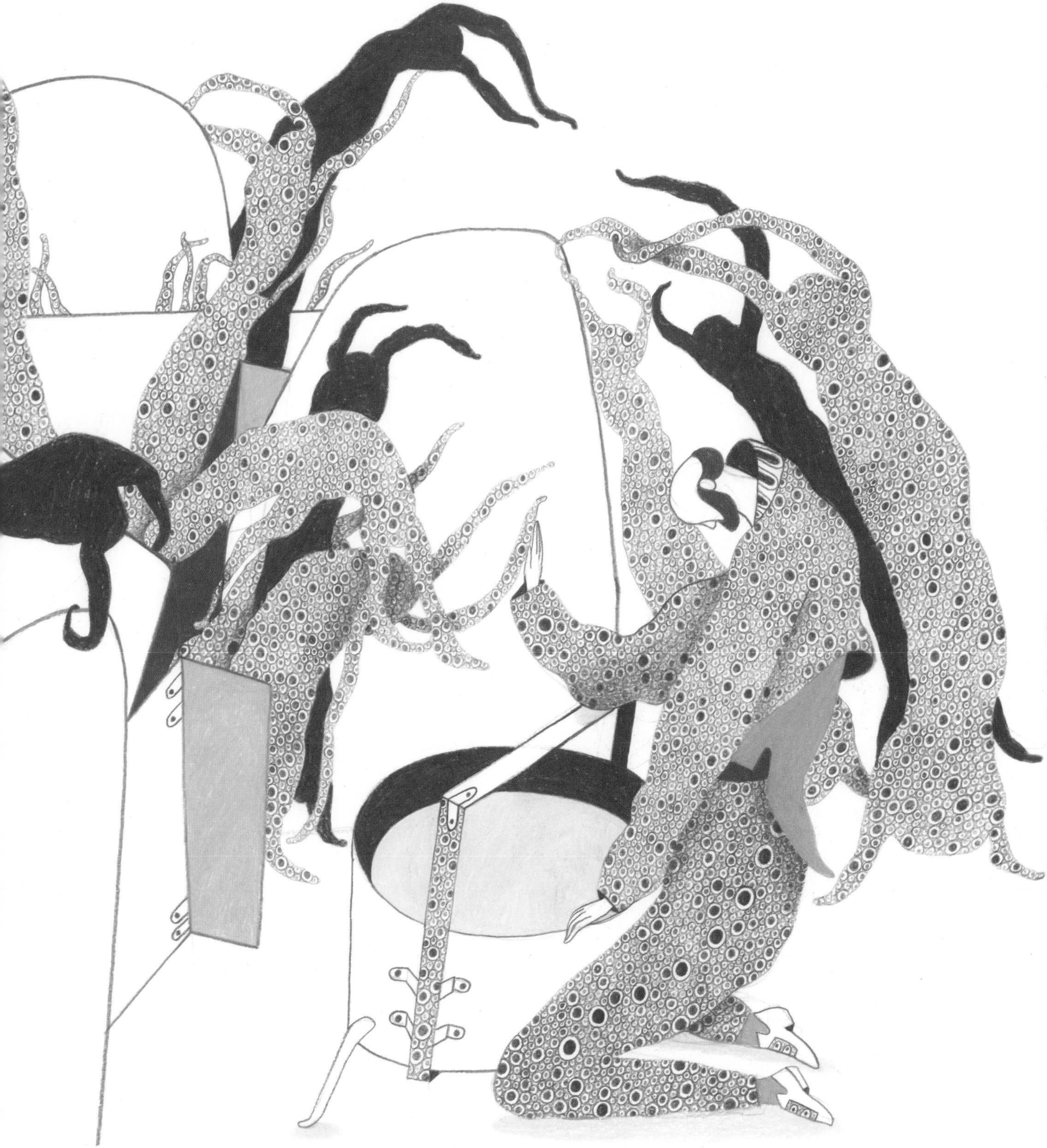

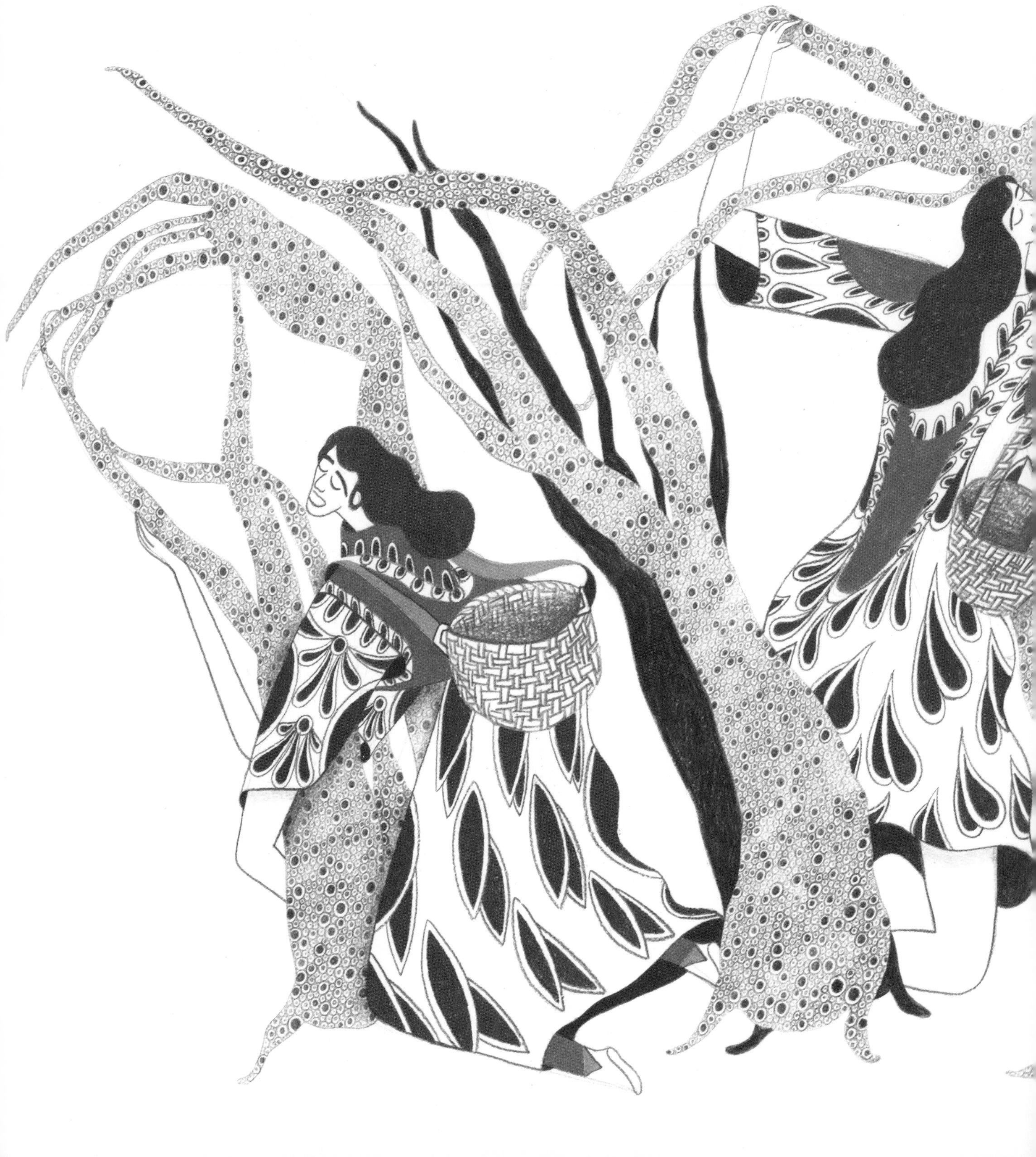

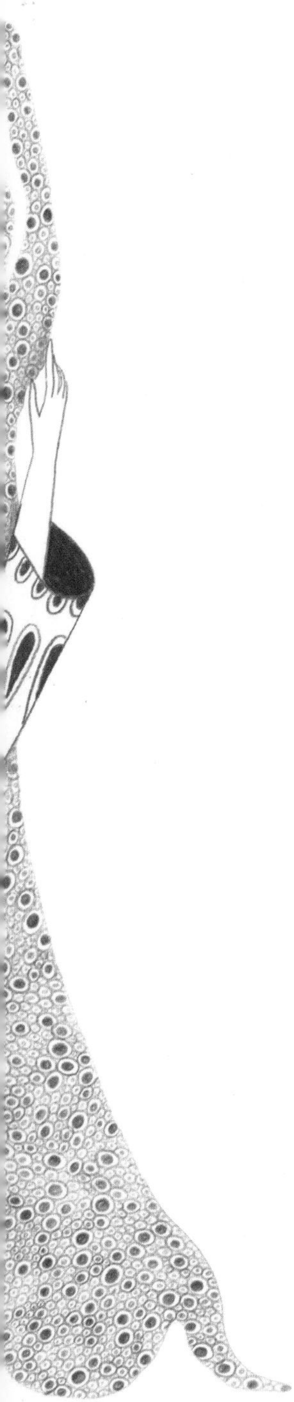

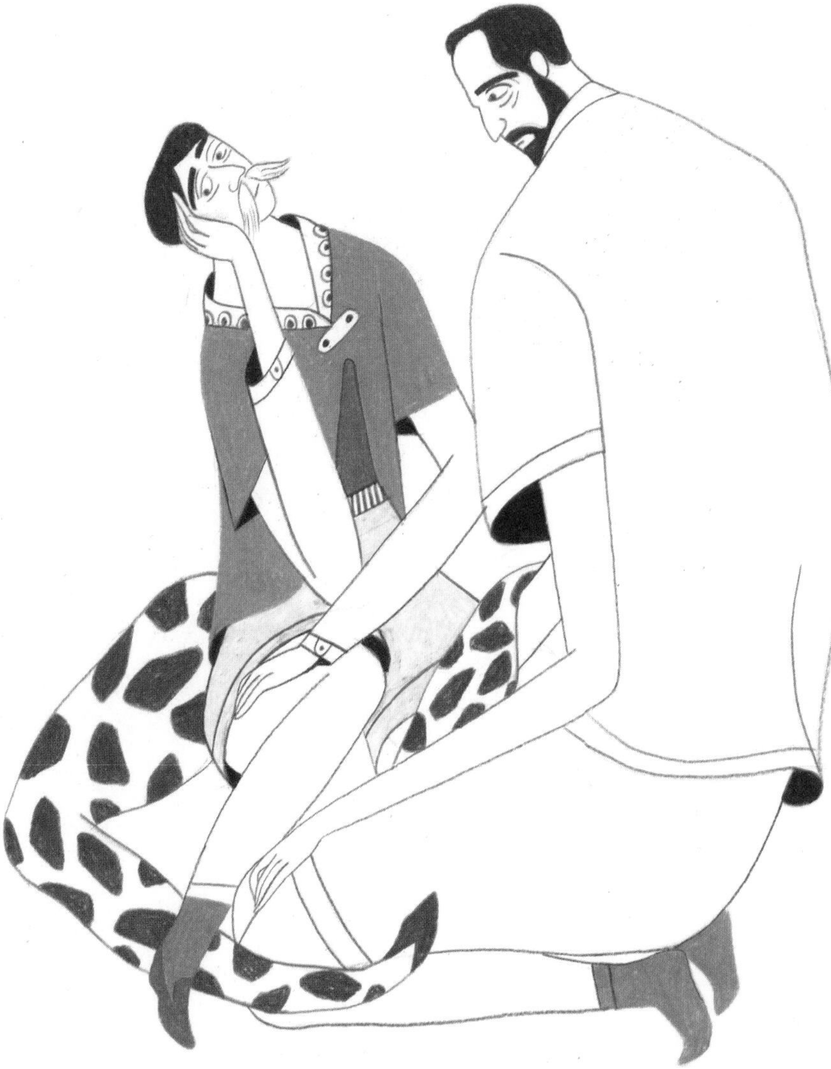

AND HOPEFULLY CARRYING
THE CORRECT PROP FOR THEIR
SCENE,

THEY REACH THEIR AUDIENCE.

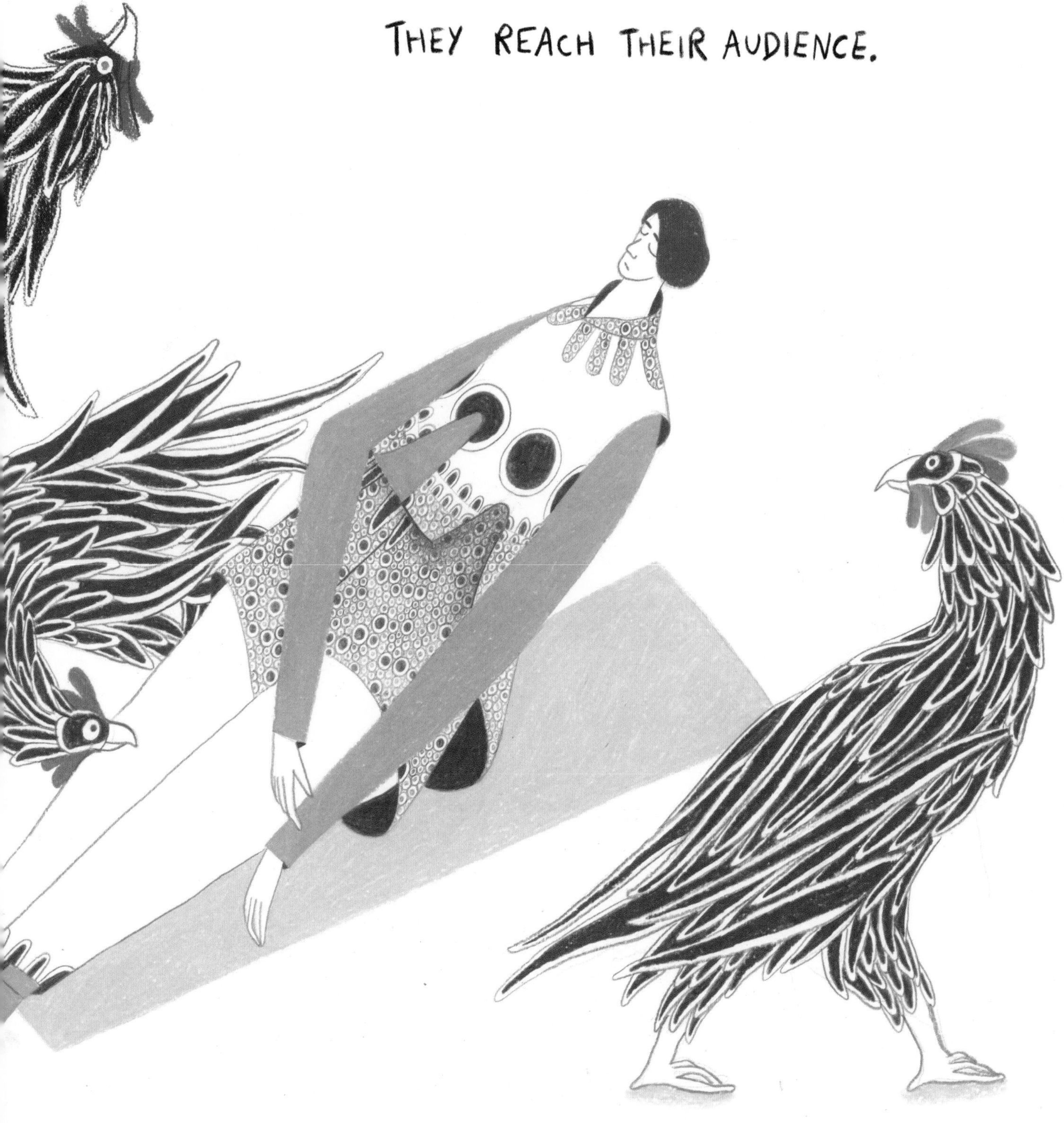

Chapter 1: MOUNT SCOPUS

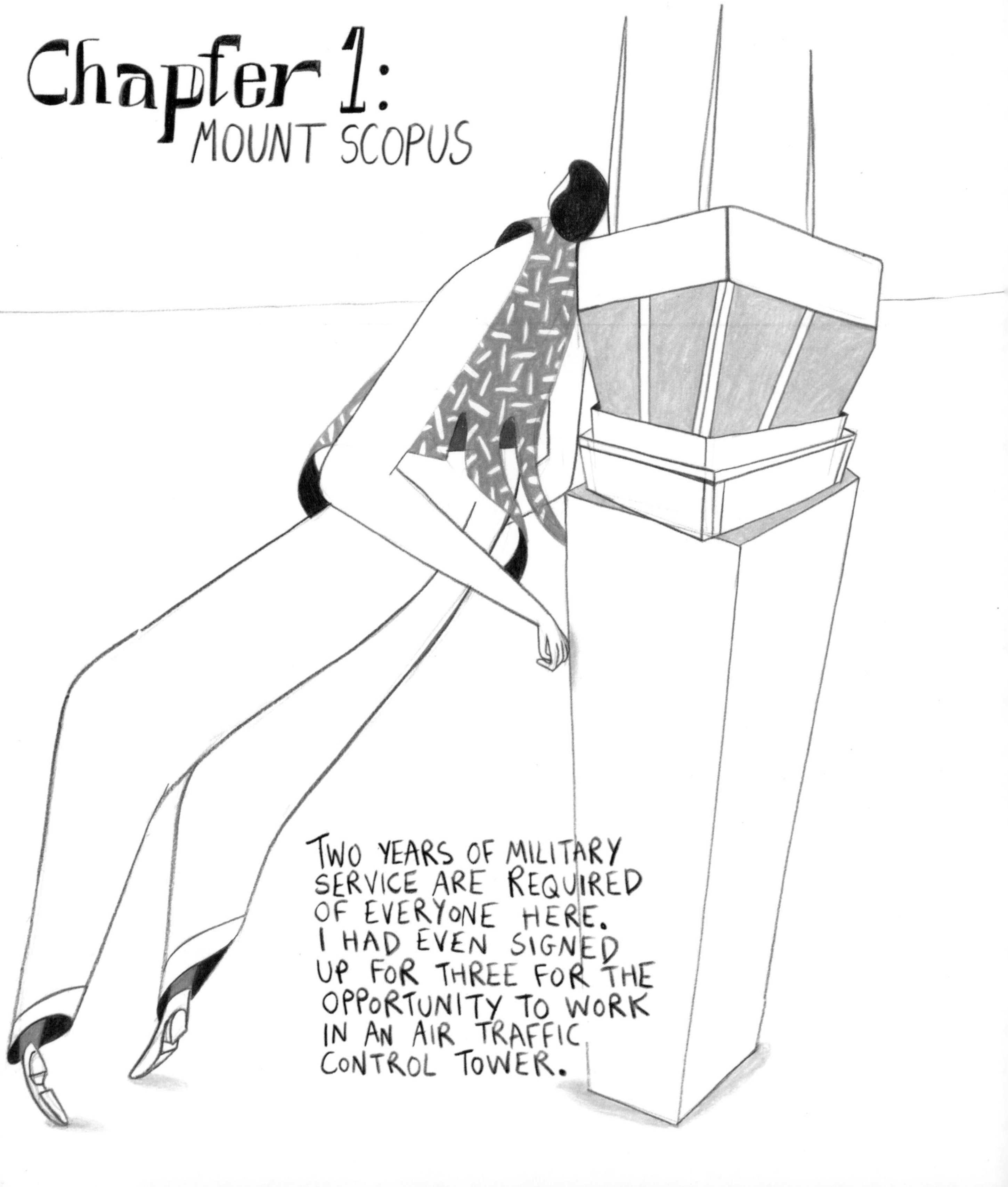
TWO YEARS OF MILITARY SERVICE ARE REQUIRED OF EVERYONE HERE. I HAD EVEN SIGNED UP FOR THREE FOR THE OPPORTUNITY TO WORK IN AN AIR TRAFFIC CONTROL TOWER.

I WAS SOON DISCHARGED
DUE TO LACK OF FOCUS.
YAKOV BROKE UP WITH
ME THE WEEK BEFORE.

I HAD NEVER MET
HIM IN PERSON.

I WOULD DESCRIBE TO
HIM HOW I SQUINT AT
THE PURPLE FIRES
THRUSTING PLANES INTO
THE DESERT NIGHT,

AND THE RATTLE OF
GLASS AND CONCRETE
AND FLESH AS DISTANT
BLIPS APPARATE THROUGH
A STORM.

WIND, THUNDER AND DUST
NEGOTIATING THEIR WAY
TO THE LANDING STRIP
IN HUMAN VOICES THROUGH
THE RADIO.

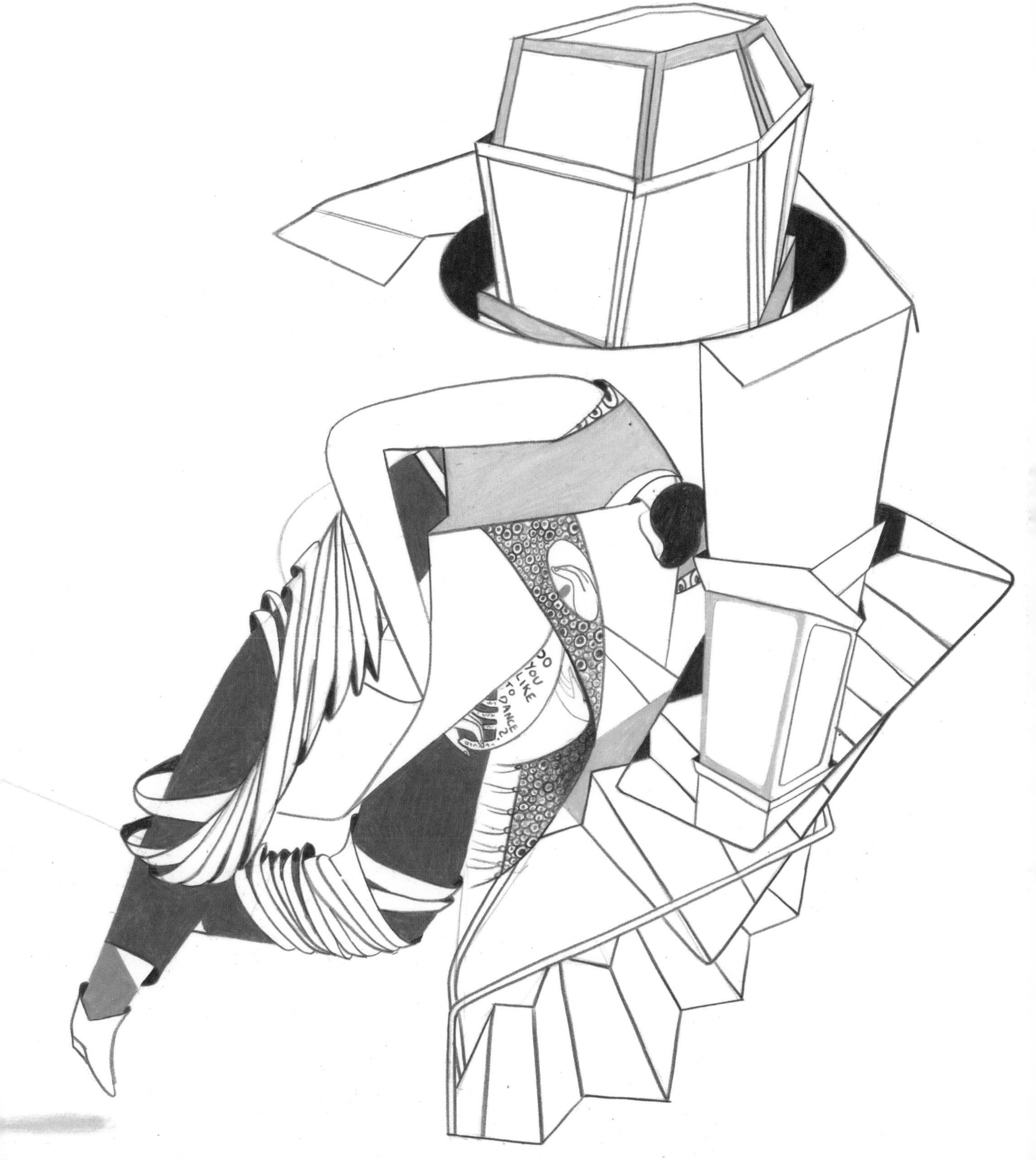
DO YOU LIKE TO DANCE?

ALL OF THIS WAS BEAUTIFUL IN FRONT OF THE LARGE GLASS TOWER WINDOWS ONLY BECAUSE IT CAME AND WENT AWAY FROM VIEW WITHIN SECONDS.

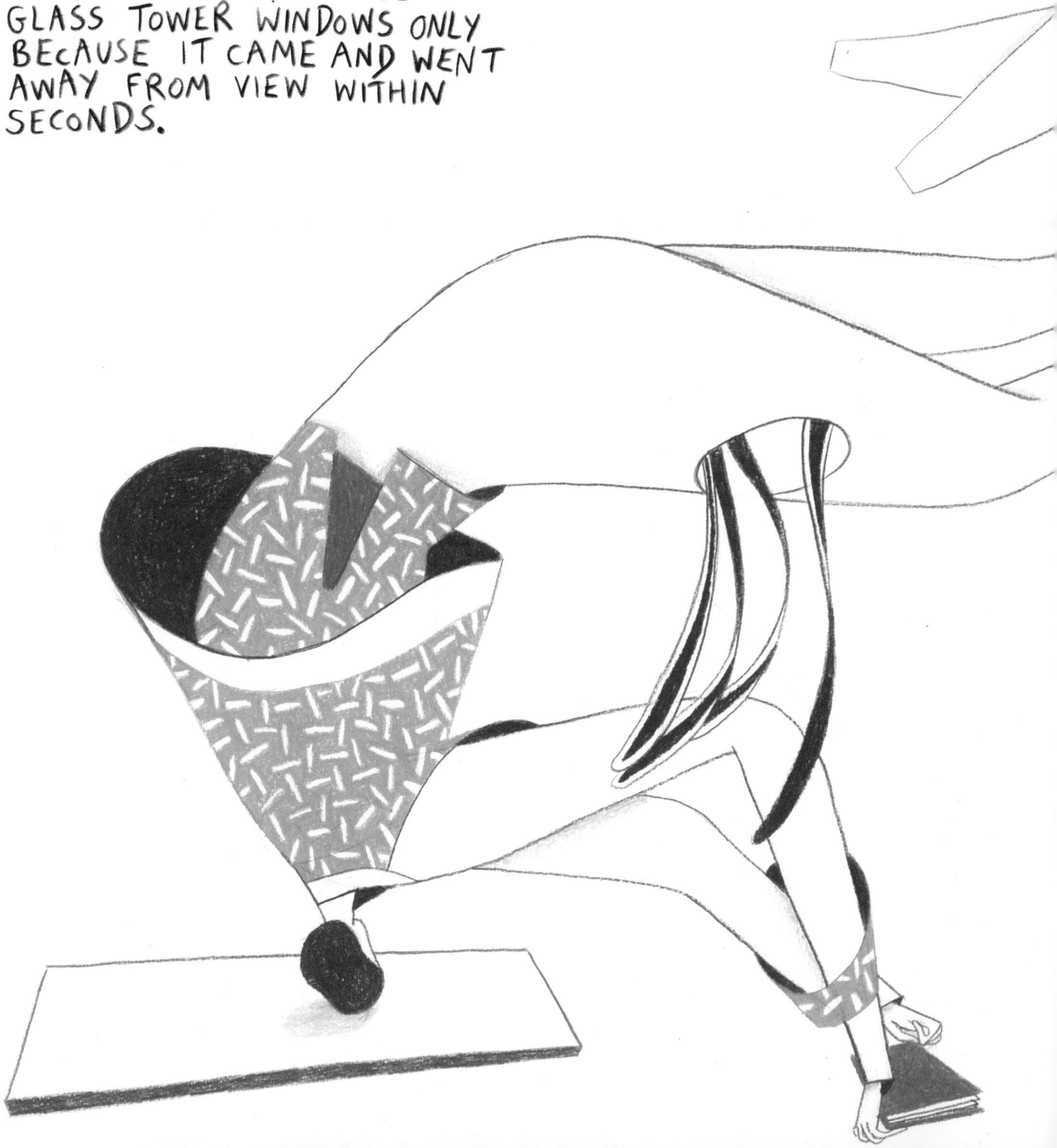

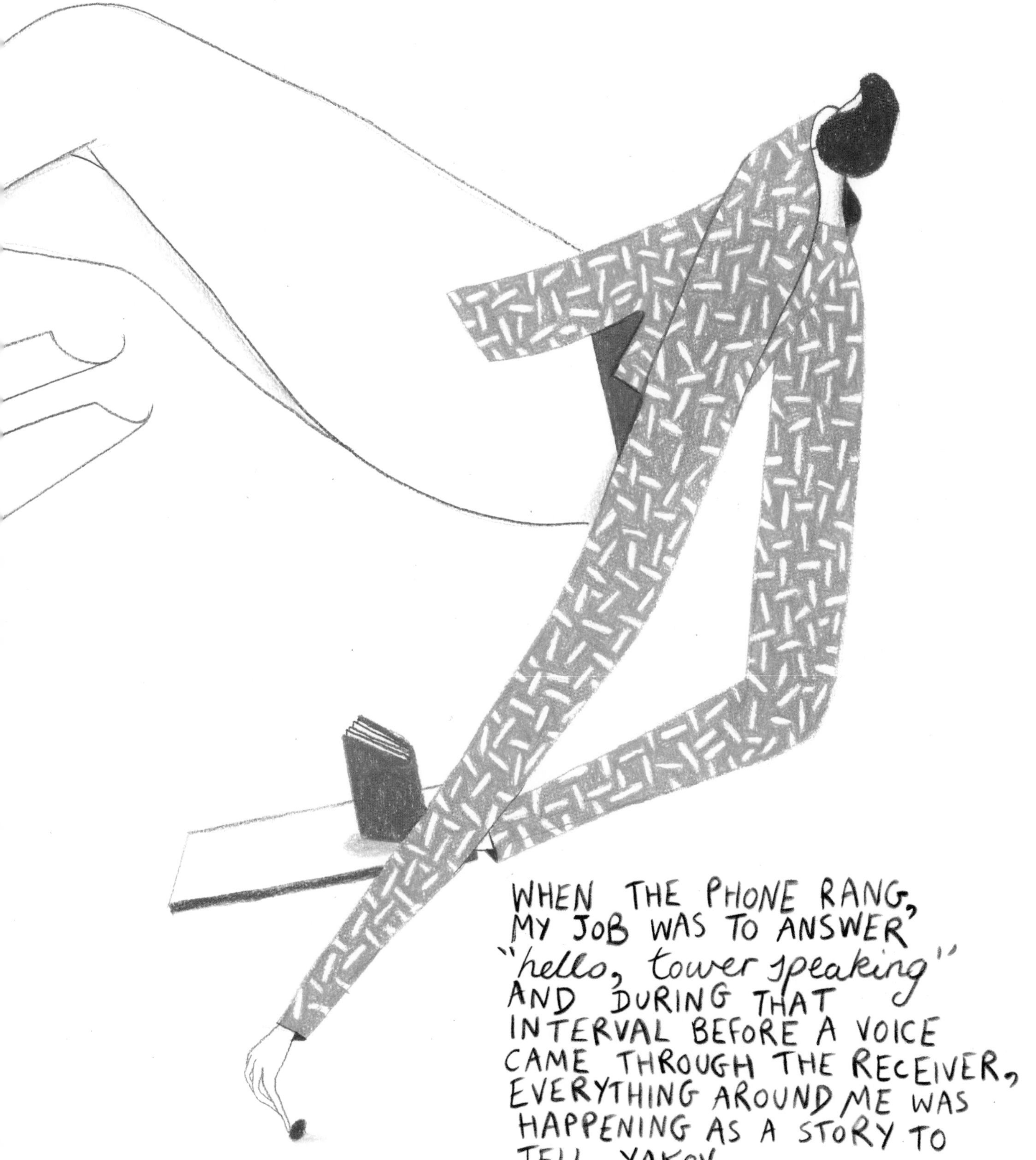
WHEN THE PHONE RANG, MY JOB WAS TO ANSWER "*hello, tower speaking*" AND DURING THAT INTERVAL BEFORE A VOICE CAME THROUGH THE RECEIVER, EVERYTHING AROUND ME WAS HAPPENING AS A STORY TO TELL YAKOV.

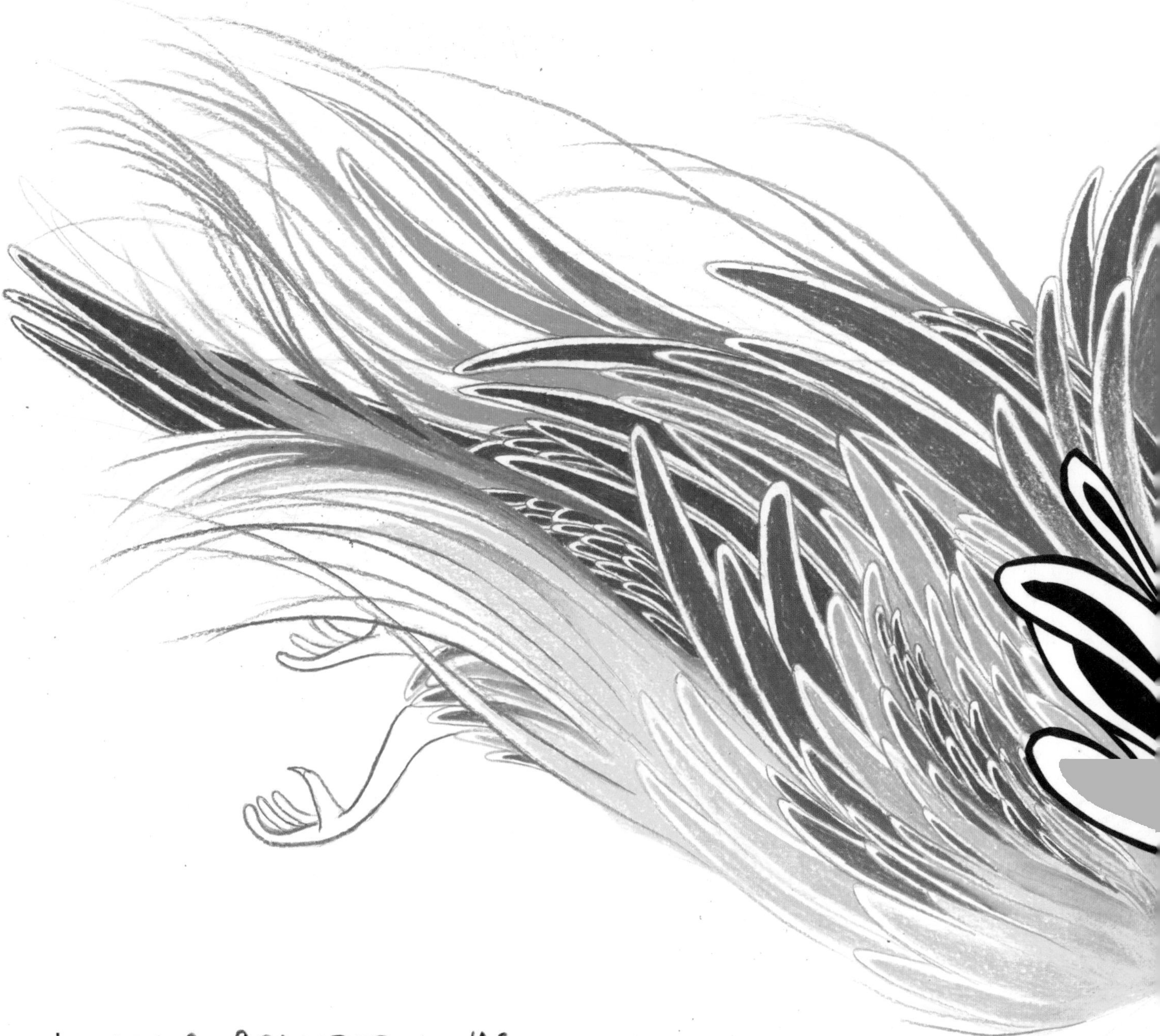

I NEVER REALIZED I WAS
SEDUCING HIM WITH
DESCRIPTIONS OF DISEMBODIED
MOMENTS OF DISTANT VIOLENCE.
THEY WERE INVISIBLE TO ME.

I ONLY SAW THE COLLAPSE OF COLOR INTO SAND AS ULTRA SONIC BLASTS CAUSED BIRDS TO PLUMMET FROM THE SKY.

WITH YAKOV GONE, ALL I HAD WITNESSED WAS LEFT TO EXPAND, UNALTERED, IN MY OWN MIND.

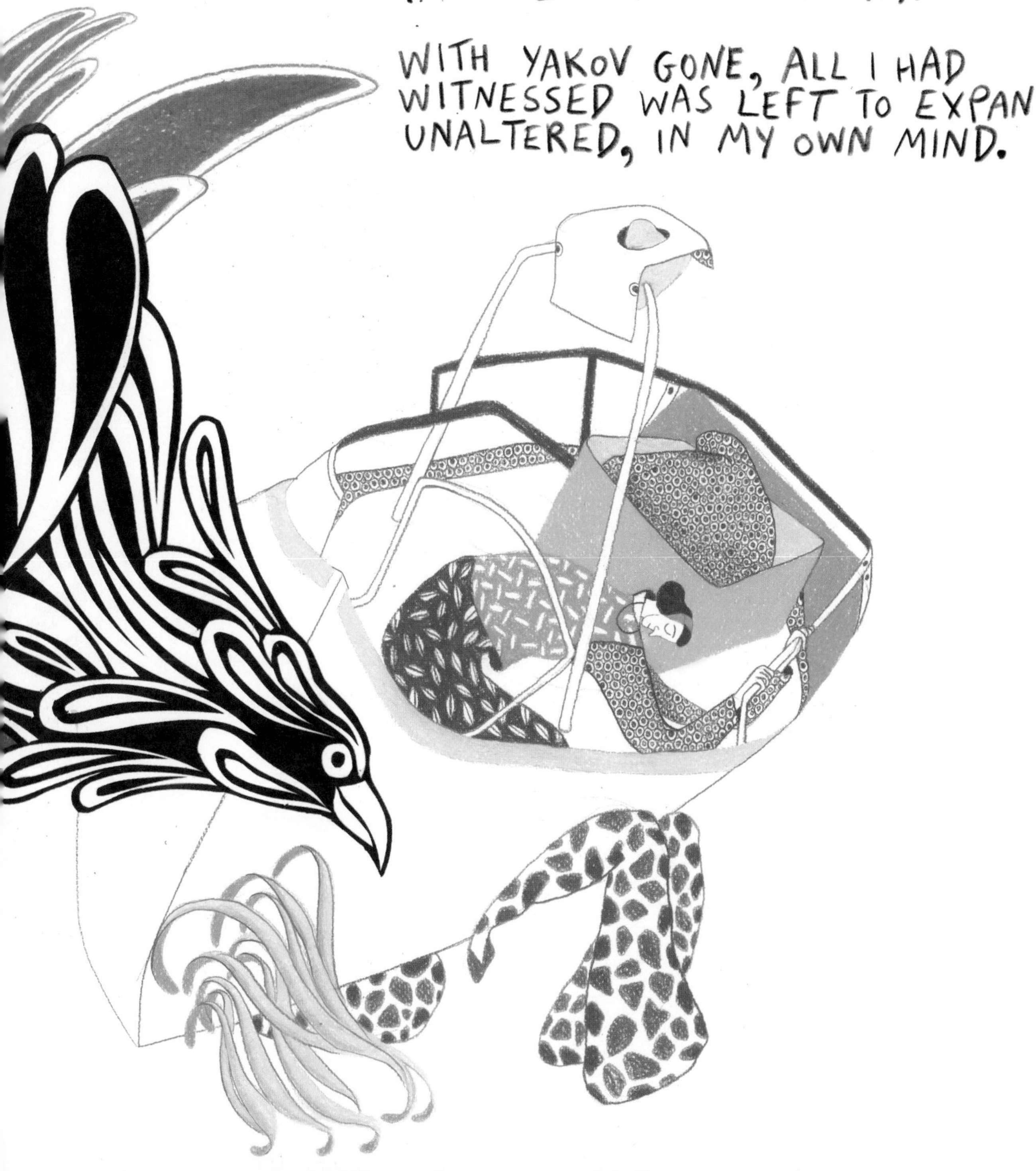

I SPENT THE NEXT MONTHS AT HOME,
UNABLE TO MOVE, UNWILLING TO
MOVE ON MY OWN BEHALF.

IN THE FALL, MY FATHER ENROLLED
ME TO MOUNT SCOPUS ACADEMY—

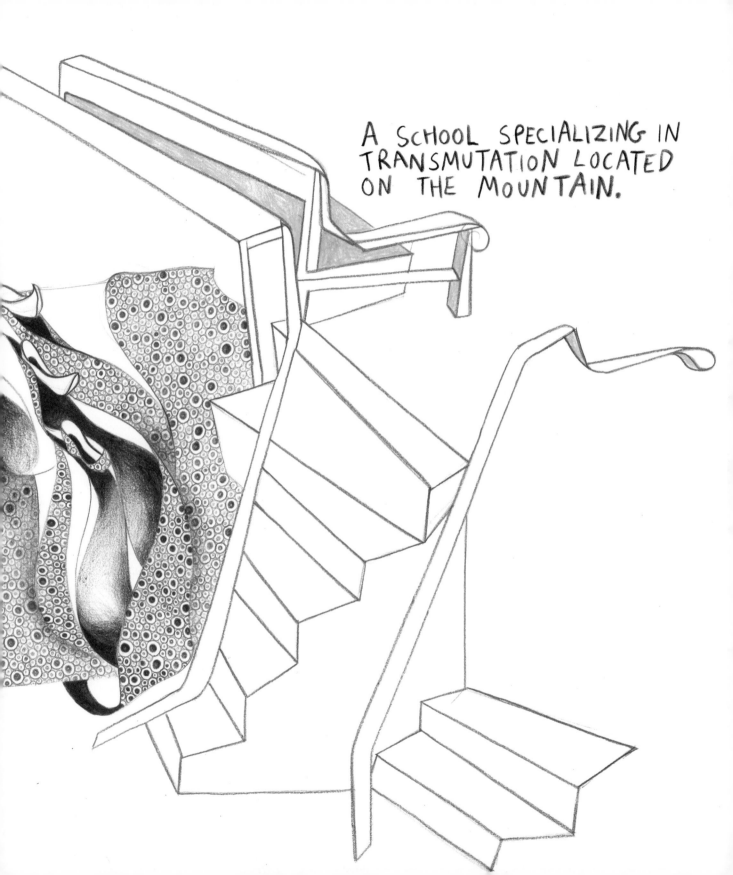

A SCHOOL SPECIALIZING IN TRANSMUTATION LOCATED ON THE MOUNTAIN.

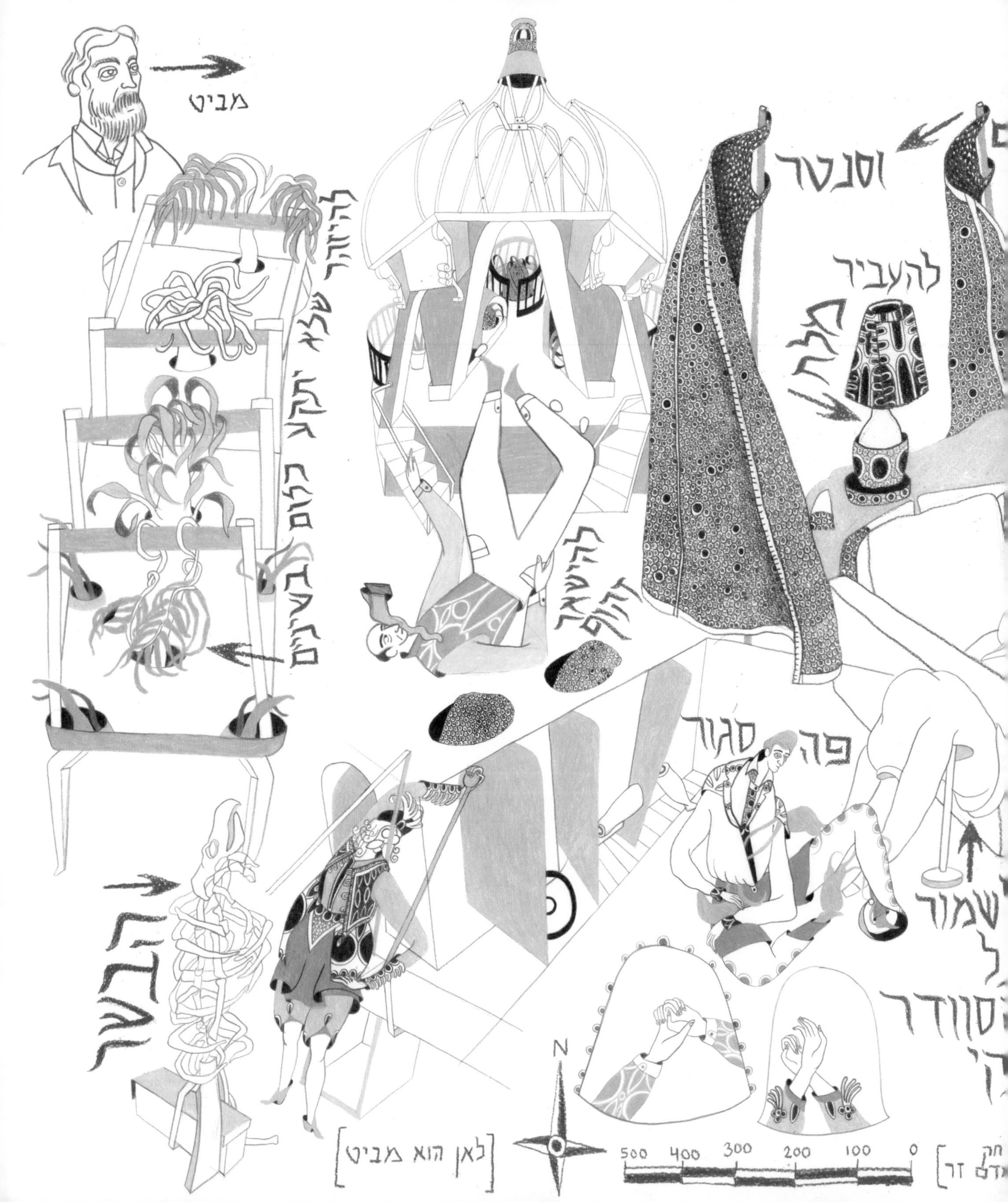

מביט
וסנטר
להעביר
מלח
להיזהר שלא יתקע חלום במעיים
להישאר
פה סגור
הרגש
שמור
ל
סוודר
N
[לאן הוא מביט]
500 400 300 200 100 0

I NEVER HEARD OF THE SCHOOL PRIOR TO RECIEVING AN ACCEPTANCE LETTER. EVENTHOUGH I HAD STUDIED MAPS OF SCOPUS MOUNTAIN DURING MY MILITARY SERVICE,

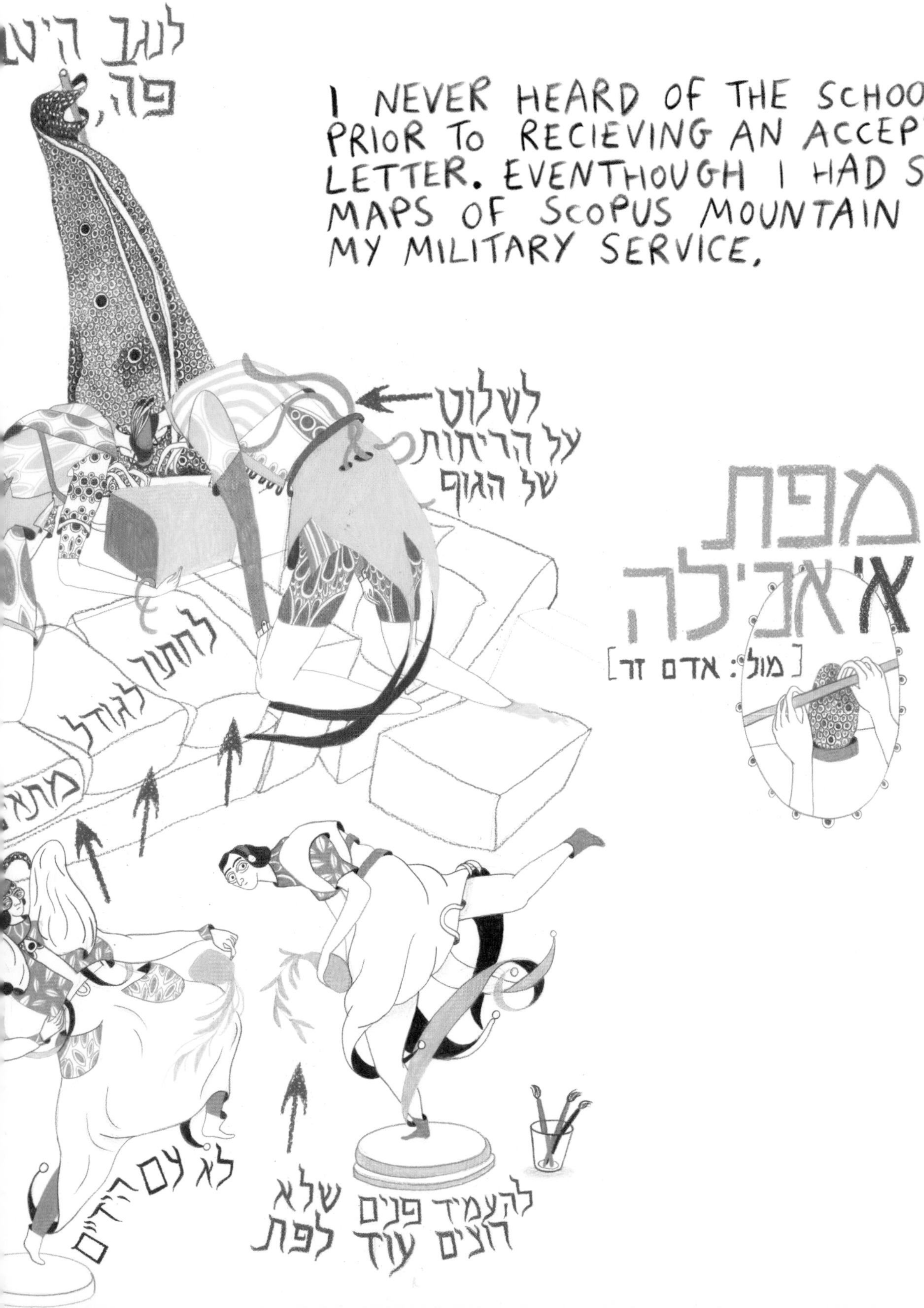

לנגב היט
פה,
לשלוט
על הריחות
של הגוף
מפת
איאכילה
[מול: אדם זר]
לחתוך
לגודל
לא עם הידיים
להעמיד פנים שלא
רוצים עוד לפת

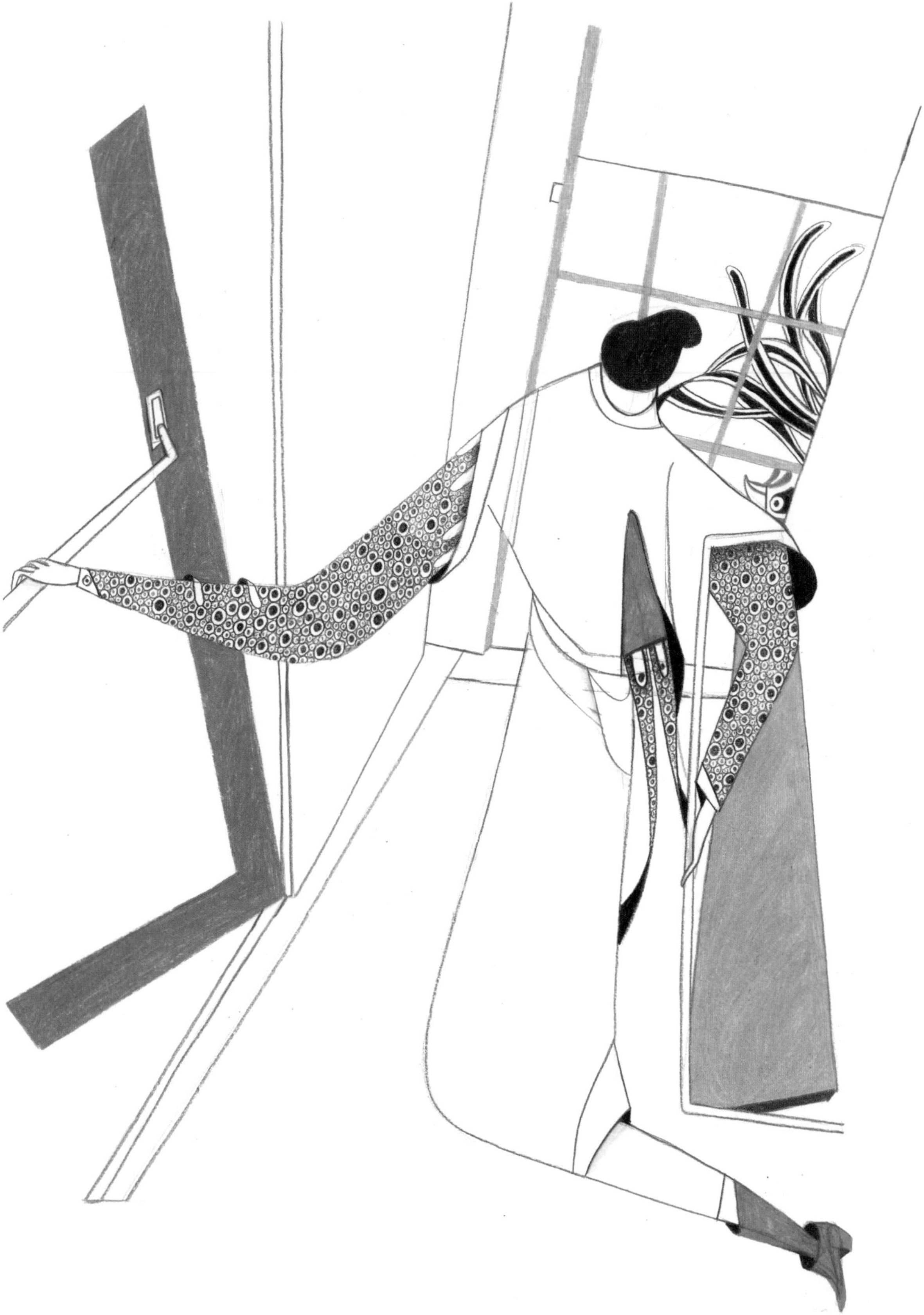

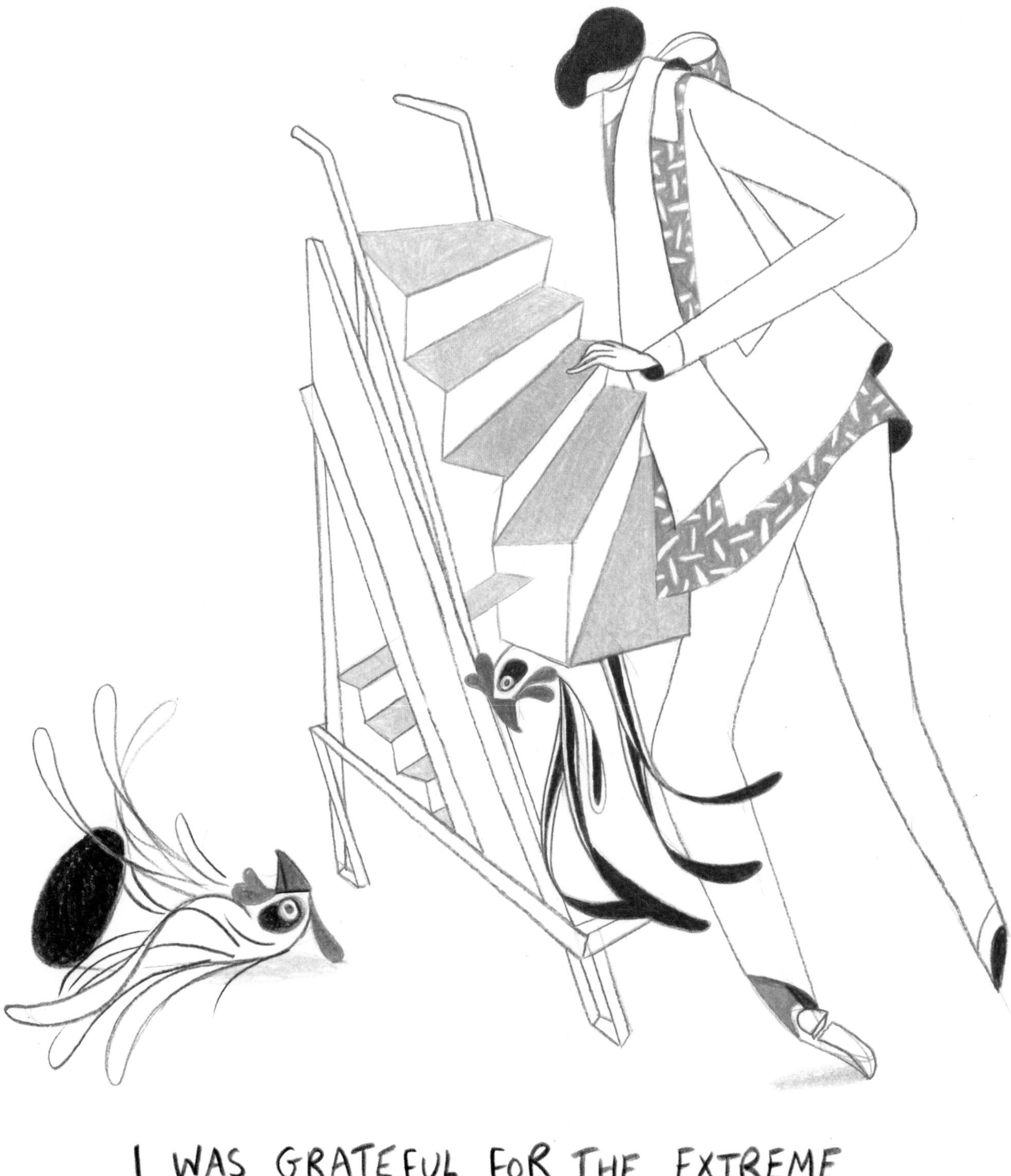

I WAS GRATEFUL FOR THE EXTREME ALERTNESS THE SCHOOL DEMANDED OF ITS STUDENTS.

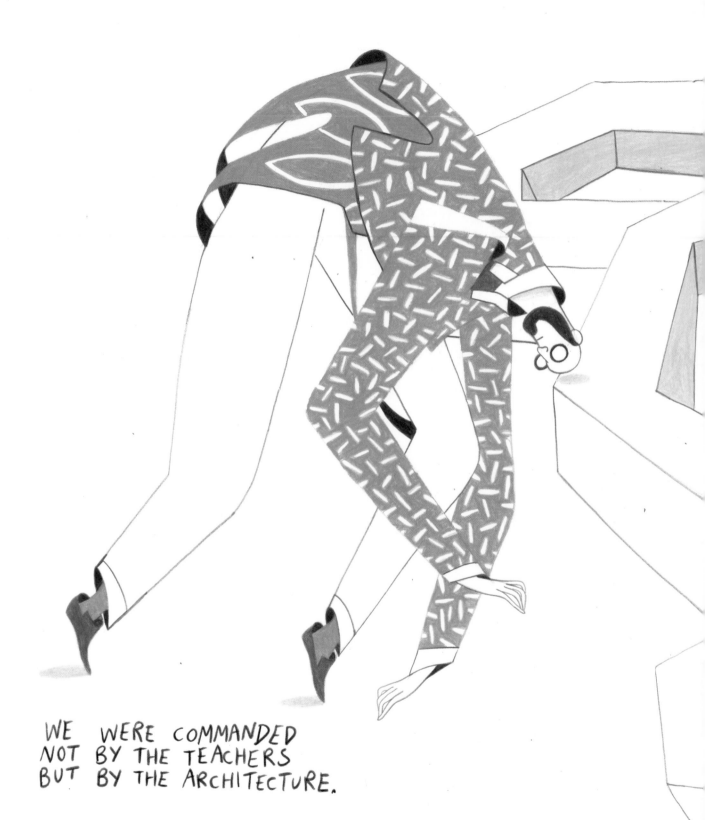

WE WERE COMMANDED
NOT BY THE TEACHERS
BUT BY THE ARCHITECTURE.

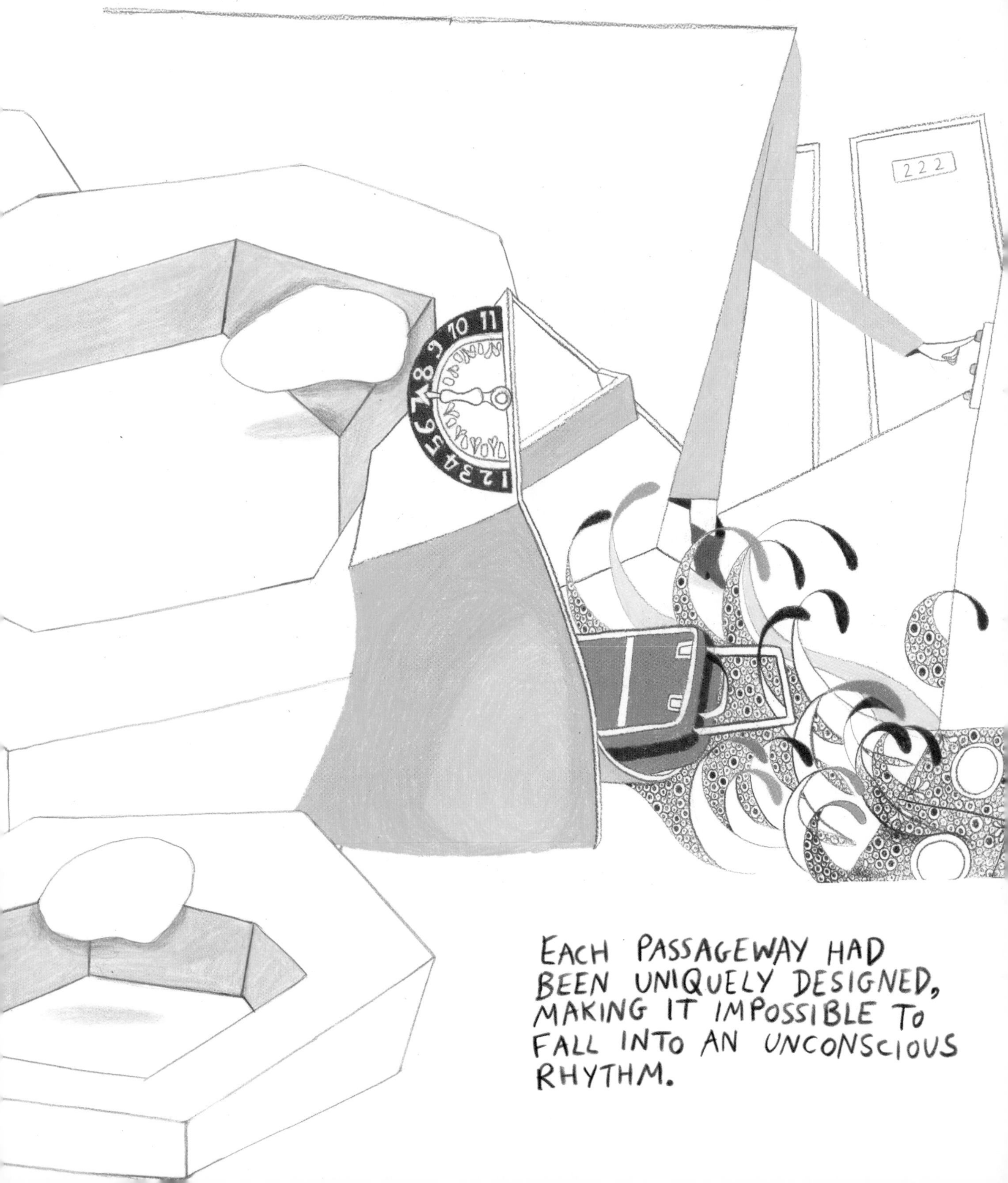
222
EACH PASSAGEWAY HAD BEEN UNIQUELY DESIGNED, MAKING IT IMPOSSIBLE TO FALL INTO AN UNCONSCIOUS RHYTHM.

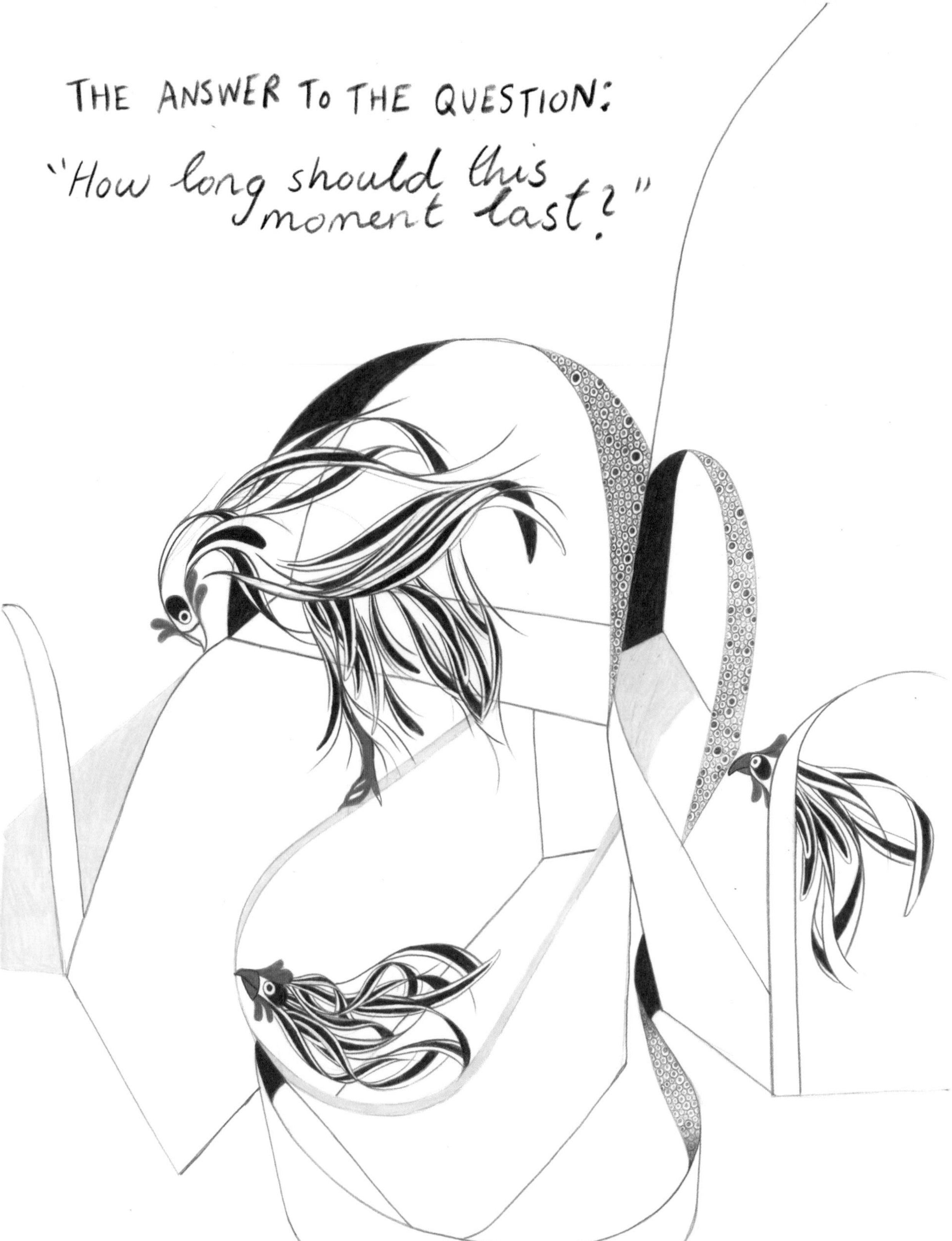
THE ANSWER TO THE QUESTION:
"How long should this moment last?"

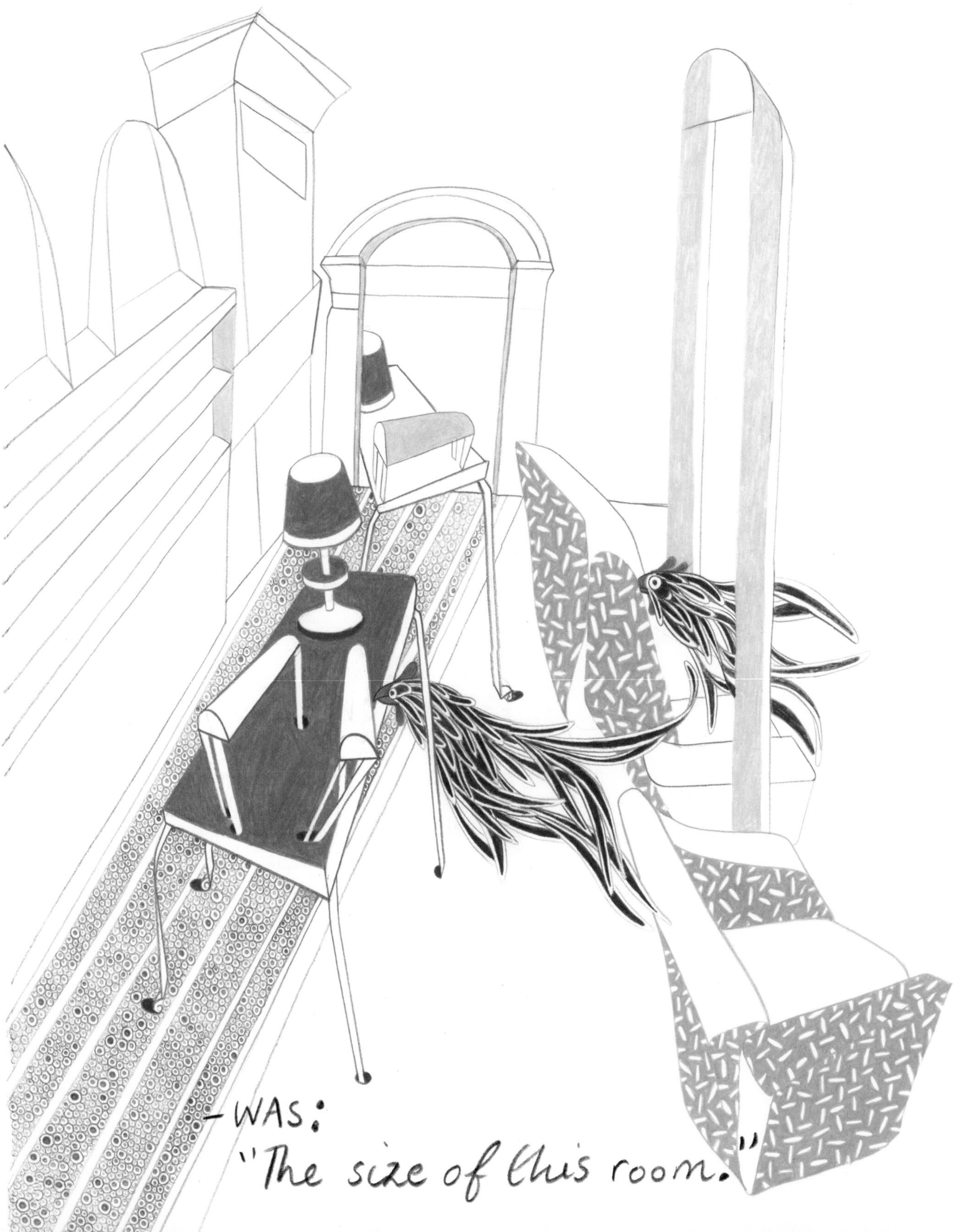
—WAS:
"The size of this room."

WE WERE ALL TEACHER'S ASSISTANTS.
WE WERE ALL EXPELLED FROM CLASSES.
WE WERE ALL LATE SOMEWHERE.

WE WERE ALL WONDERING IF
THE CHAIRS ARE BEING USED.

WE ONLY MET FELLOW STUDENTS IN PASSING.

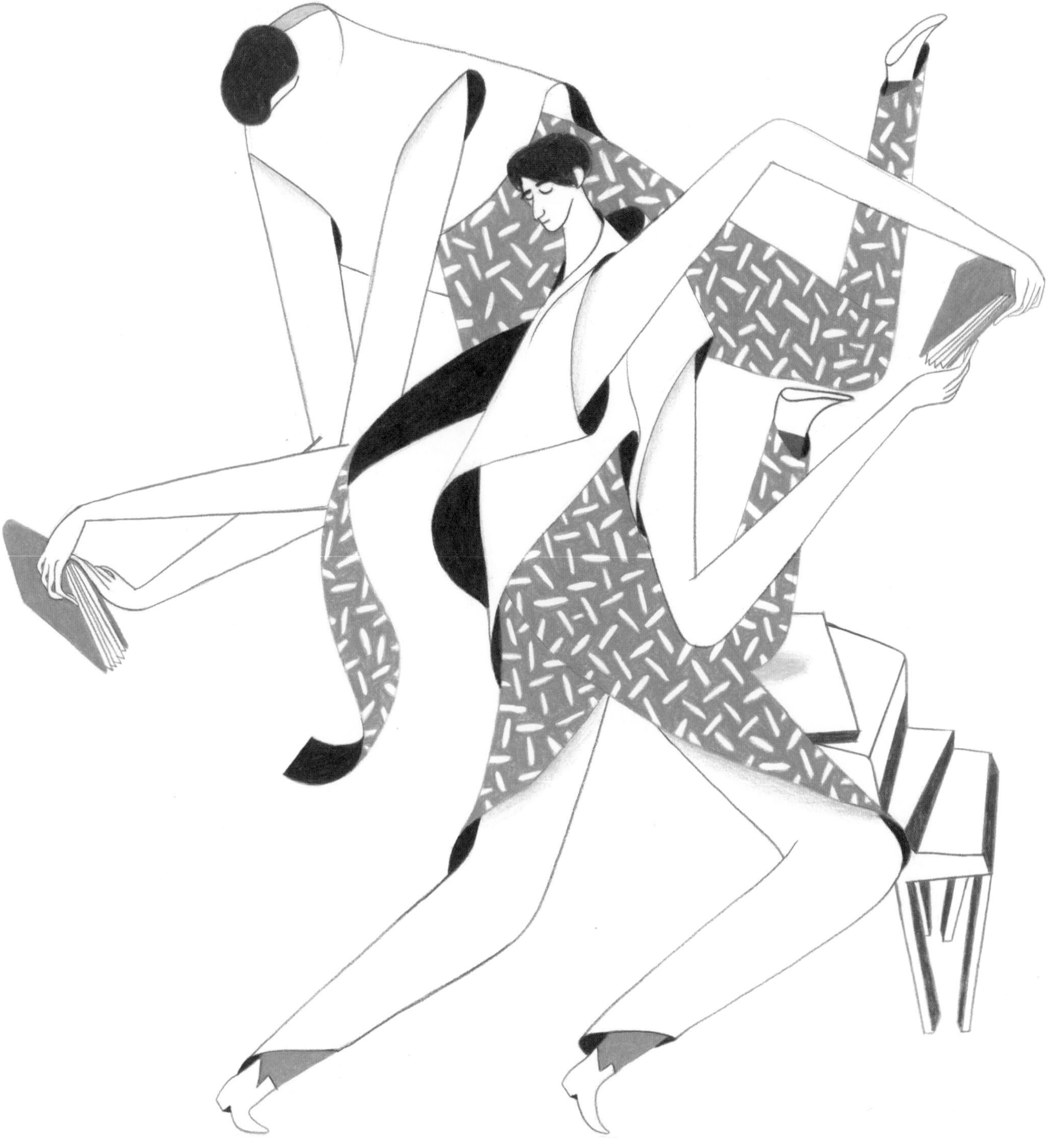

COLLECTING LIBRARY STICKERS OR LABELS FROM DISCARDED FRUIT OR TICKET STUBS OR LEAVES DRYING IN THE PAGES.

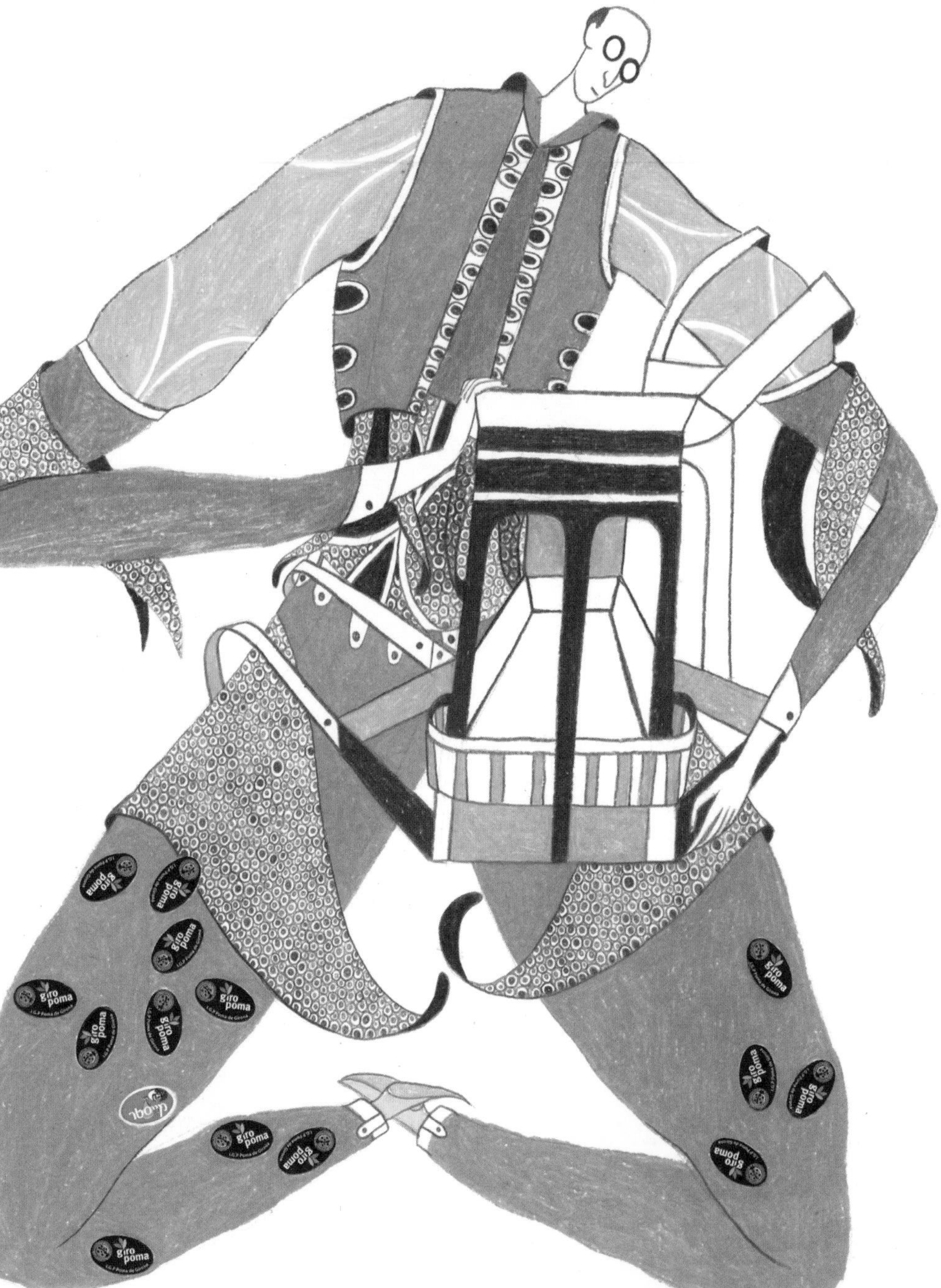
giro poma

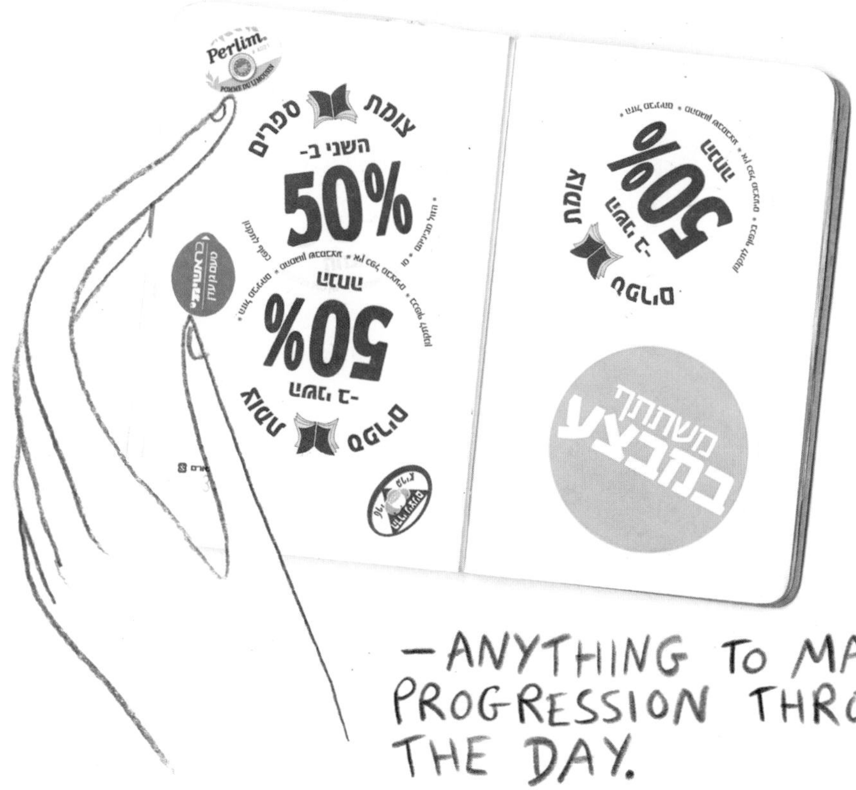
Perlim
צומת ספרים
השני ב-
50%
משתתף במבצע

—ANYTHING TO MARK OUR PROGRESSION THROUGH THE DAY.

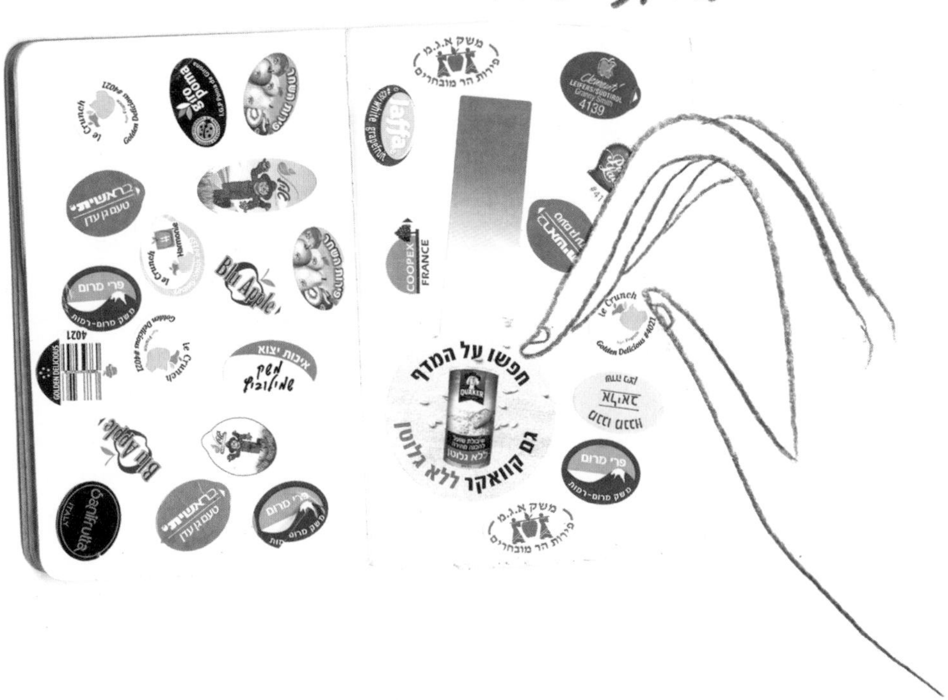
le Crunch
Golden Delicious #4021
Bio Poma
בראשית
טעם גן עדן
פרי מרום
משק מרום-רמות
Blu Apple
איכות יצוא
משק שמולביץ
4021
Fanfrutta
ITALY
משק א.ג.מ
פירות הר מובחרים
Jaffa
4139
COOPEX
FRANCE
חפשו על המדף
QUAKER
ללא גלוטן
גם קוואקר ללא גלוטן

SIGNS OF SPATIAL HESITATION
MANIFESTED IN OUR BODIES.

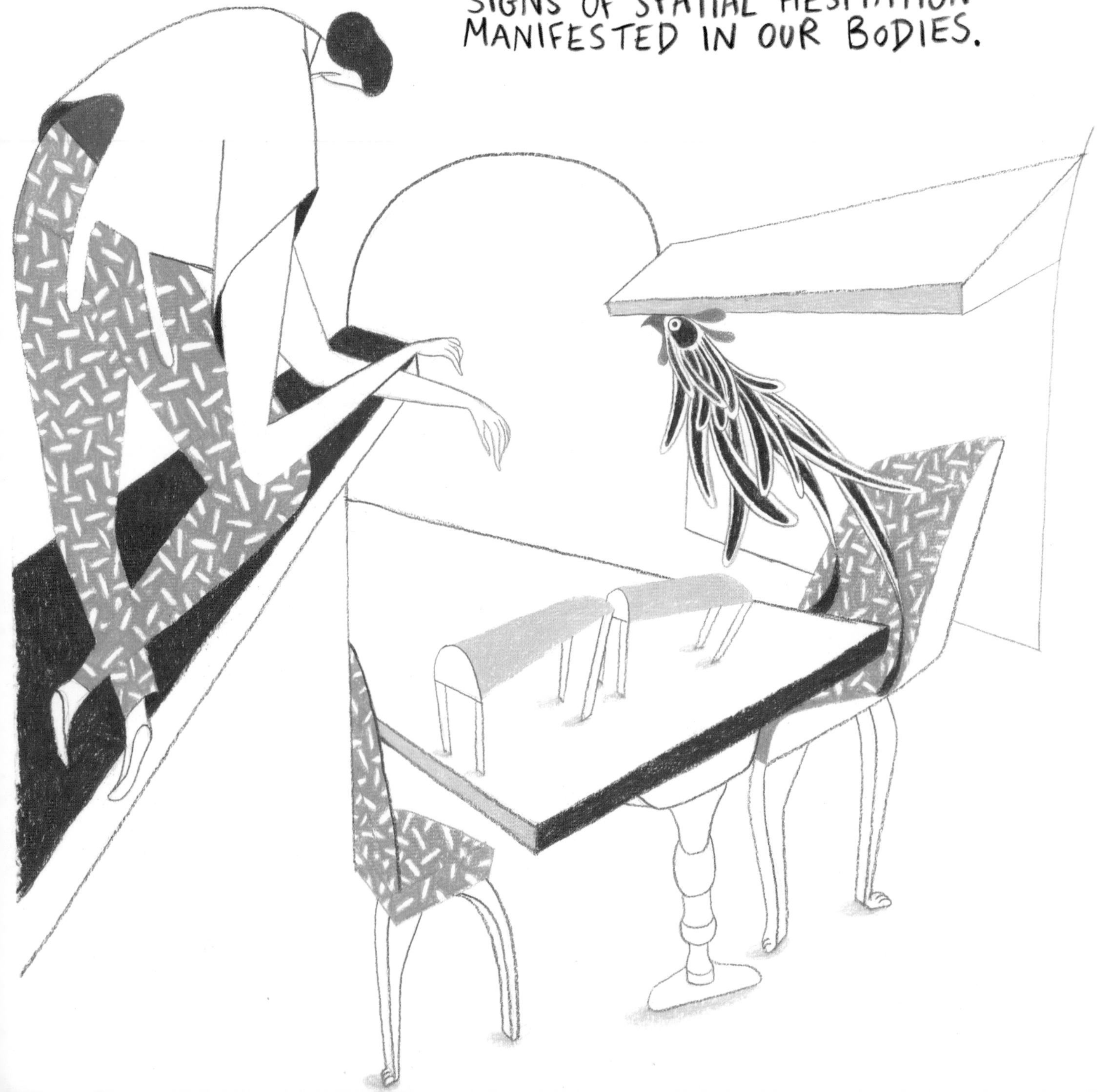

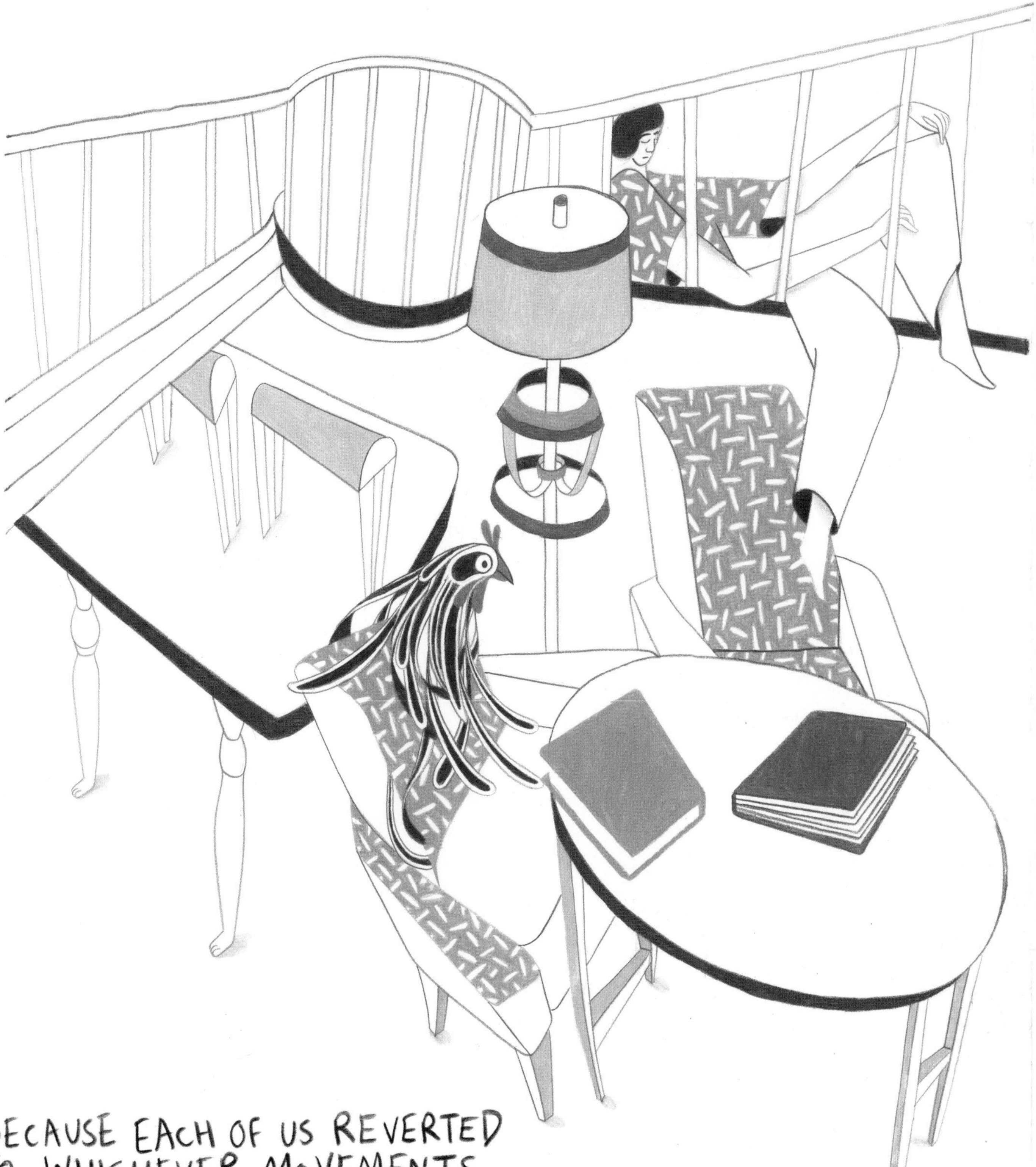

BECAUSE EACH OF US REVERTED
TO WHICHEVER MOVEMENTS
HAD BELONGED TO US BEFORE
WE BECAME STUDENTS.

THE ONE I RETURNED TO MOST WAS LYING ON THE ROOF OF THE CONTROL TOWER ON THE DAY THE SKY WAS SEIZED BY CENTRAL COMMAND AND WE WERE OUT OF COMMISSION FOR SEVERAL HOURS, LEFT TO WITNESS THE ONCE FAMILIAR AIR FIELD SWARM WITH INDECIPHERABLE ROUTES.

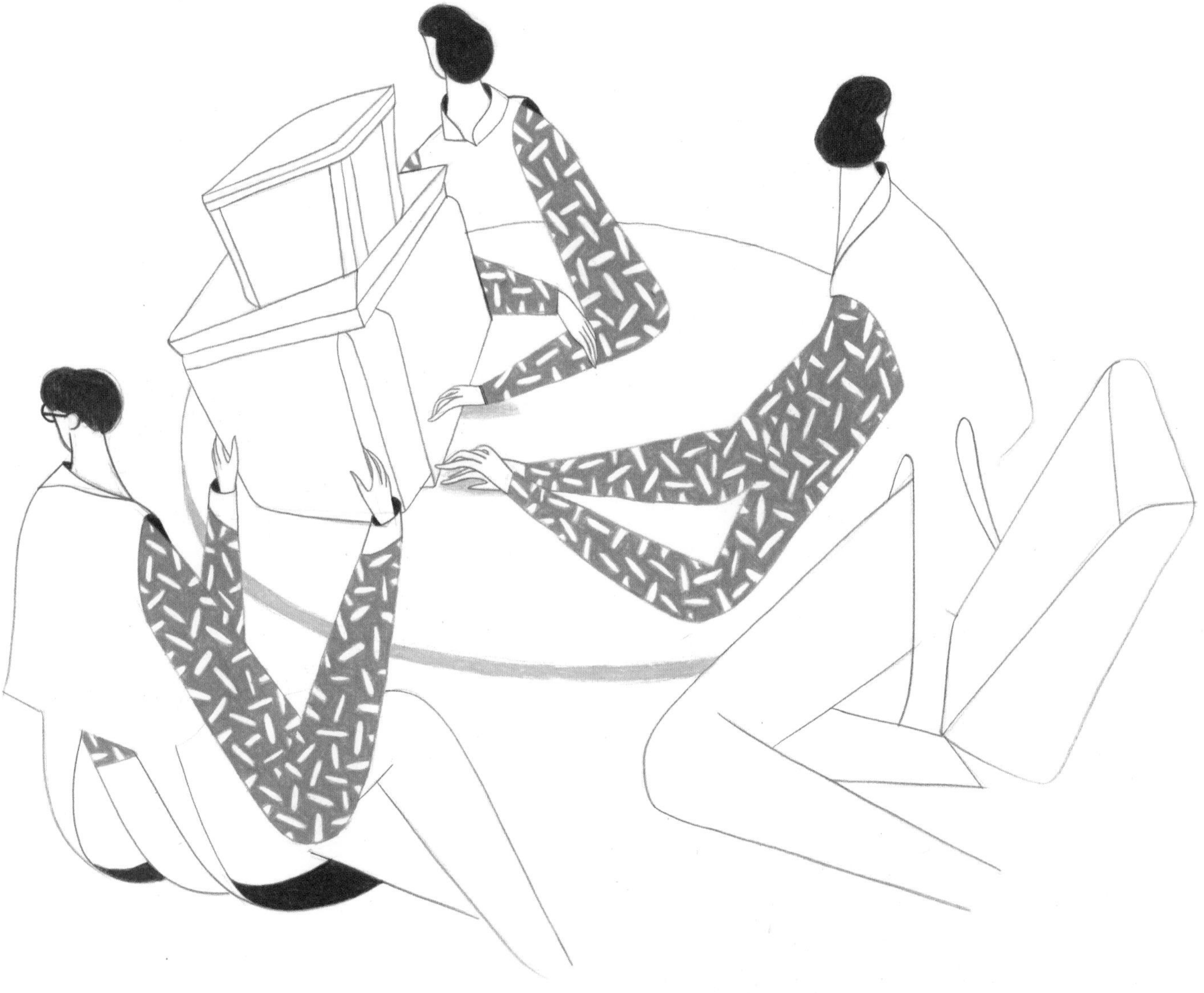

IF I WERE TO DATE SOMEONE HERE, I HAD TO ASSIGN MY ARSENAL OF MOVEMENTS TO NEW STORIES.

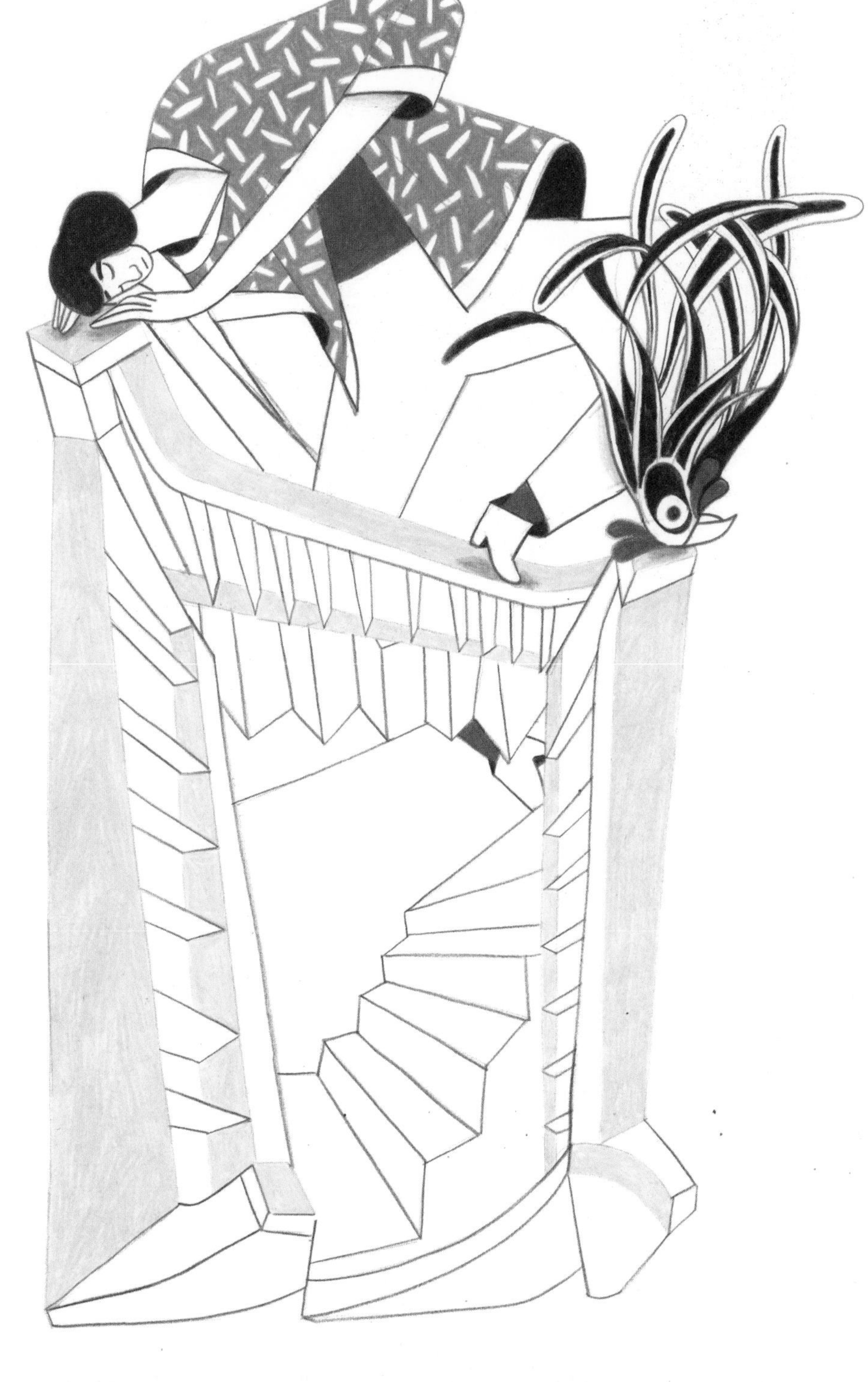

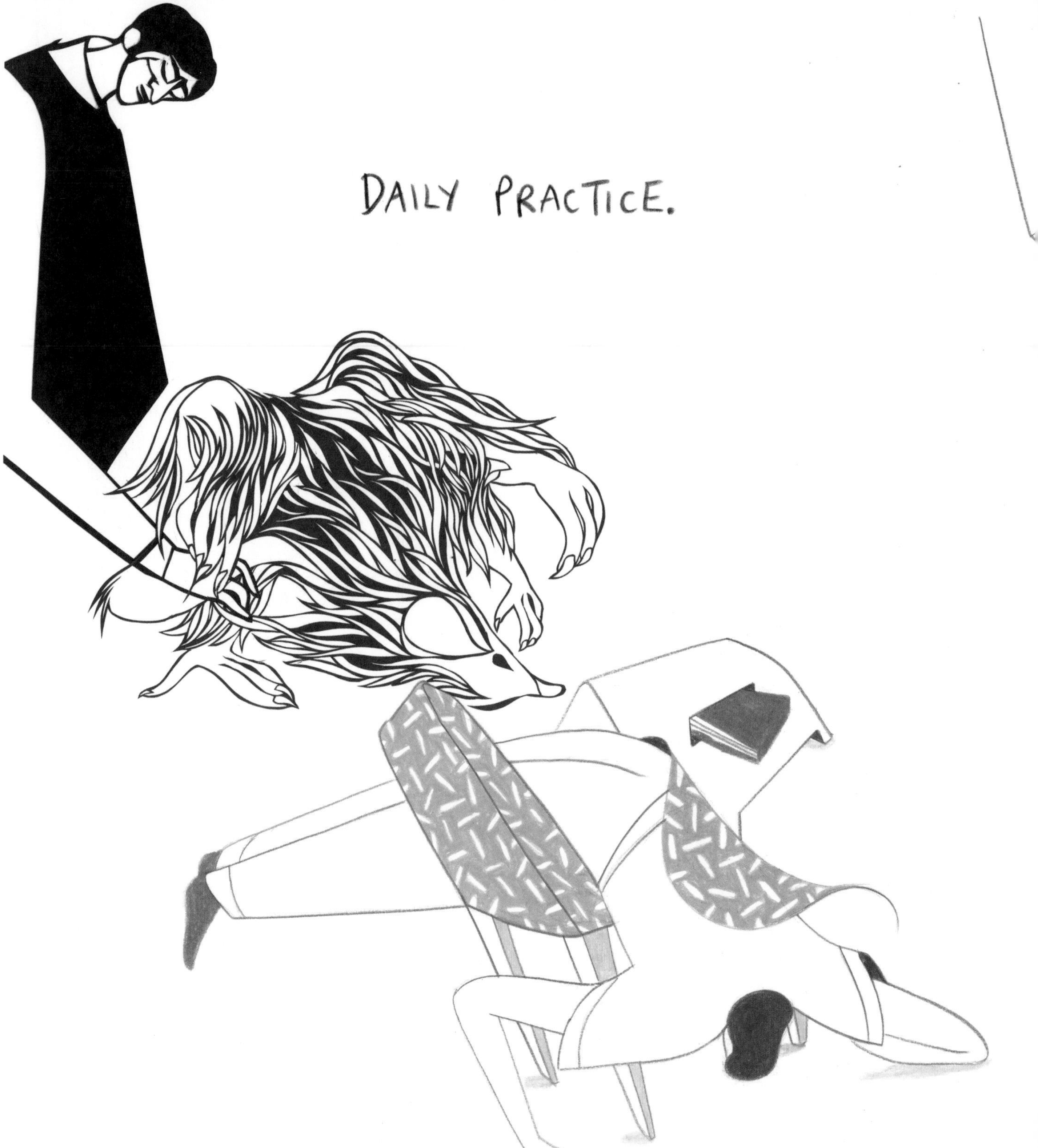
DAILY PRACTICE.

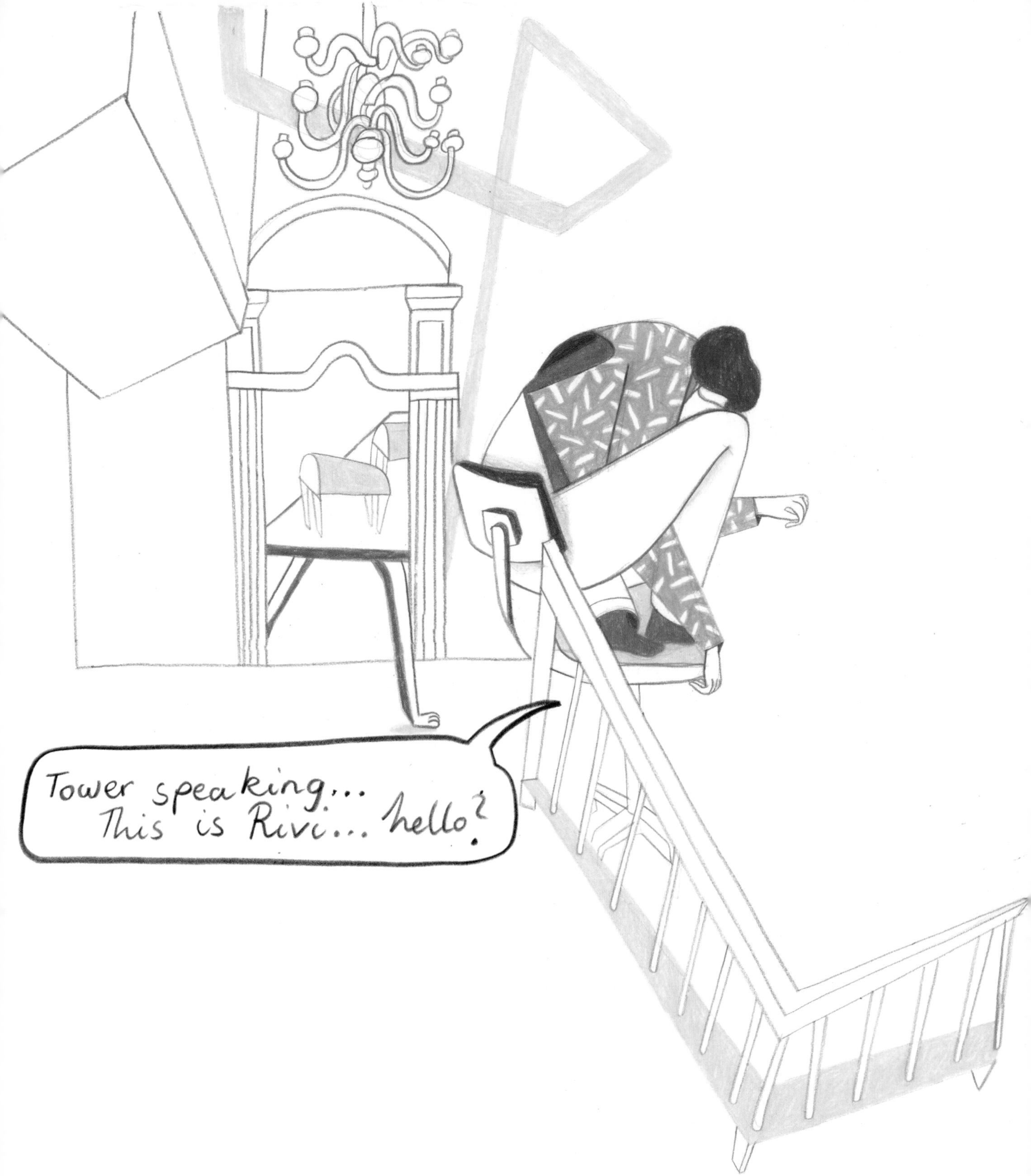
Tower speaking... This is Rivi... hello?

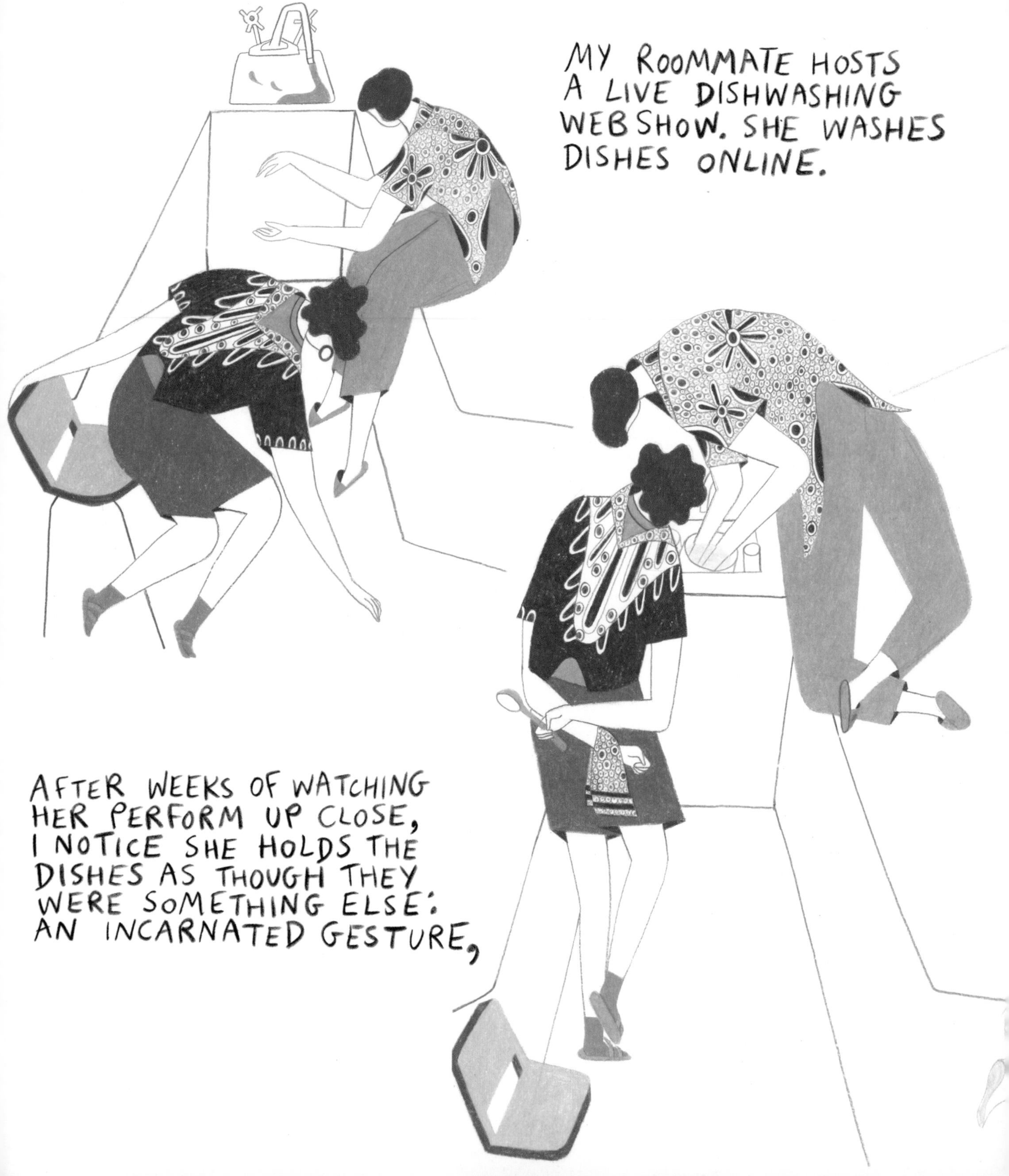
MY ROOMMATE HOSTS A LIVE DISHWASHING WEBSHOW. SHE WASHES DISHES ONLINE.
AFTER WEEKS OF WATCHING HER PERFORM UP CLOSE, I NOTICE SHE HOLDS THE DISHES AS THOUGH THEY WERE SOMETHING ELSE: AN INCARNATED GESTURE,

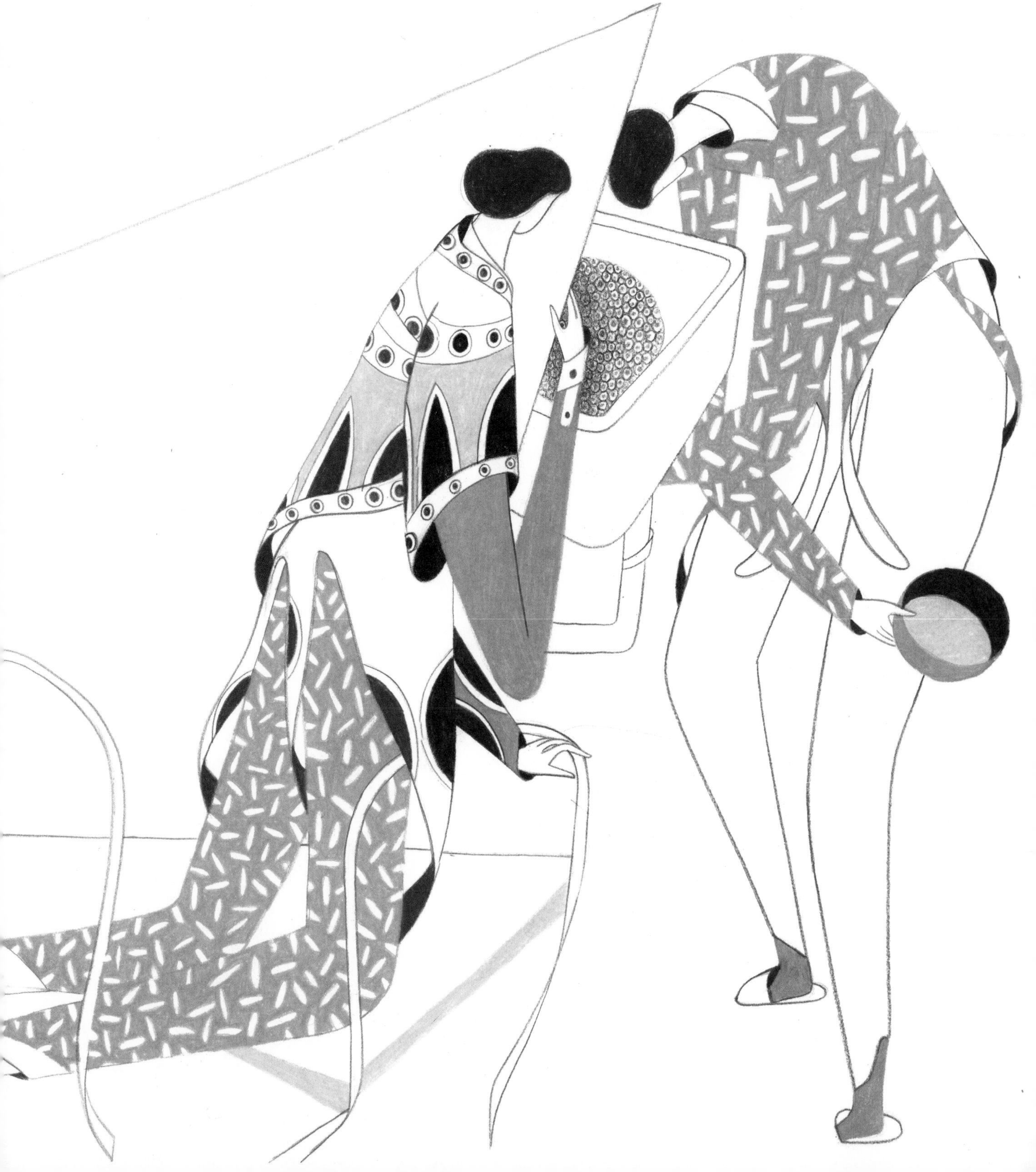

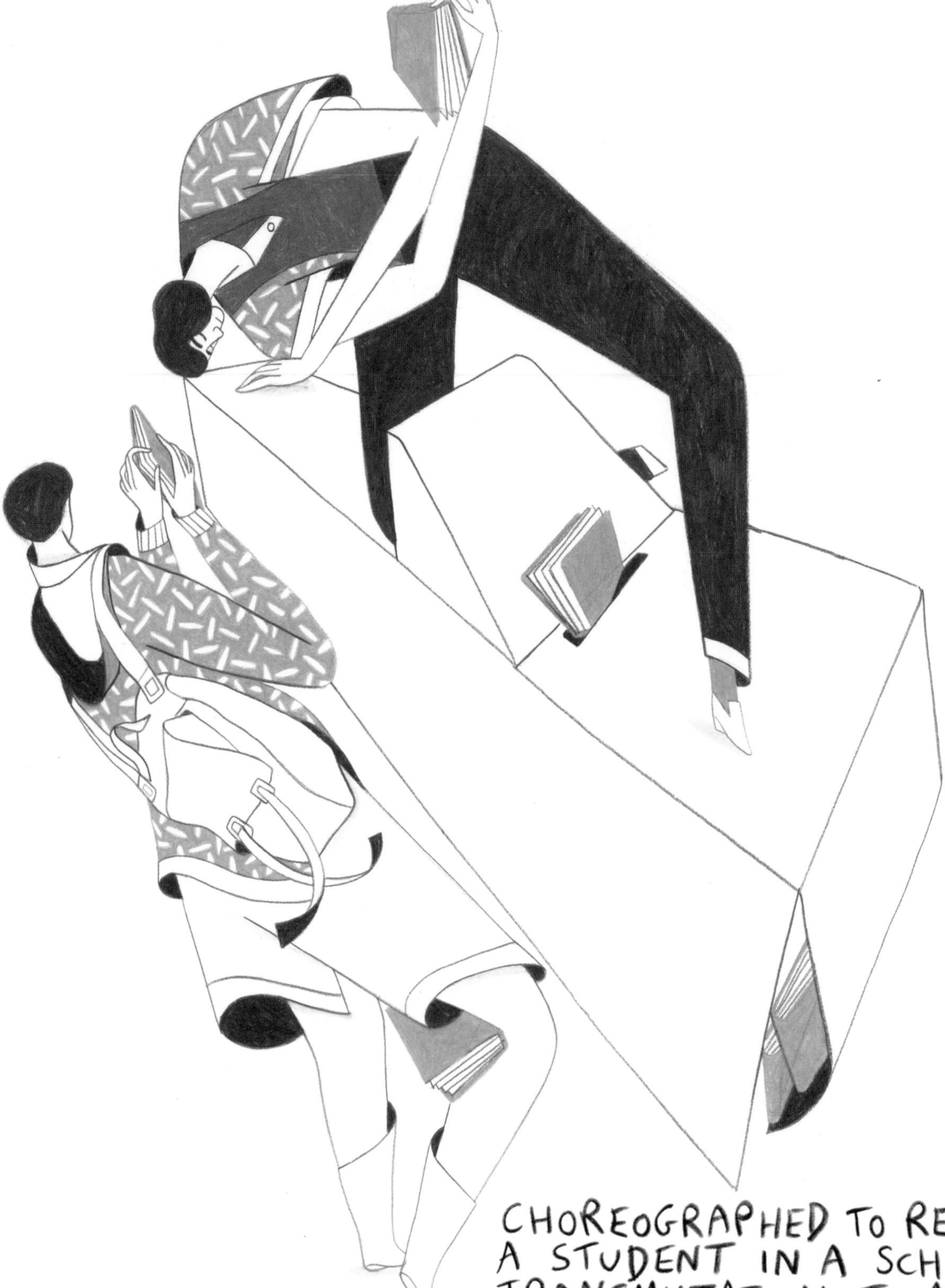

CHOREOGRAPHED TO RESEMBLE
A STUDENT IN A SCHOOL FOR
TRANSMUTATION. TO AN AUDIENCE
OF ANYONE WAITING TO JOIN.

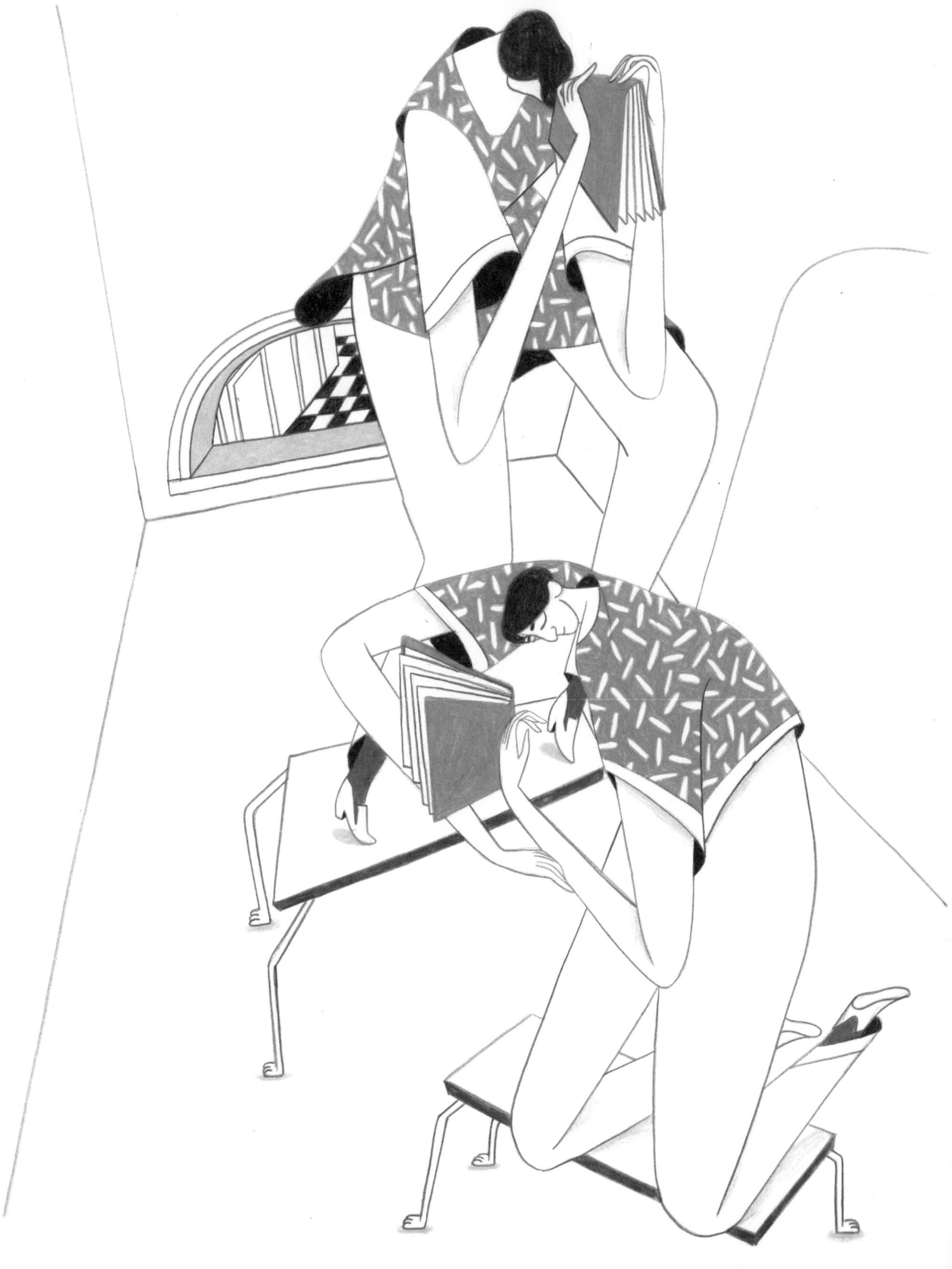

chapter 2:

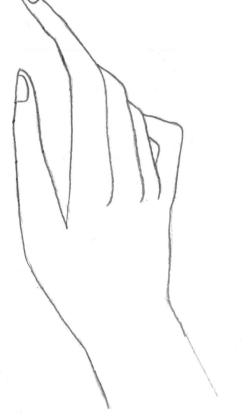

A DISHWASHING LIVE
STREAM WEBSHOW

THE WEBCAM IS POSITIONED
OVER THE SINK, CAPTURING
ONLY THE HANDS.

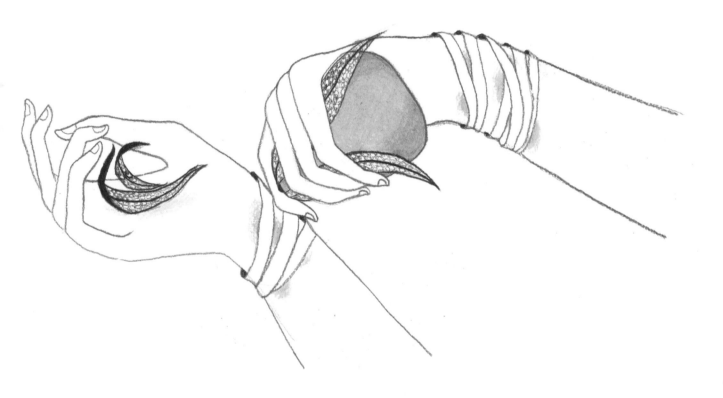

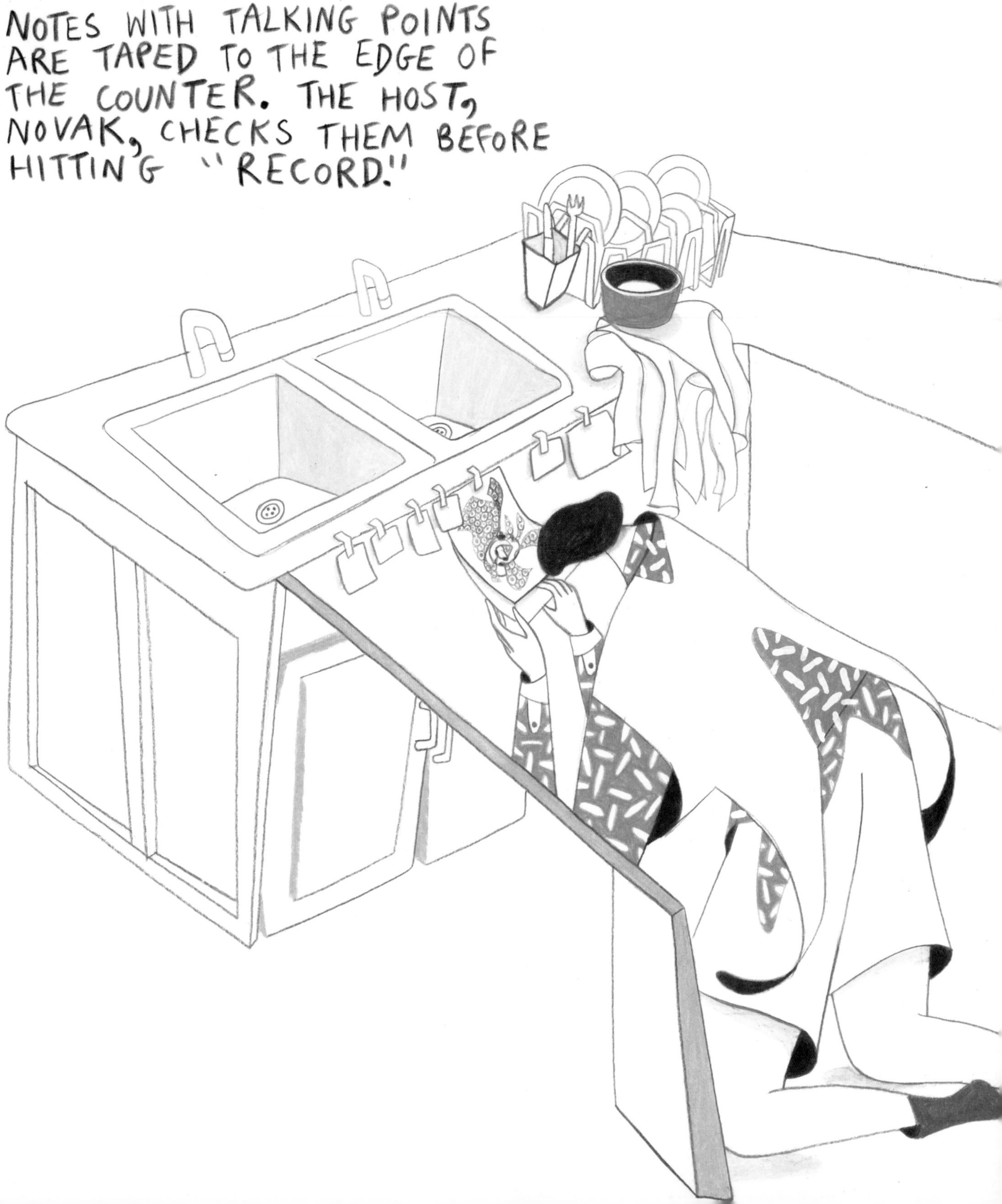
NOTES WITH TALKING POINTS ARE TAPED TO THE EDGE OF THE COUNTER. THE HOST, NOVAK, CHECKS THEM BEFORE HITTING "RECORD."

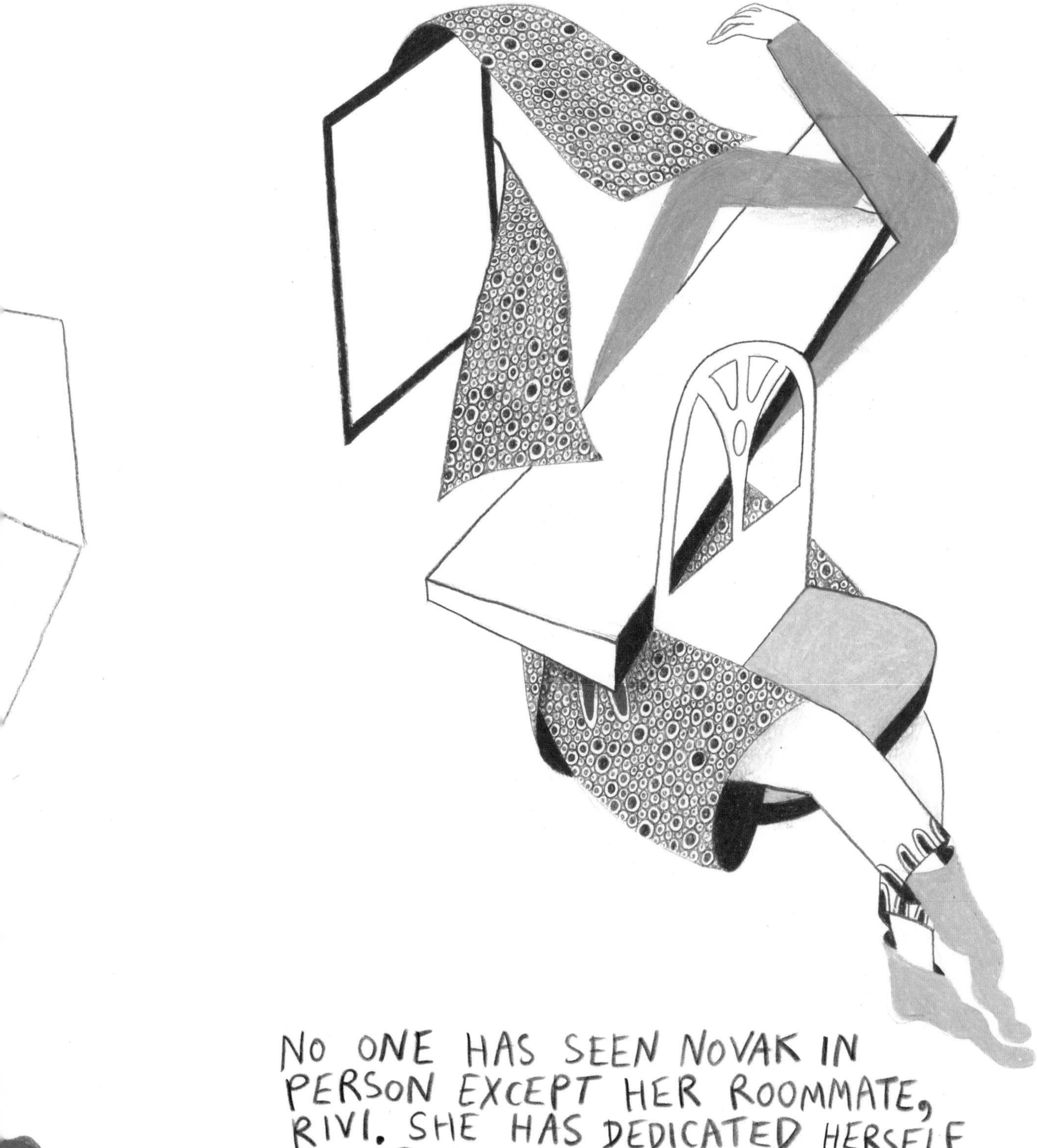

NO ONE HAS SEEN NOVAK IN PERSON EXCEPT HER ROOMMATE, RIVI. SHE HAS DEDICATED HERSELF TO THE SHOW AND WITHDRAWN FROM CAMPUS LIFE.

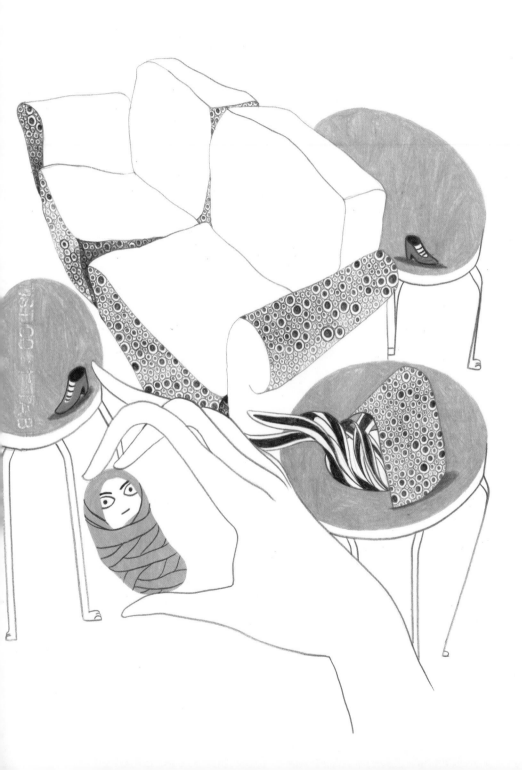

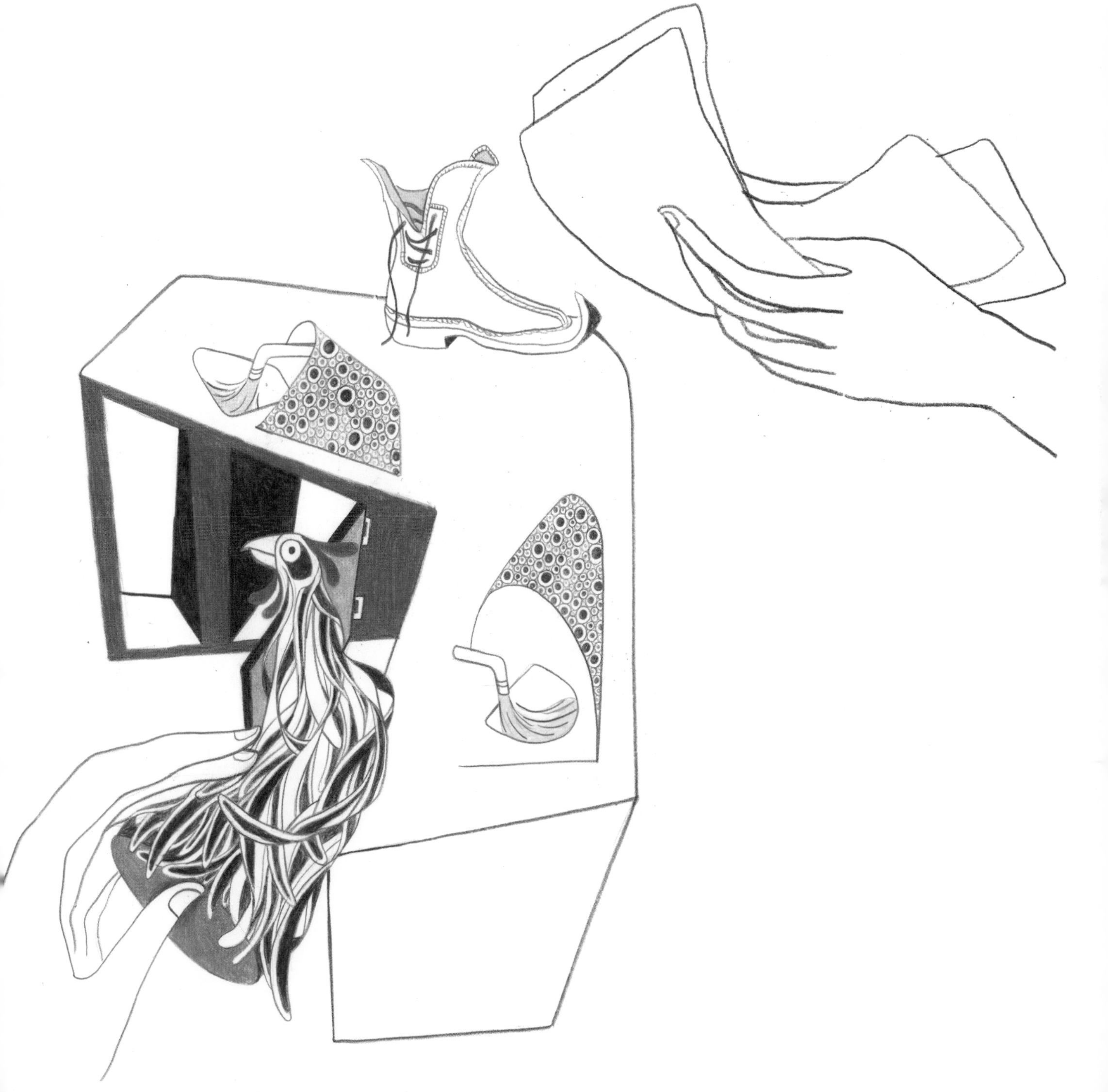

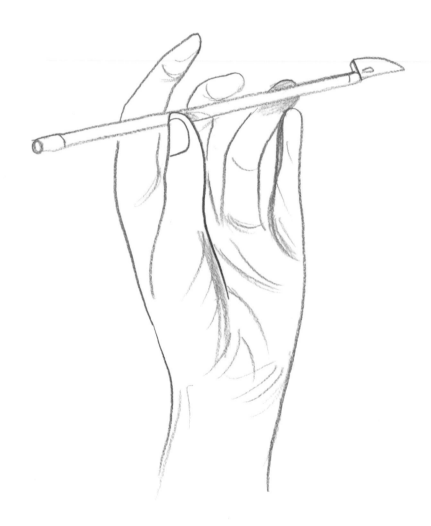

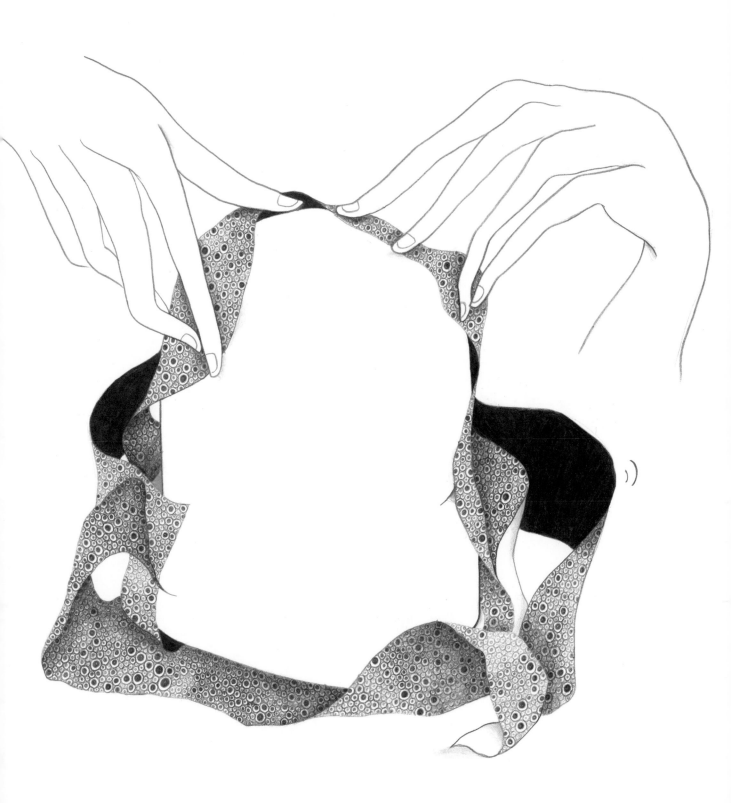

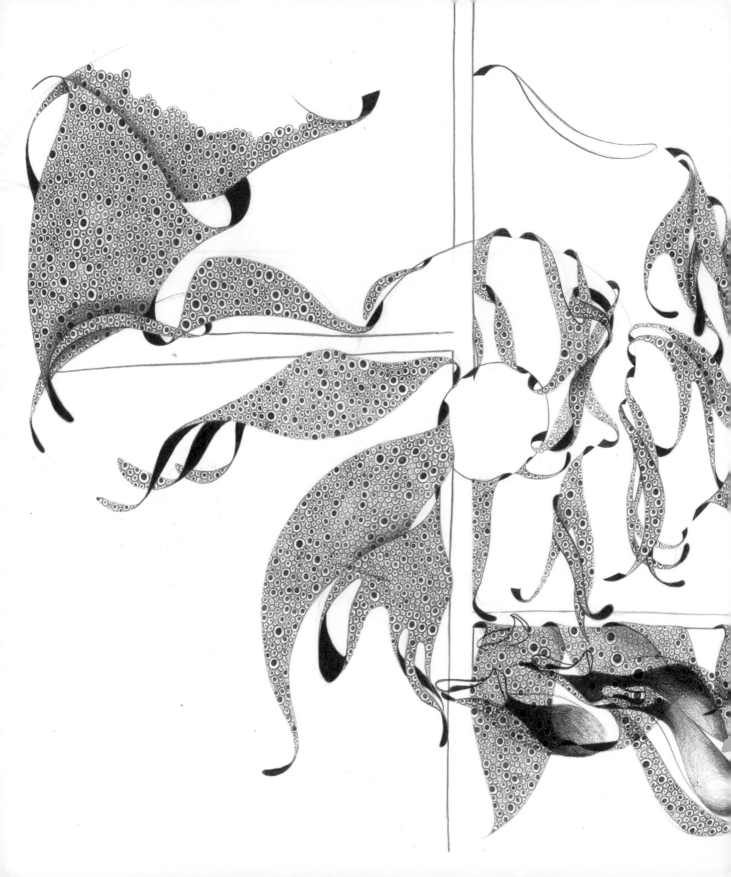

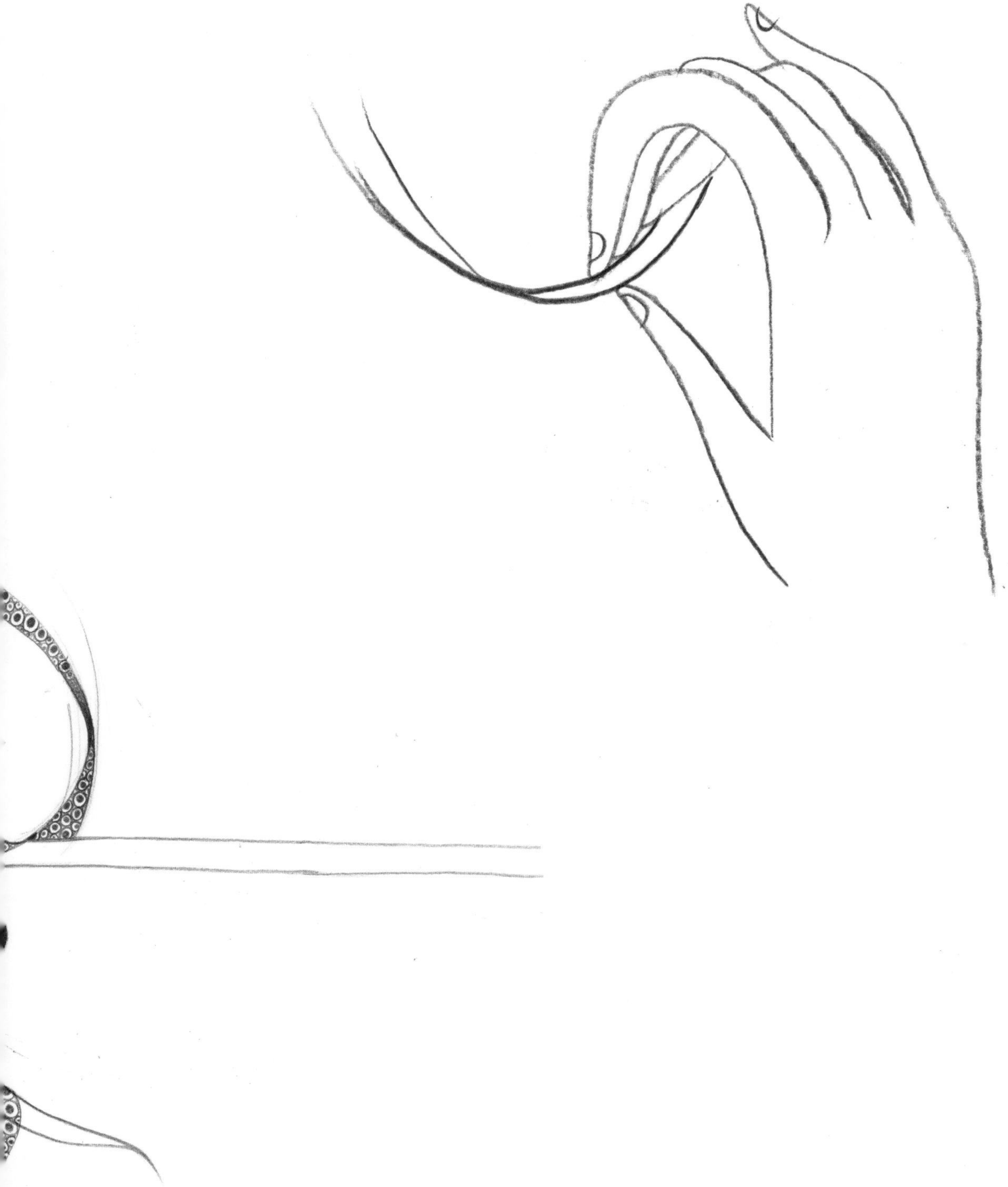

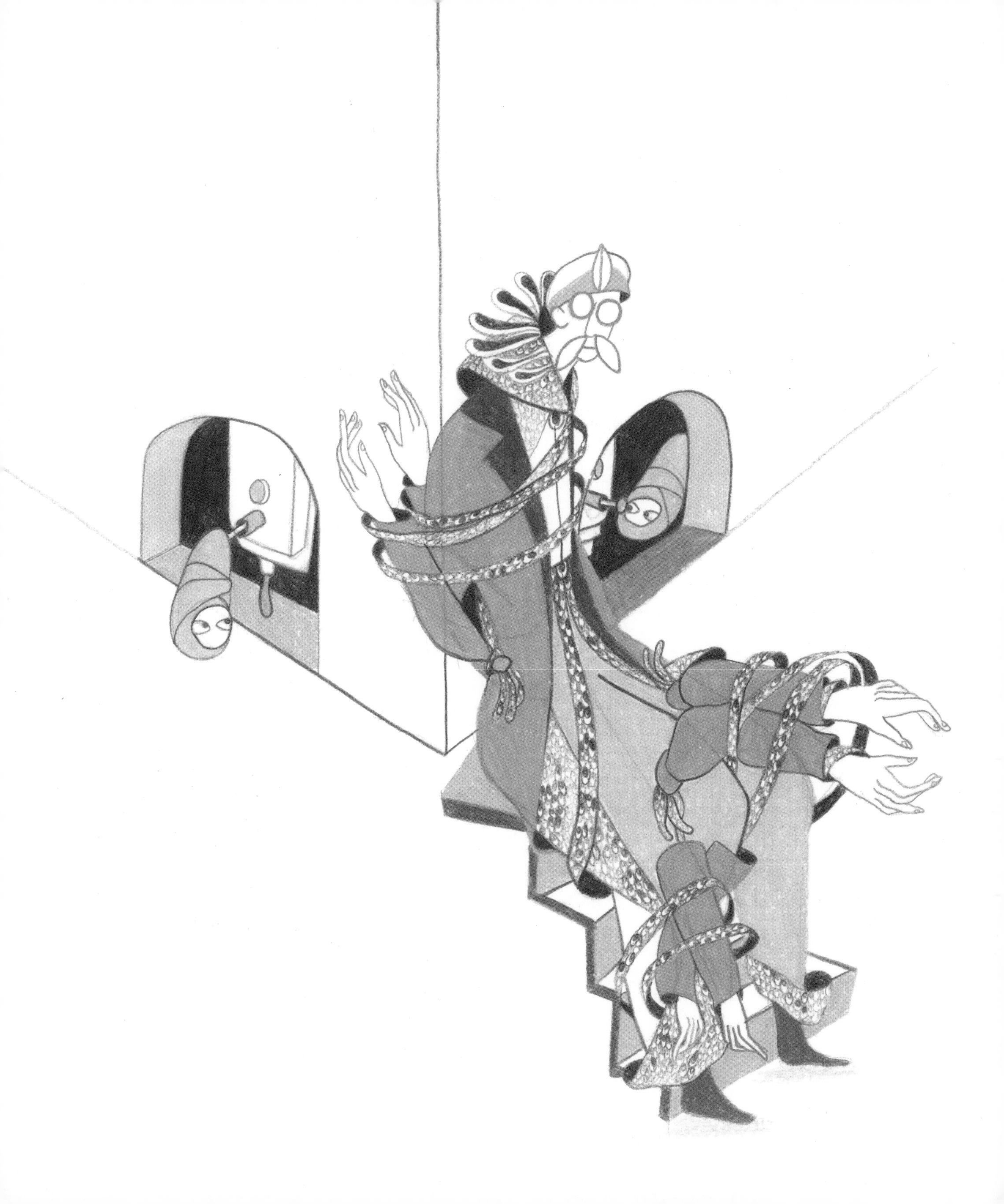

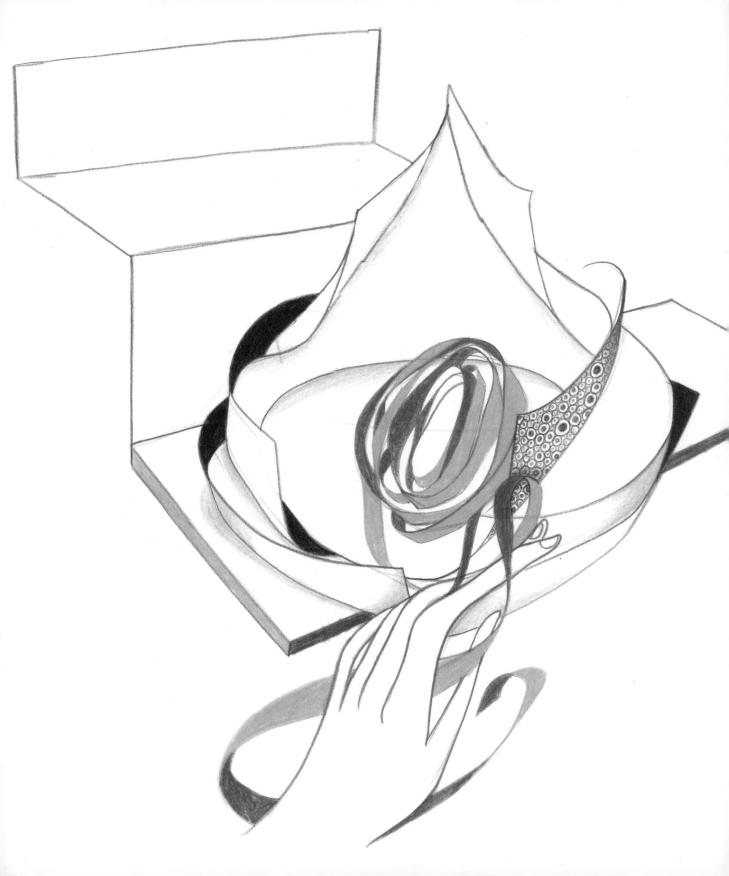

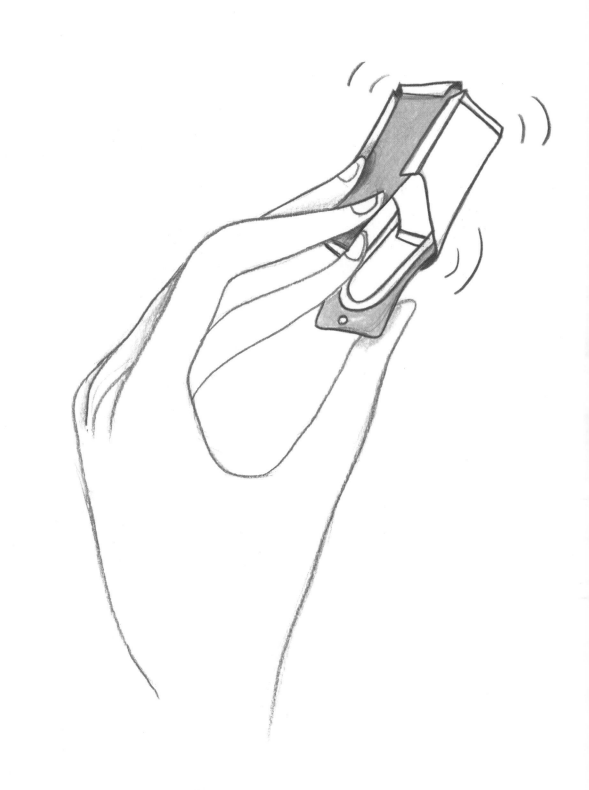

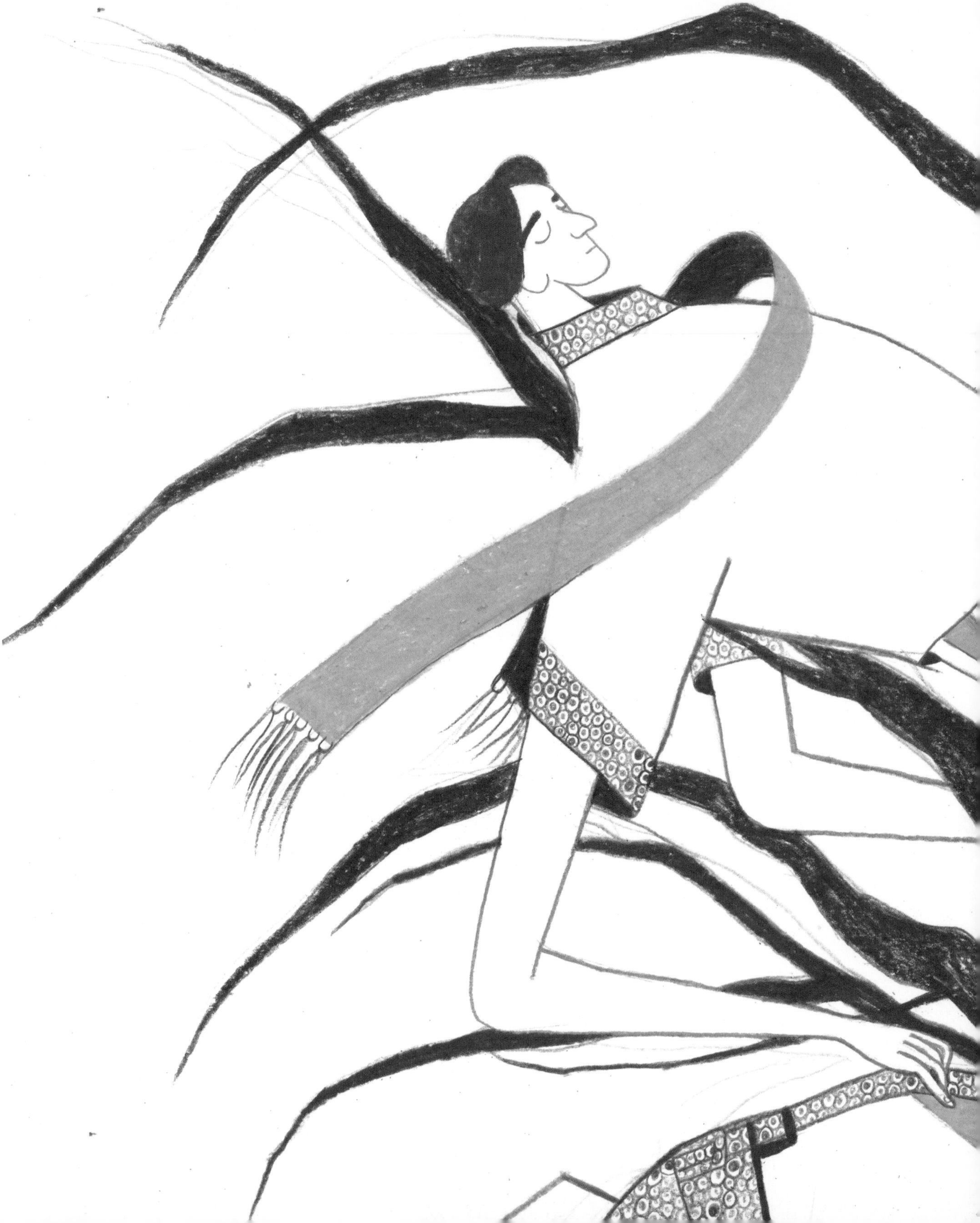

chapter 3: YAKOV

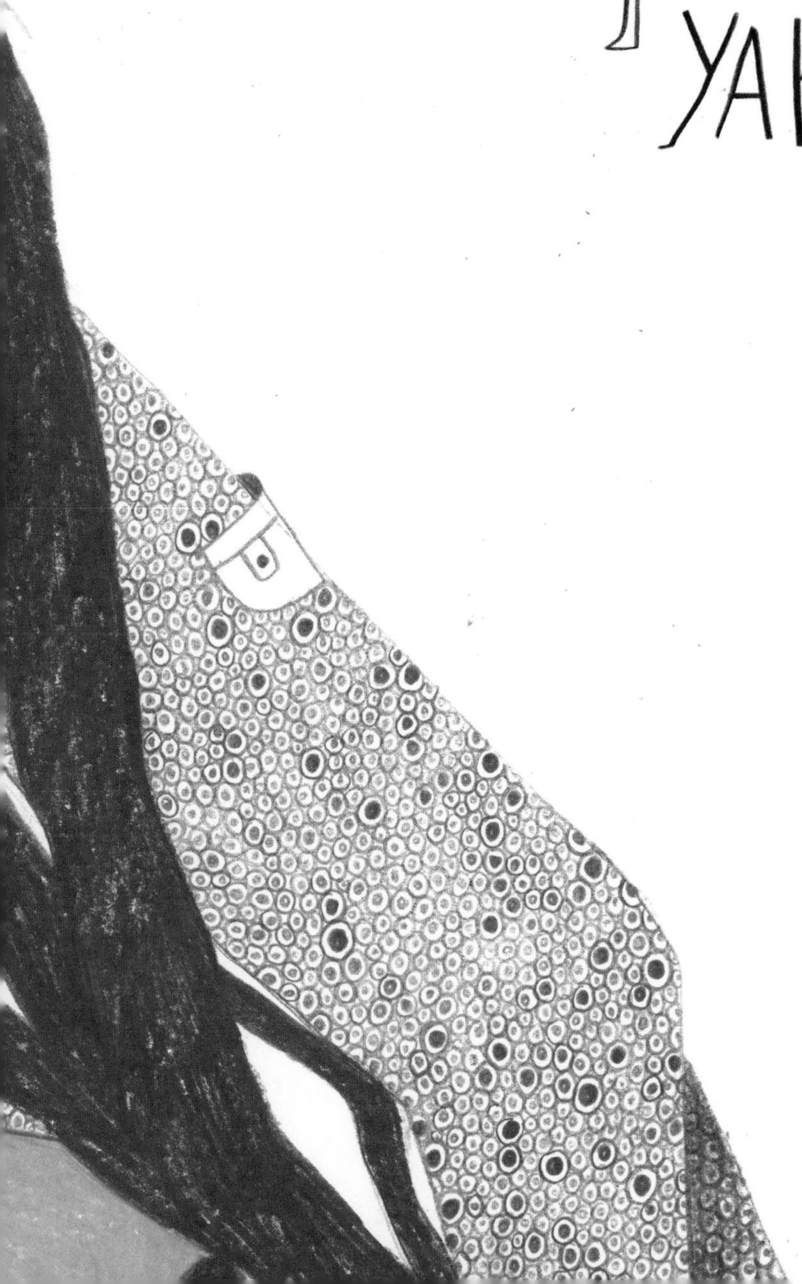

YAKOV LIVES NEXTDOOR TO NOVAK AND RIVI AND HAS BEEN A FAN OF THE SHOW SINCE DAY ONE.

SEASON 01 : EPISODE 01

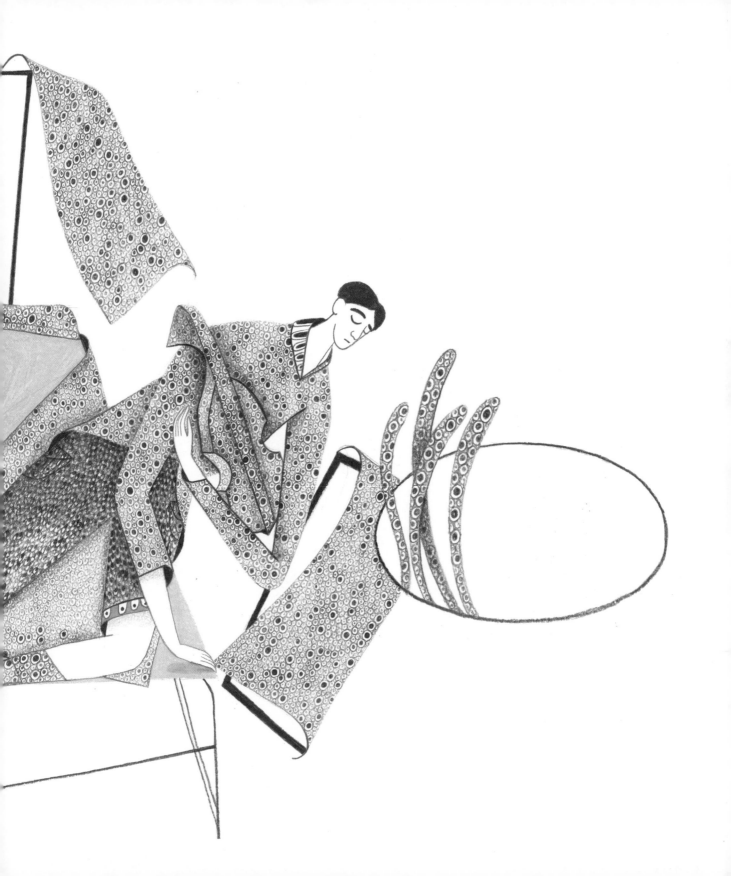

HE DOESN'T EVEN HAVE TO GO ONLINE, HE CAN LISTEN TO THE SHOW BY LEANING AGAINST HIS BEDROOM WALL.

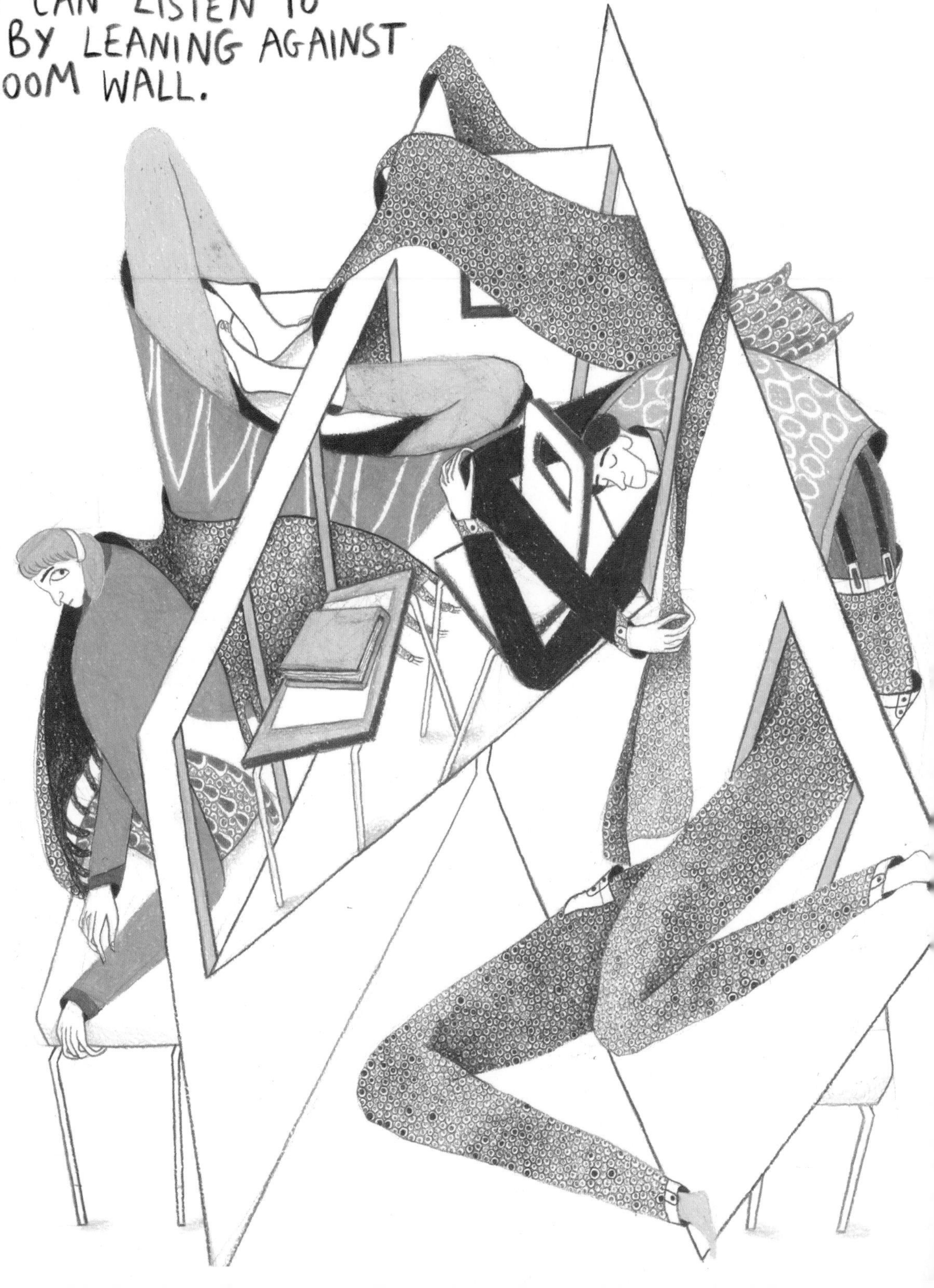

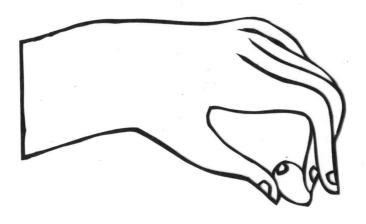

EACH BROADCAST BEGINS WITH
A SEGMENT TITLED: "THE GRAPE
DIARIES'.' THE VIEWERS ARE DARED
TO SWALLOW STRANDED GRAPES
THAT THEY FIND AROUND CAMPUS
AND SEND PICTURES OF THE
LOCATIONS TO NOVAK.

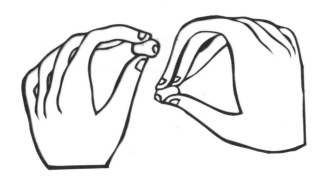

NOVAK MARKS THE LOCATIONS
ON A MAP AND PROMISES TO
RACE THROUGH THEM BAREFOOT
ONCE A HUNDRED GRAPES ARE
EATEN.

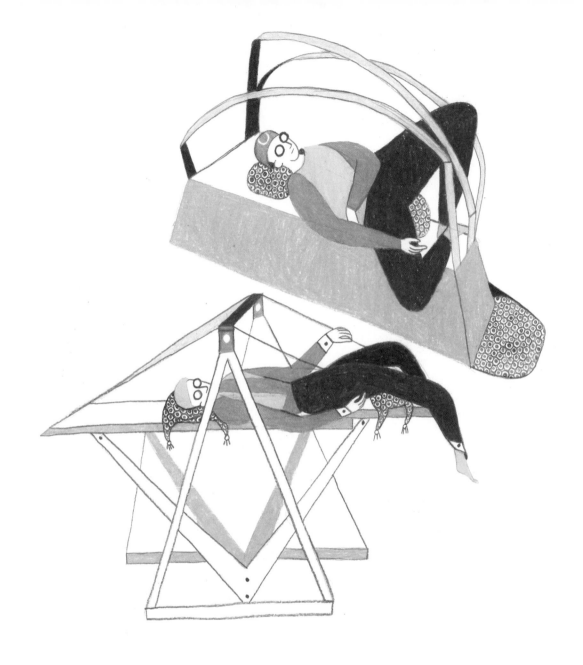

HER FANS LAY STREWN ACROSS
CAMPUS, CLUTCHING THEIR
ACHING BELLIES AND WAITING
FOR HER FOOTSTEPS.

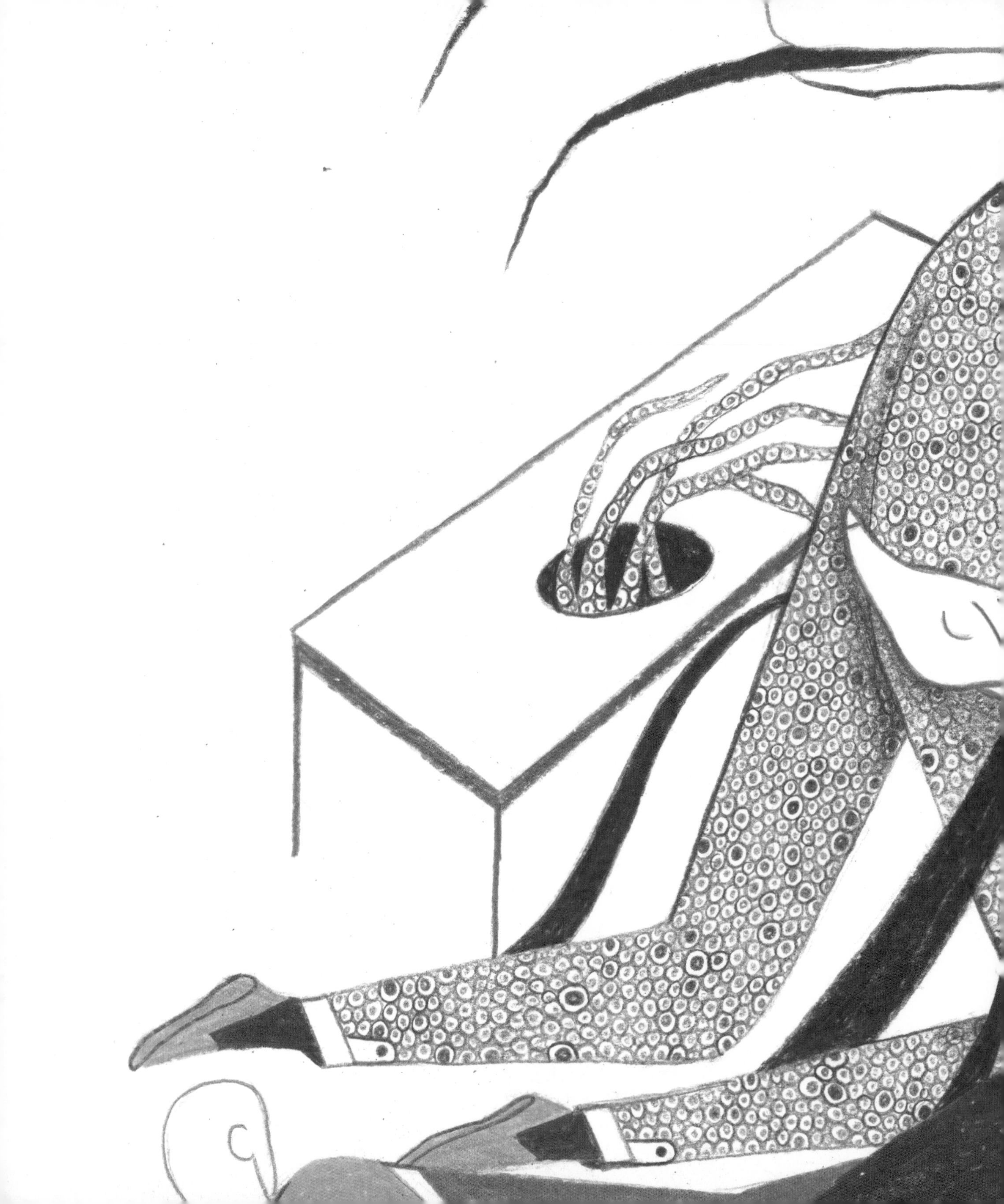

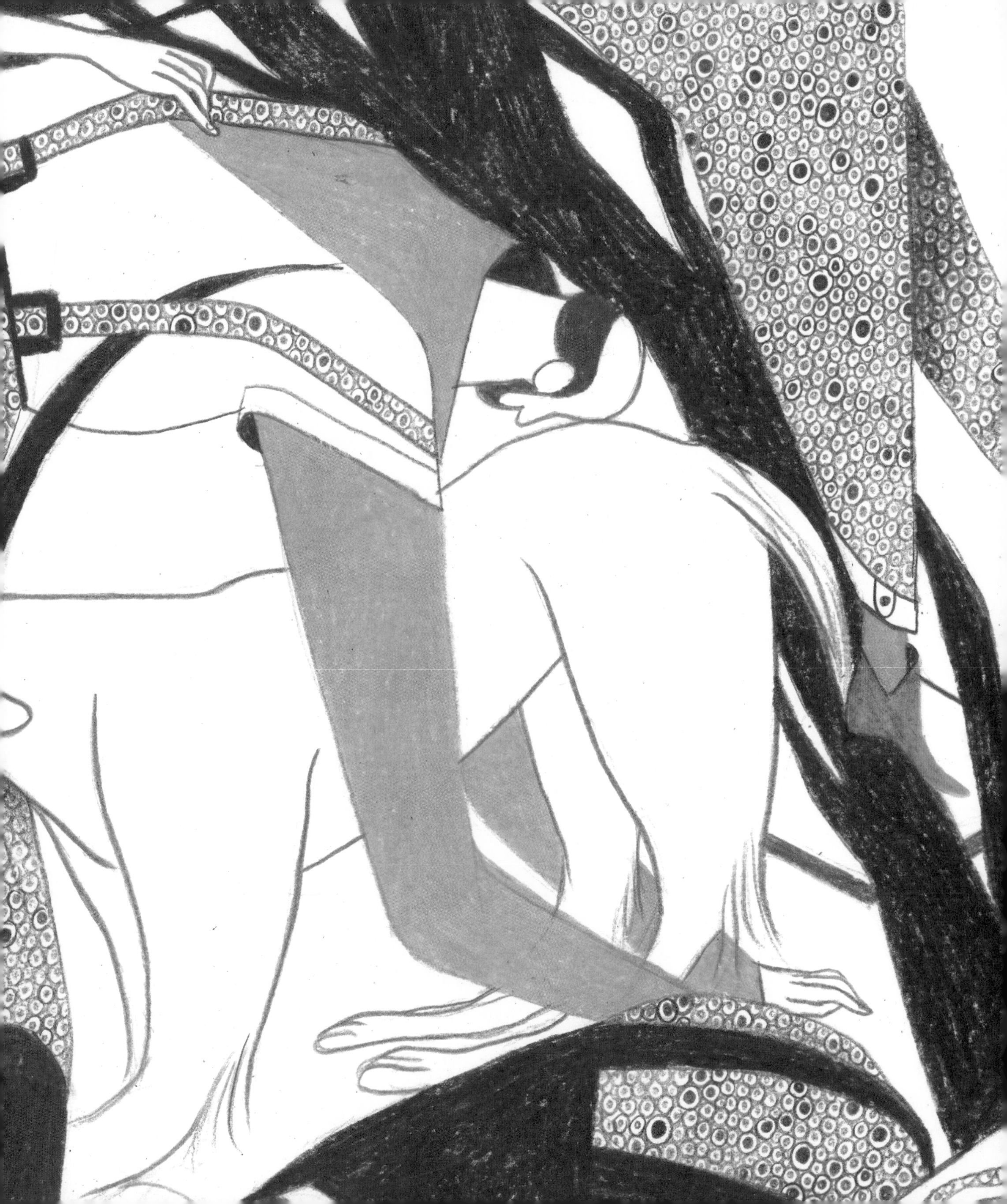

ON HIS WAY TO AND FROM SCHOOL, YAKOV SEARCHES FOR GRAPES ON THE GROUND.

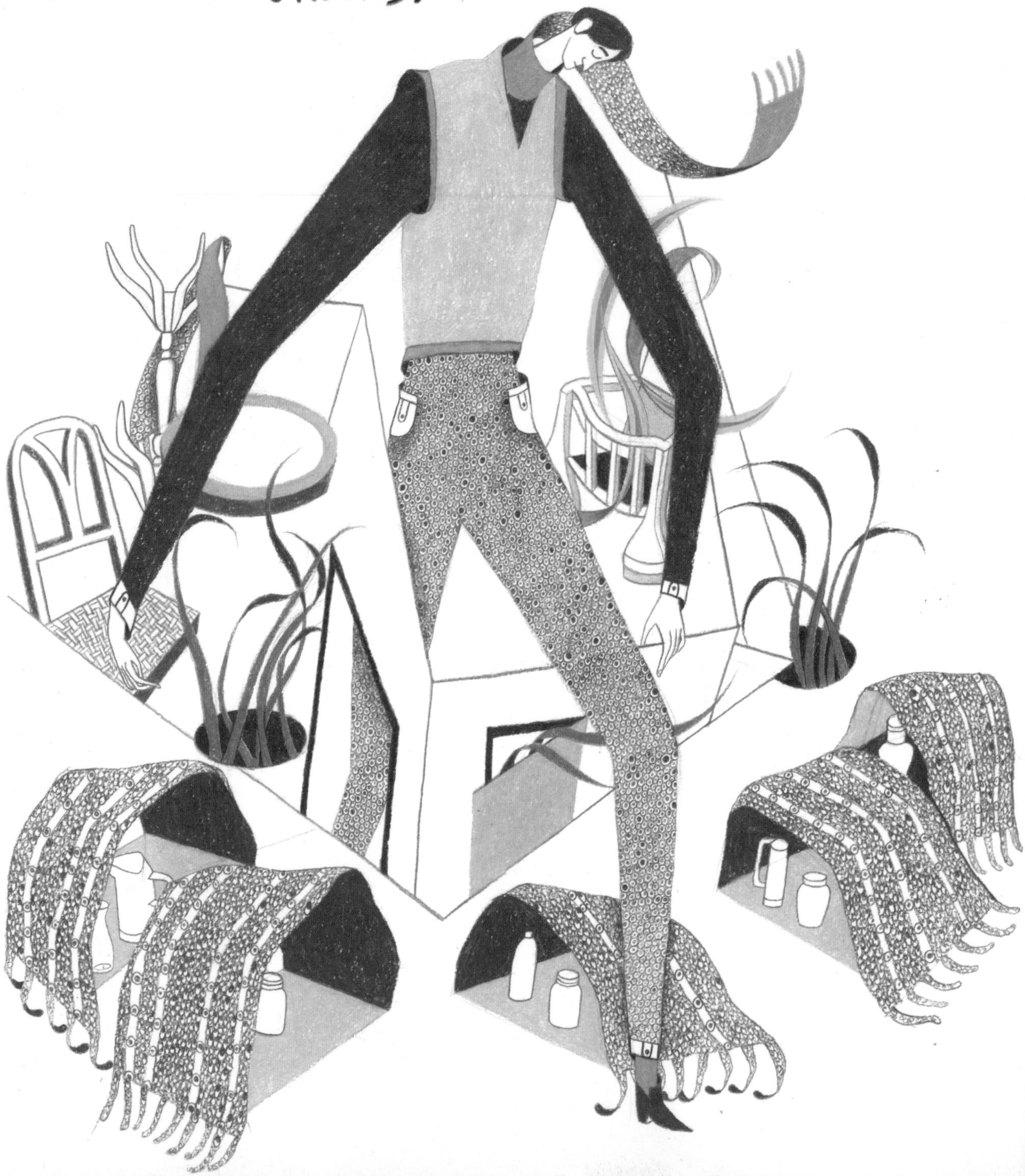

AT THE SAME TIME, HE
DREADS HER LEAVING HER ROOM.

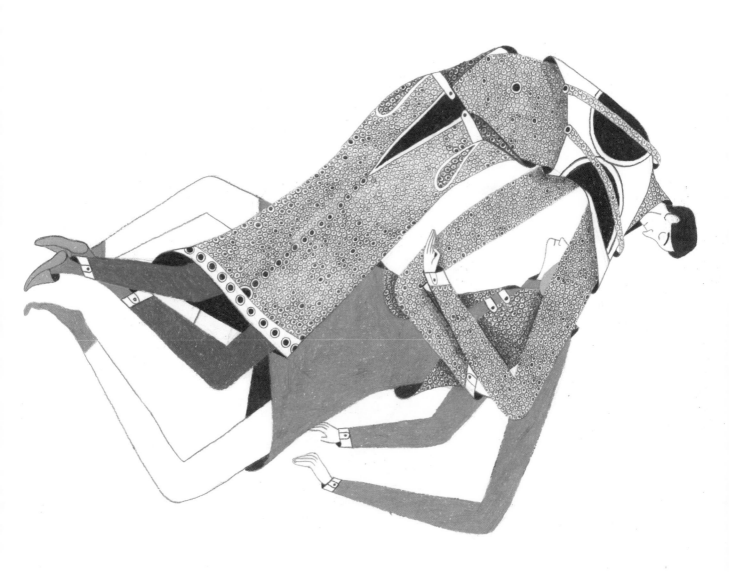

AS THOUGH THE ONLY WAY OUT
IS THROUGH HIS.

PILES OF HIS UNWASHED DISHES
LINE THE WALLS OF HIS DORM,

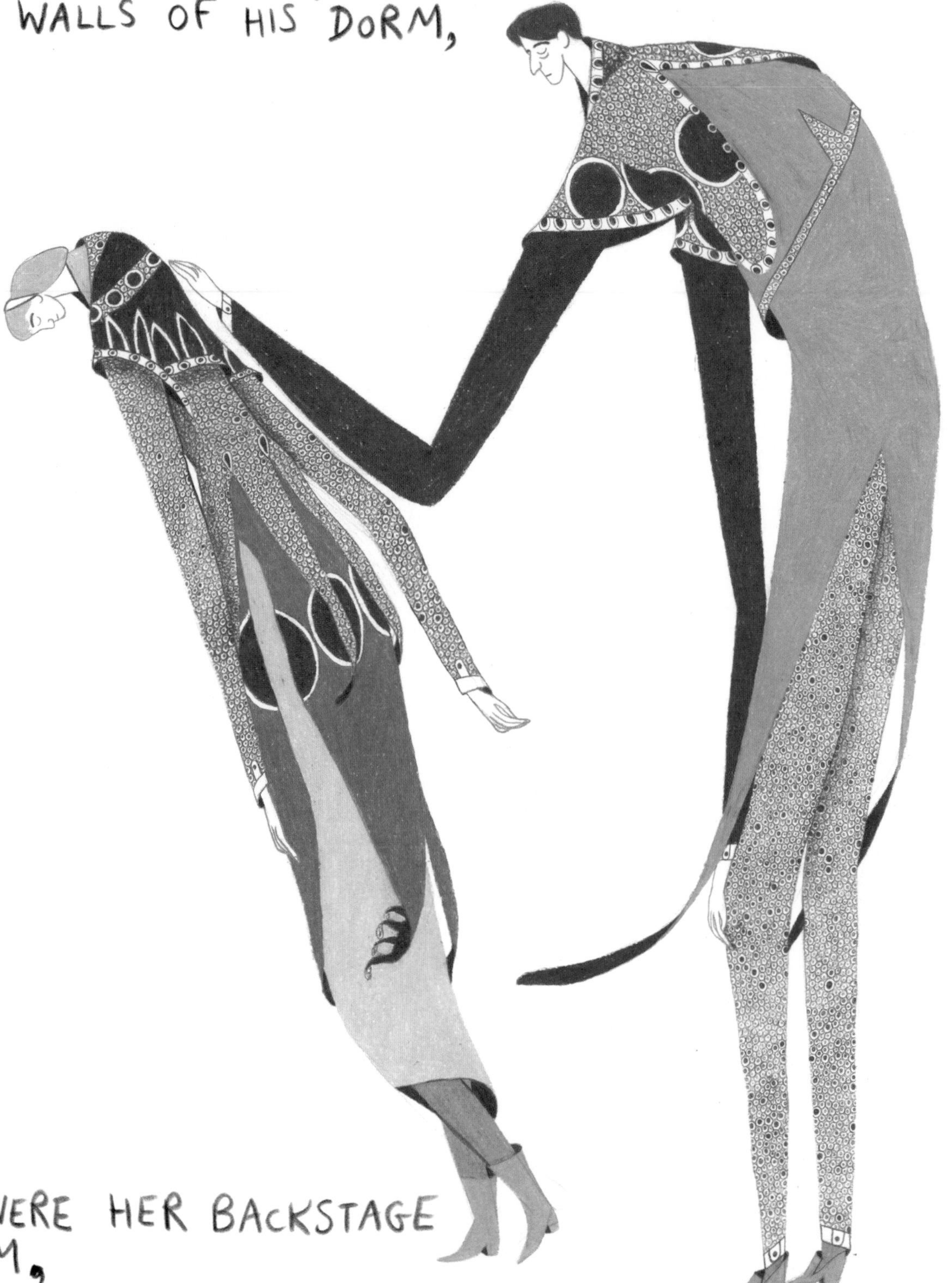

AS IF IT WERE HER BACKSTAGE
PROP ROOM,

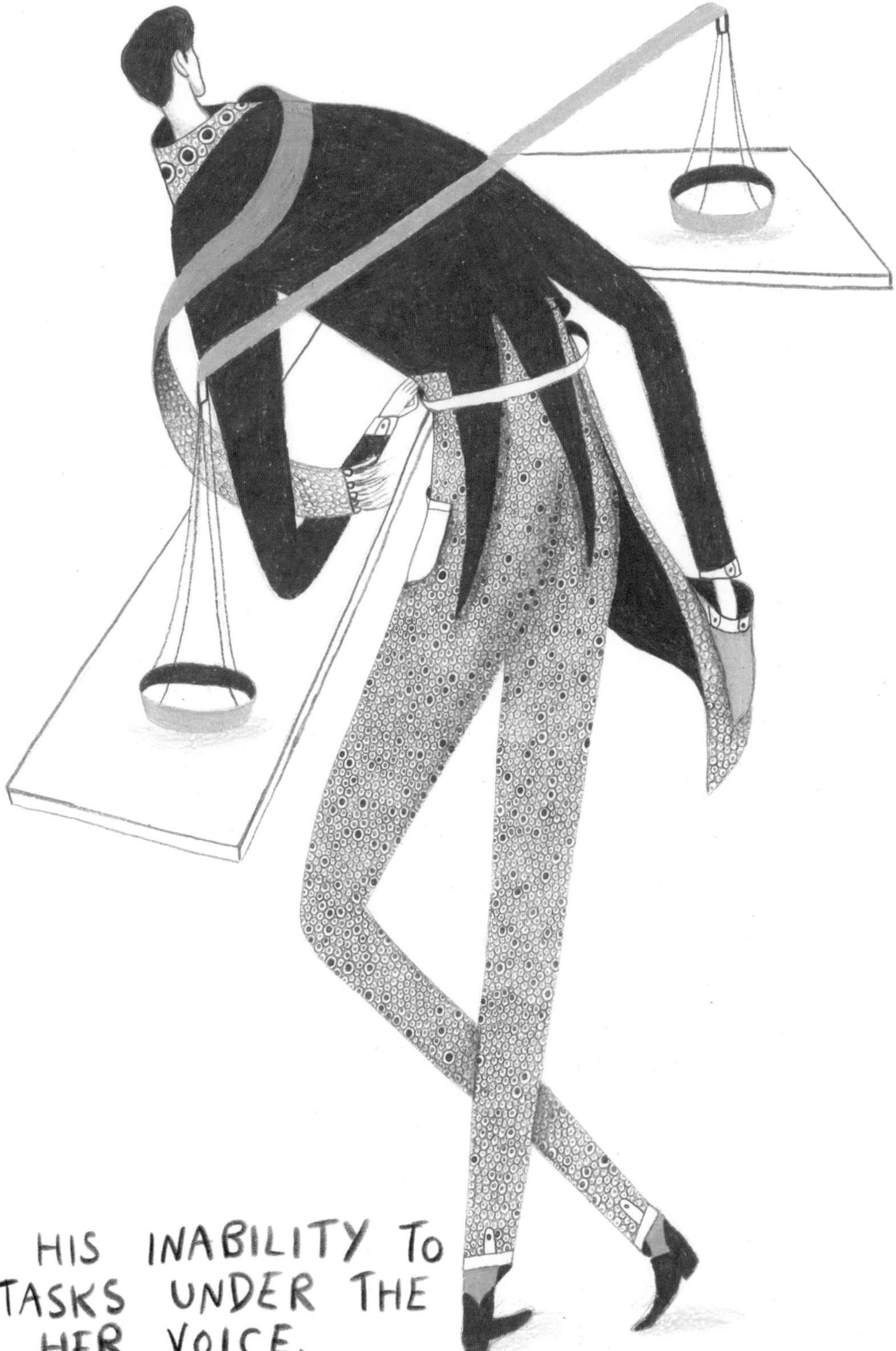

BETRAYING HIS INABILITY TO
PERFORM TASKS UNDER THE
SPELL OF HER VOICE.

ALL THE BOOKS HE HELD WHEN
HE RETURNED FROM SCHOOL AND
FROZE IN THE DOORWAY, LISTENING—

—THOSE HE COULD NEVER READ

FEARING THAT BY DOING SO,
HE WOULD DISASSOCIATE
THE SOUND OF RUNNING WATER
FROM THEIR WEIGHT ON HIS BACK.

THEY WERE BOOKS ABOUT A
LOVE FORGED IN CHILDHOOD.
HE KNEW THAT FROM
READING THE BACK COVER.

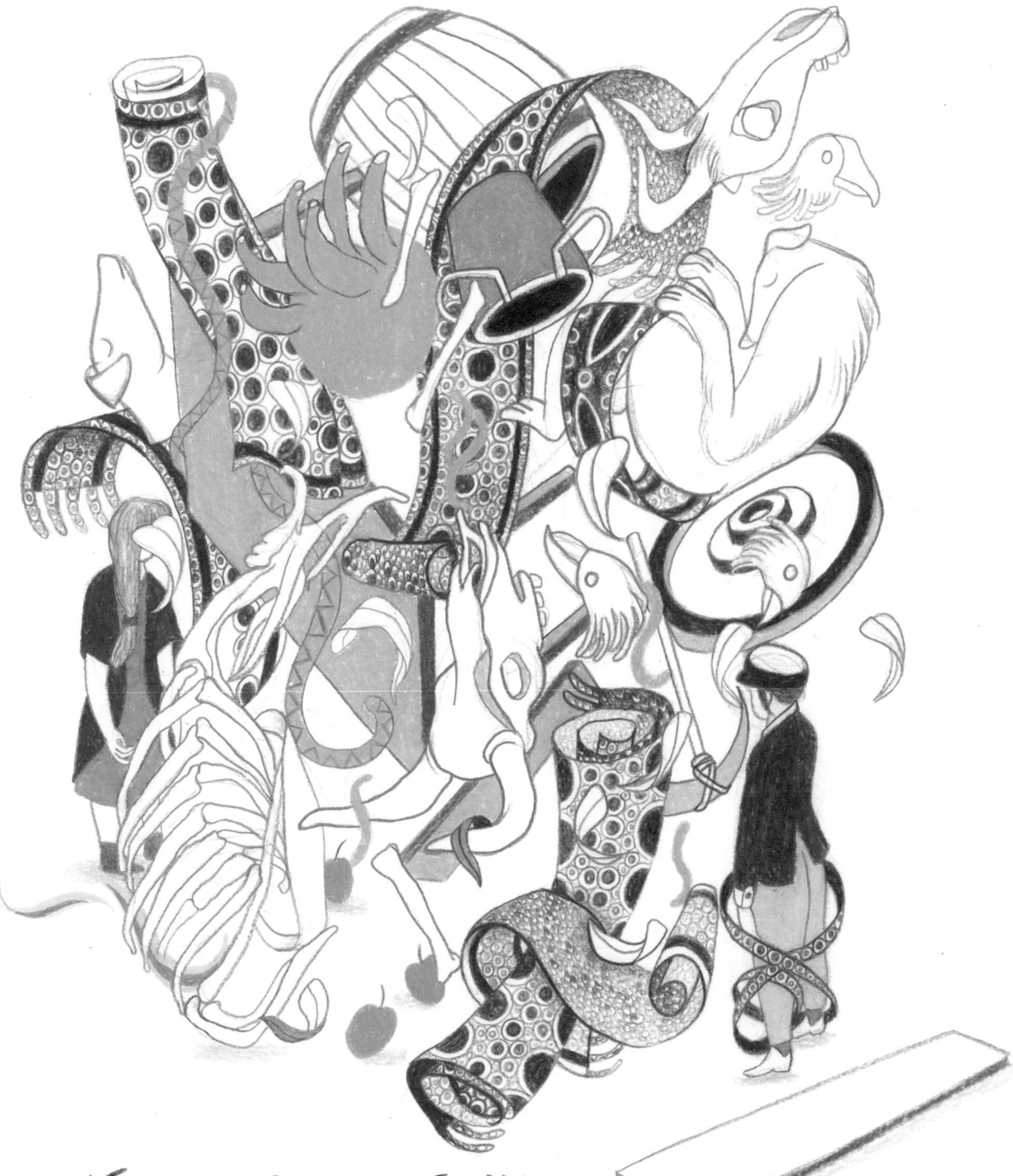

IT WAS ENOUGH TO MAKE
THOSE BOOKS HIS FAVORITES.

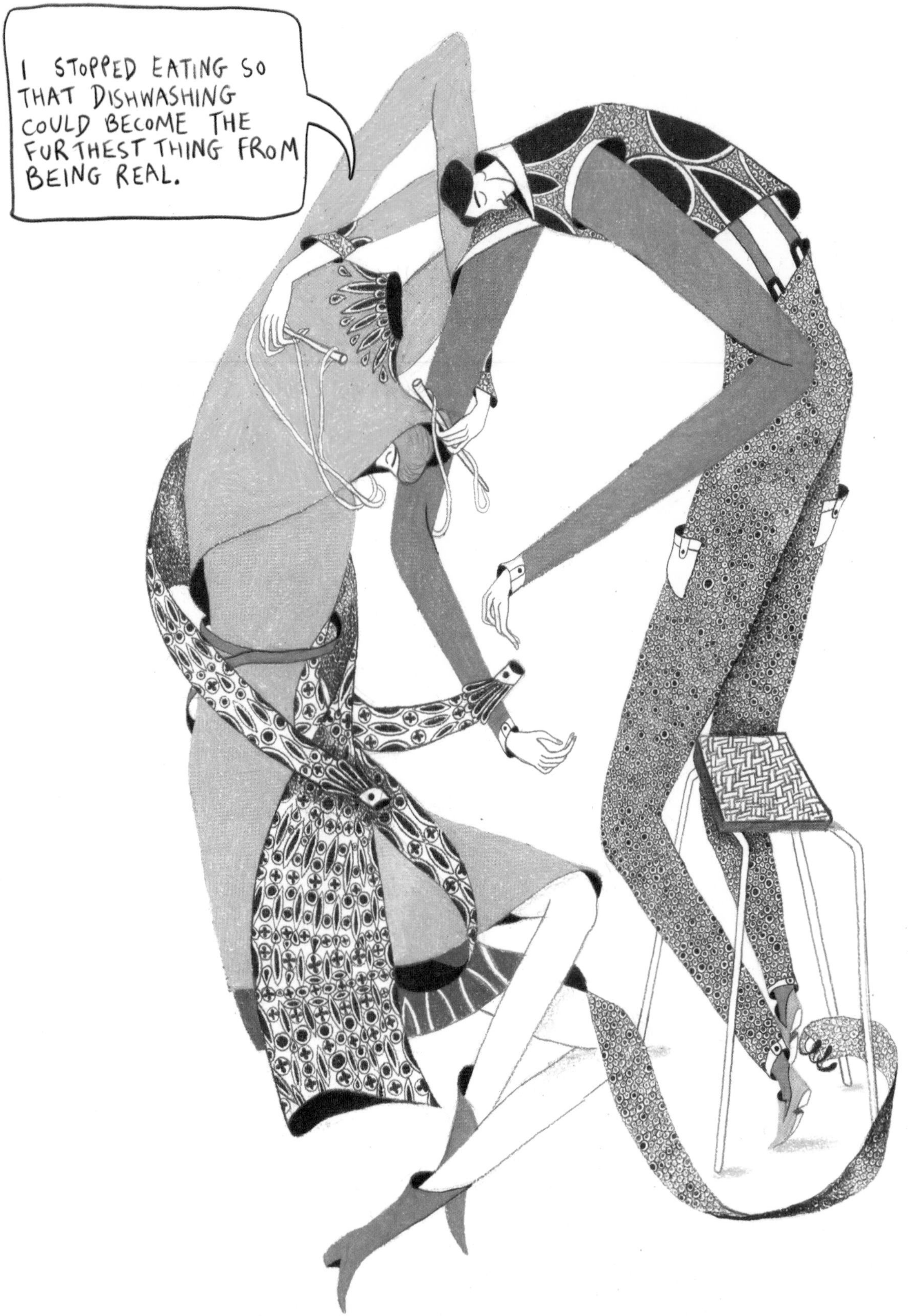
I STOPPED EATING SO THAT DISHWASHING COULD BECOME THE FURTHEST THING FROM BEING REAL.

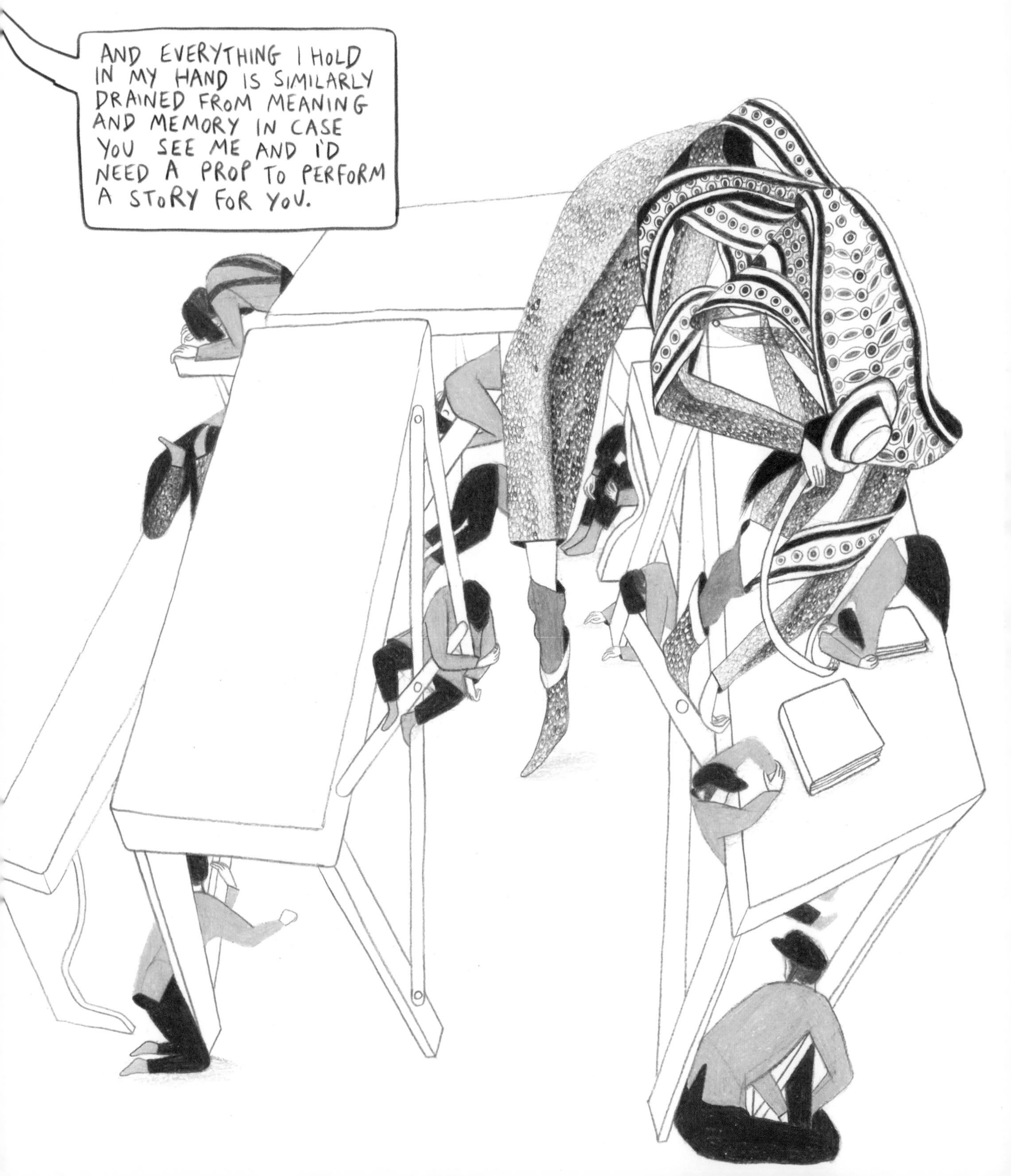
AND EVERYTHING I HOLD IN MY HAND IS SIMILARLY DRAINED FROM MEANING AND MEMORY IN CASE YOU SEE ME AND I'D NEED A PROP TO PERFORM A STORY FOR YOU.

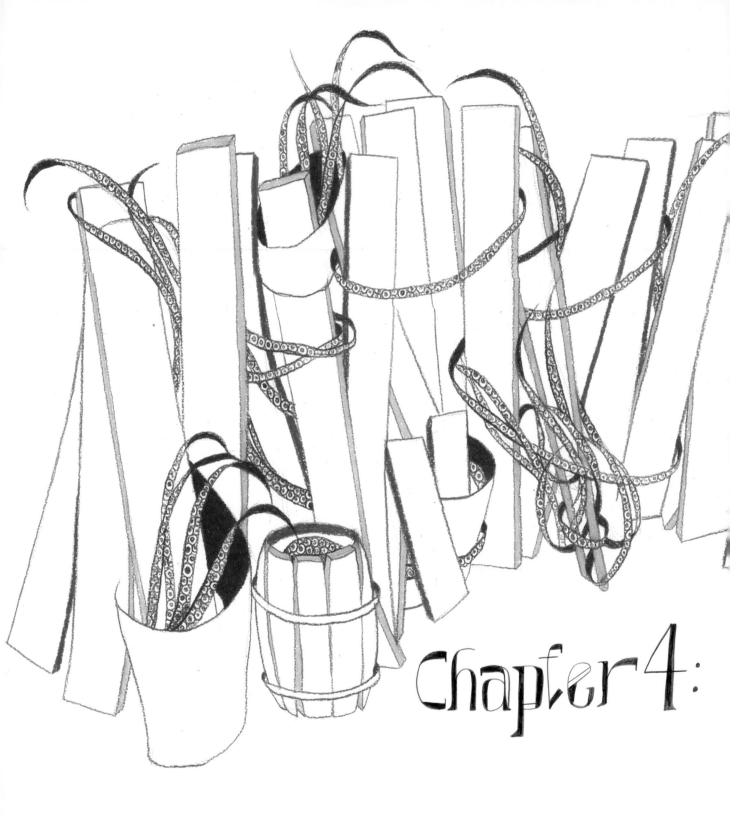

Chapter 4:

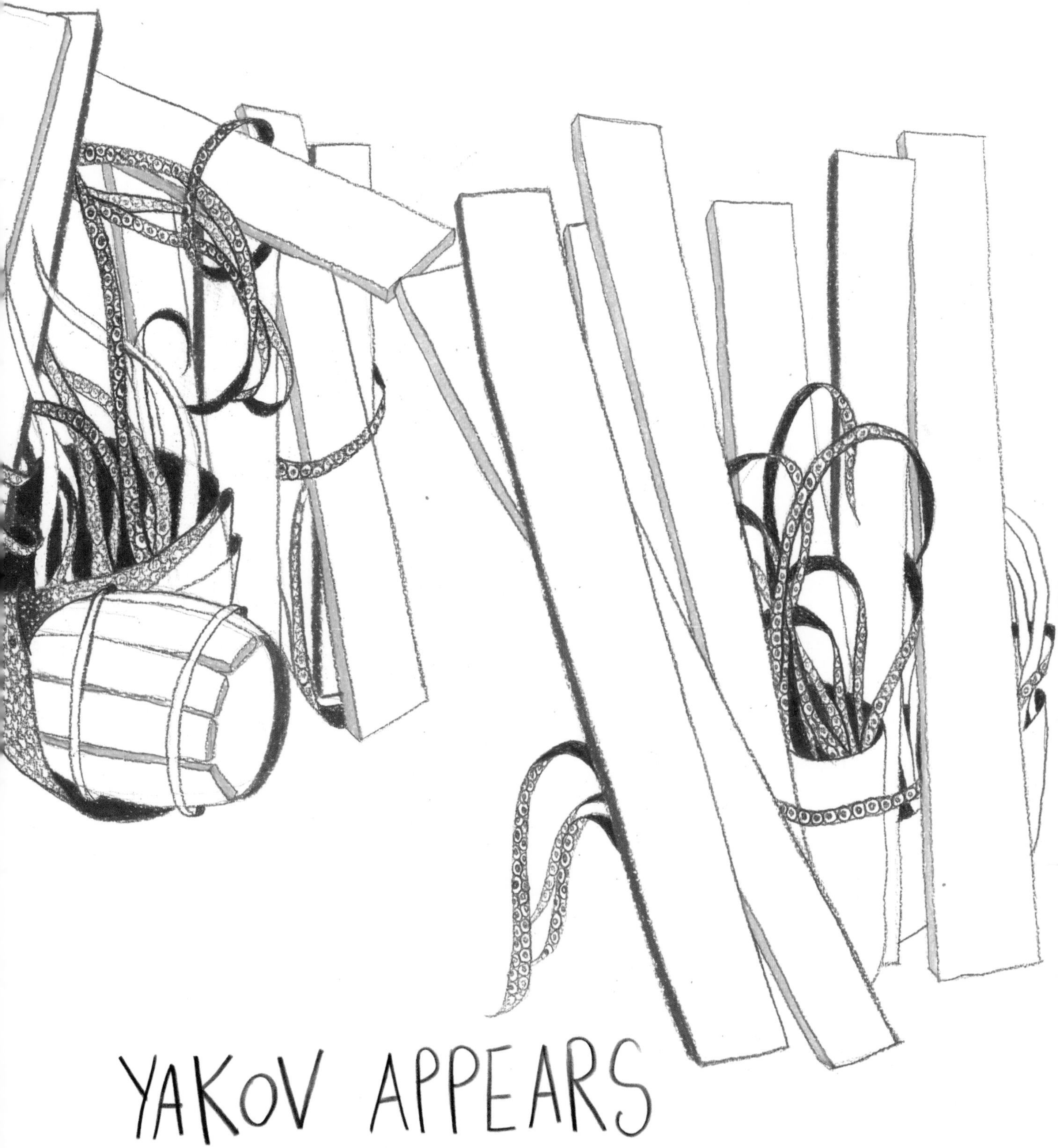

YAKOV APPEARS

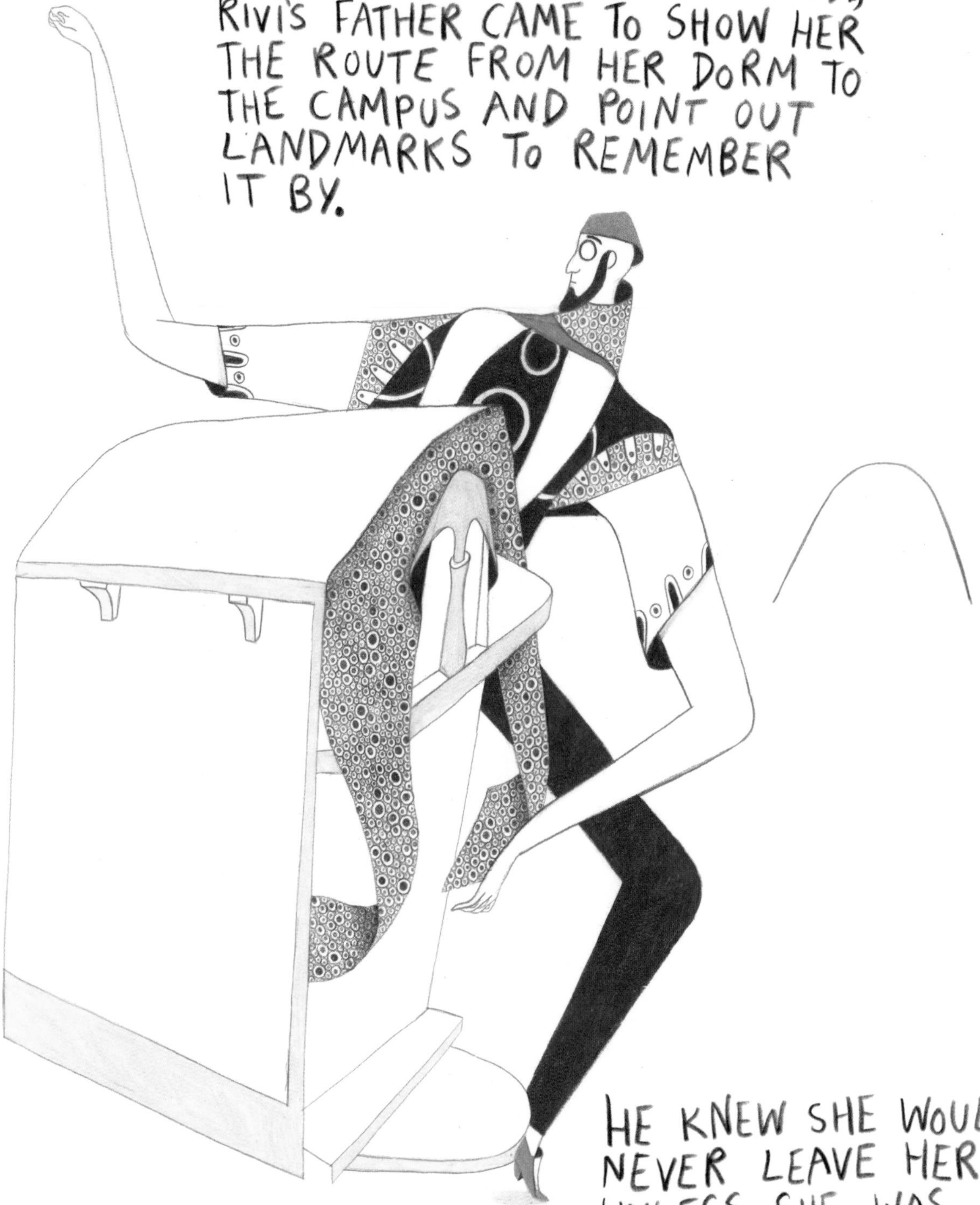
THE DAY BEFORE SCHOOL STARTED, RIVI'S FATHER CAME TO SHOW HER THE ROUTE FROM HER DORM TO THE CAMPUS AND POINT OUT LANDMARKS TO REMEMBER IT BY.
HE KNEW SHE WOULD NEVER LEAVE HER ROOM UNLESS SHE WAS ABSOLUTELY CERTAIN OF WHERE SHE WAS GOING.

RIVI TRIED TO PAY ATTENTION TO HER FATHER'S DIRECTIONS BY MIMICKING HIS MOVEMENTS BUT THEY ONLY CARRIED HER AWAY FROM HIS WORDS.

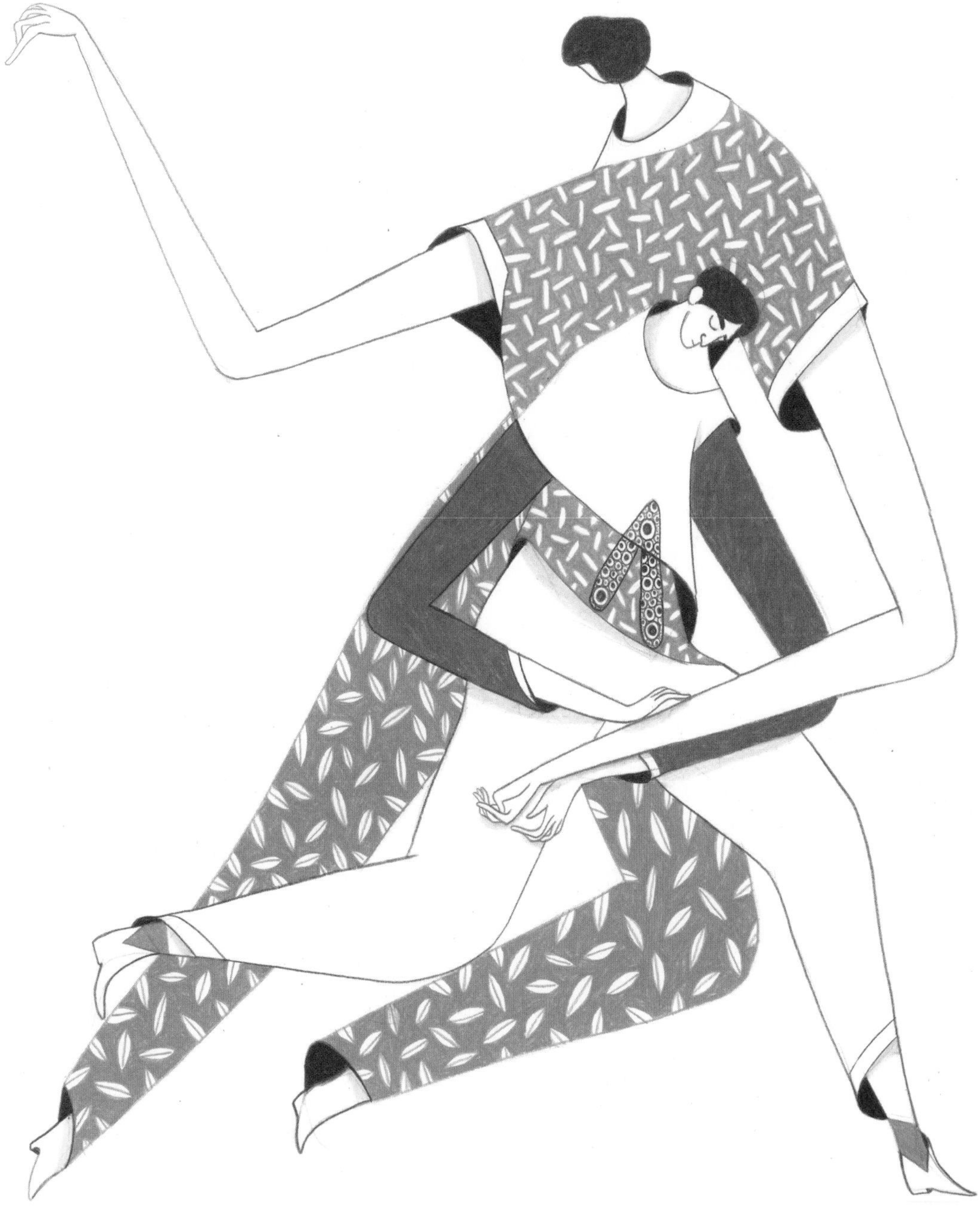

SHE WAS SHOWING THE WAY TO SOMEONE ELSE WHO BEGAN FOLLOWING THEM.

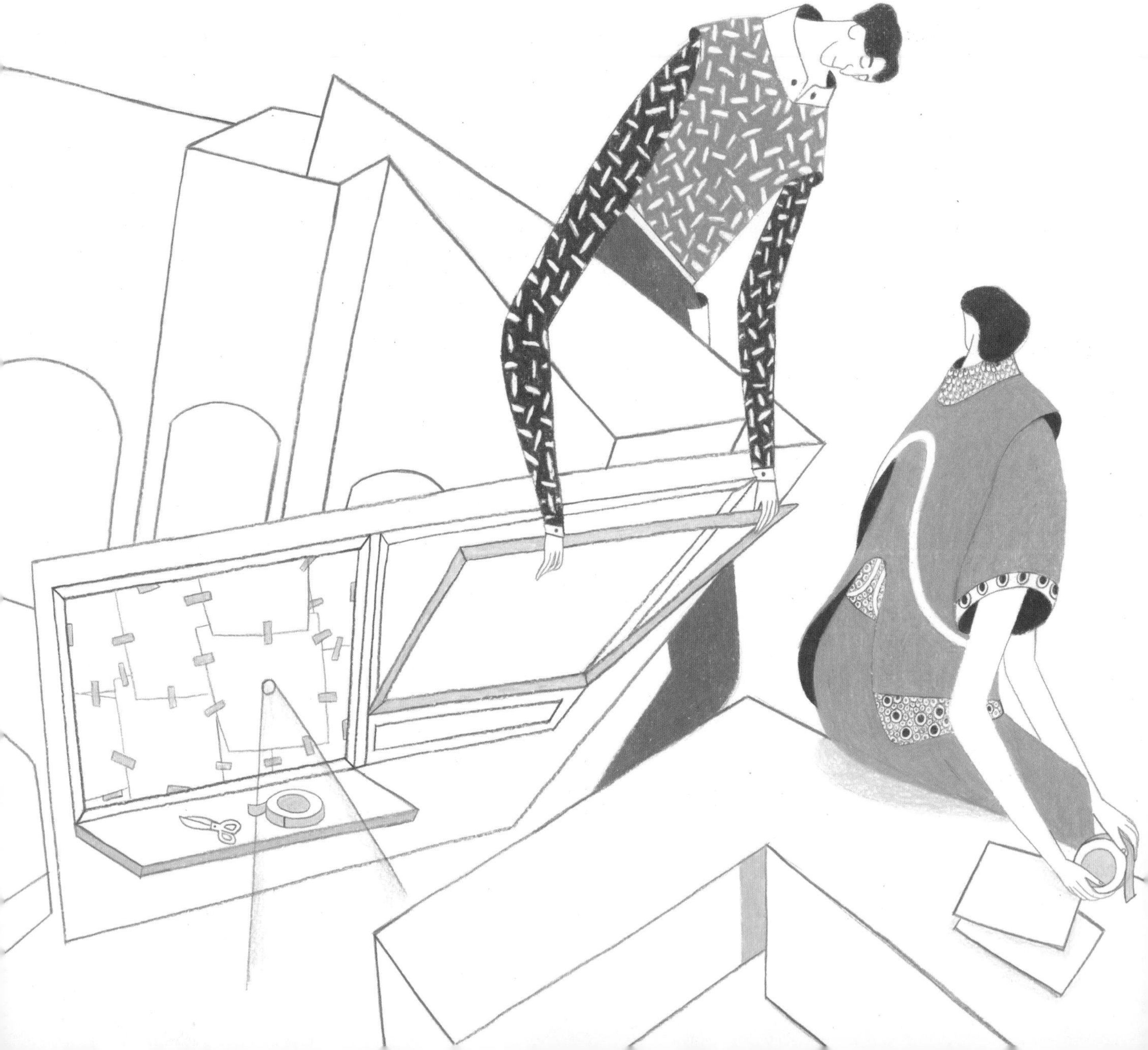

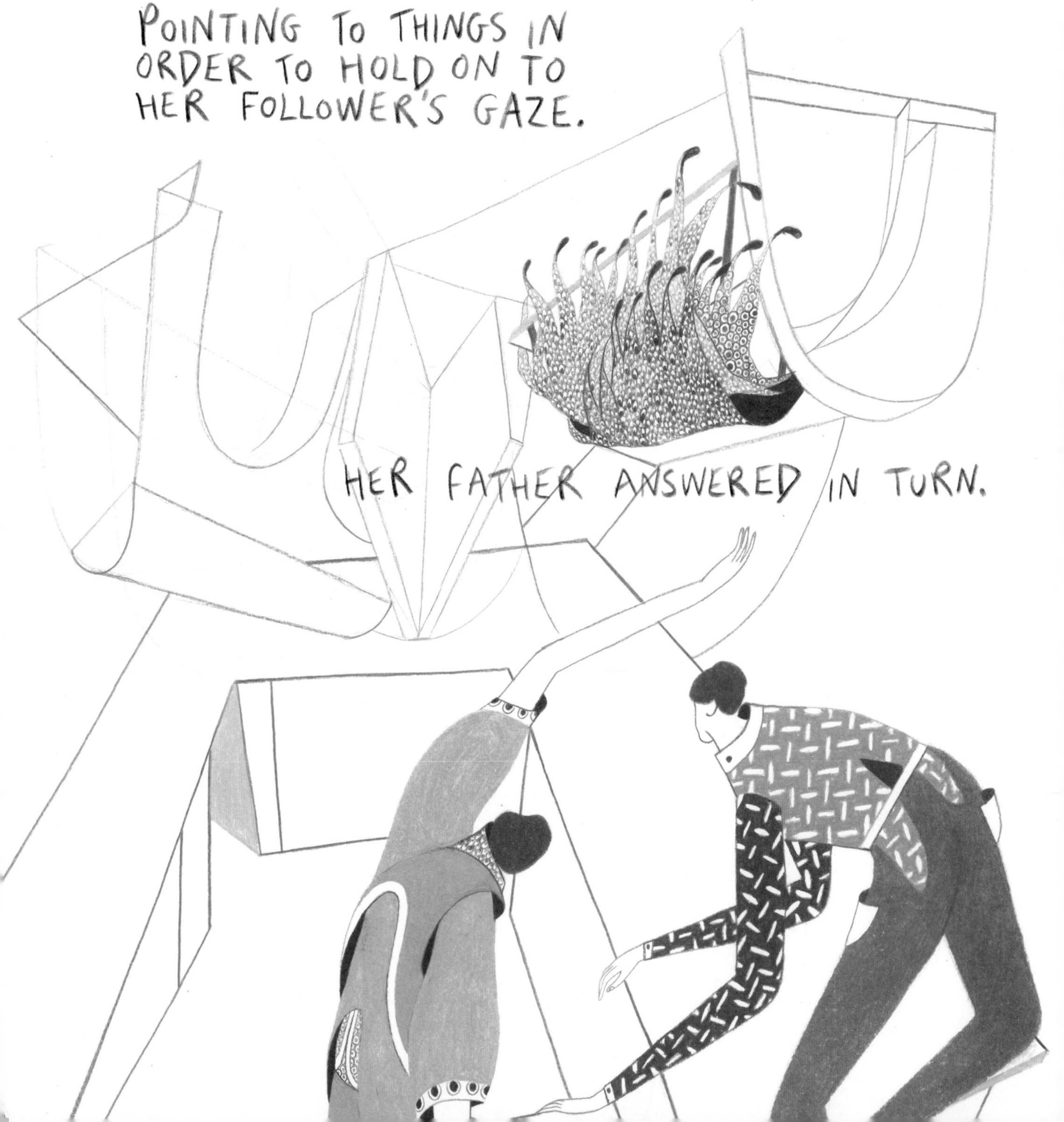
POINTING TO THINGS IN ORDER TO HOLD ON TO HER FOLLOWER'S GAZE.
HER FATHER ANSWERED IN TURN.

SHE DARED NOT LOOK BEHIND
HER AT THE STRANGER BECAUSE
SHE COULD ONLY IMAGINE HIM
AS YAKOV...

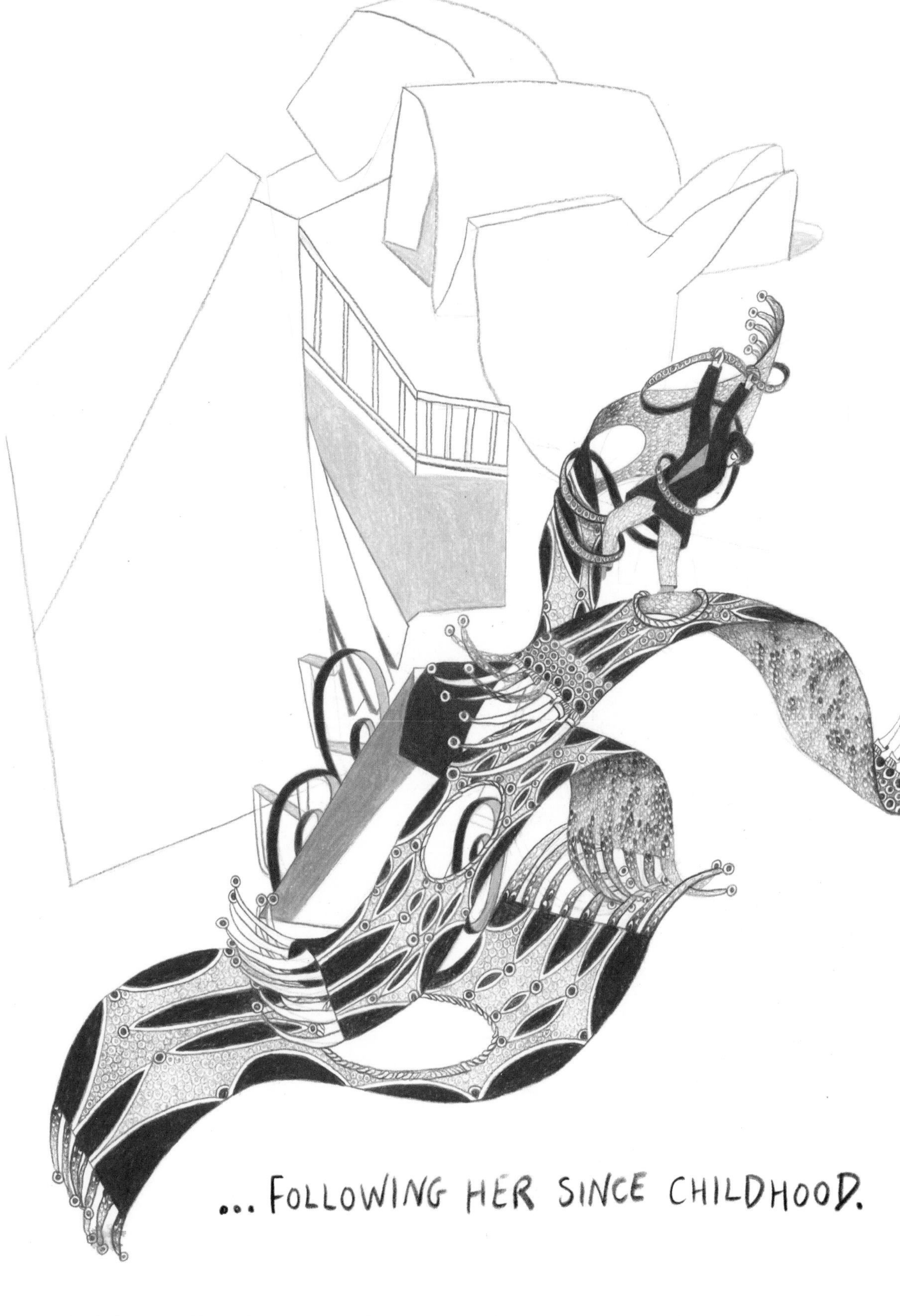
...FOLLOWING HER SINCE CHILDHOOD.

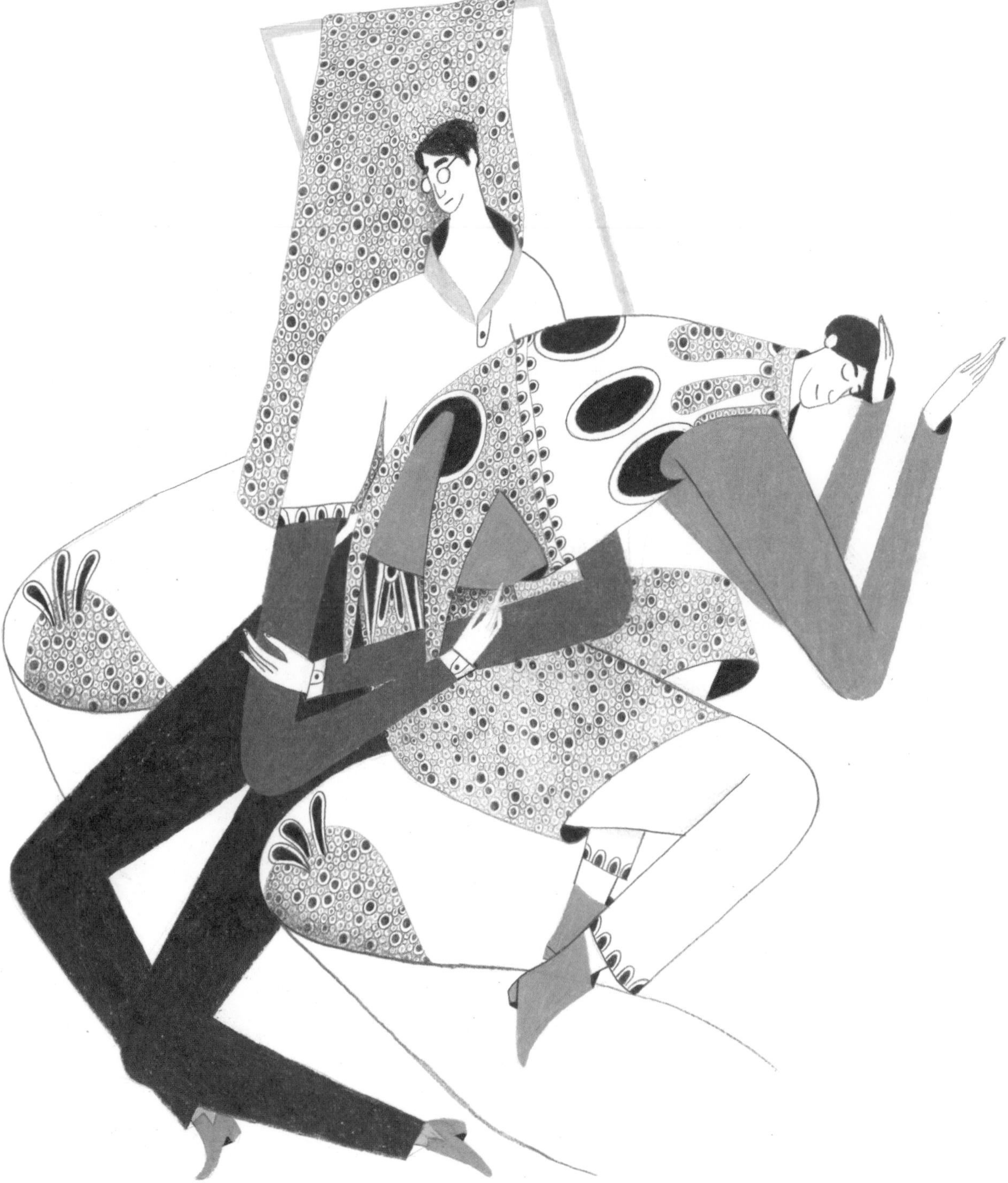

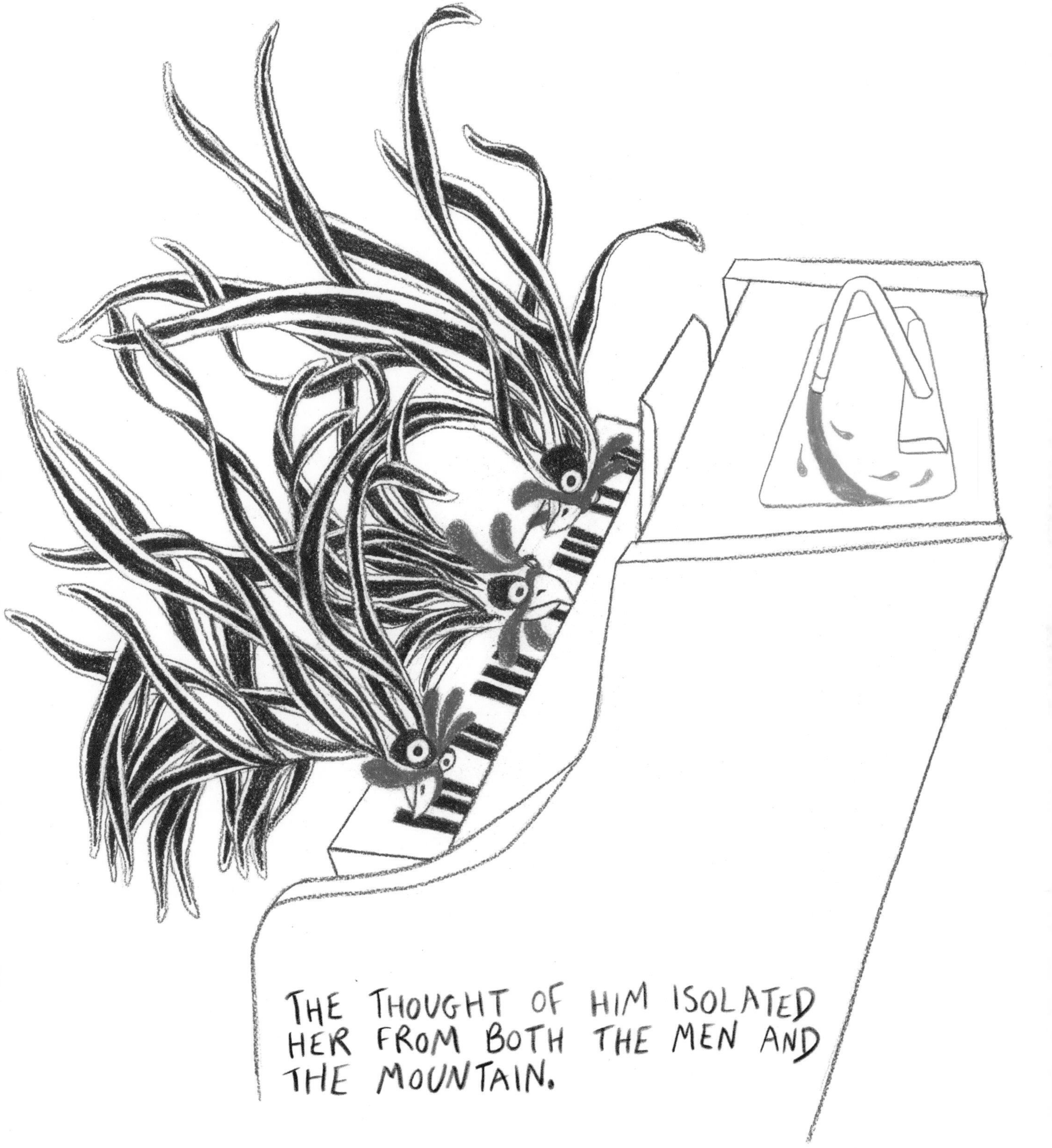
THE THOUGHT OF HIM ISOLATED HER FROM BOTH THE MEN AND THE MOUNTAIN.

ELEVATORS KICKED THE STUDENTS OUT TO SEA.

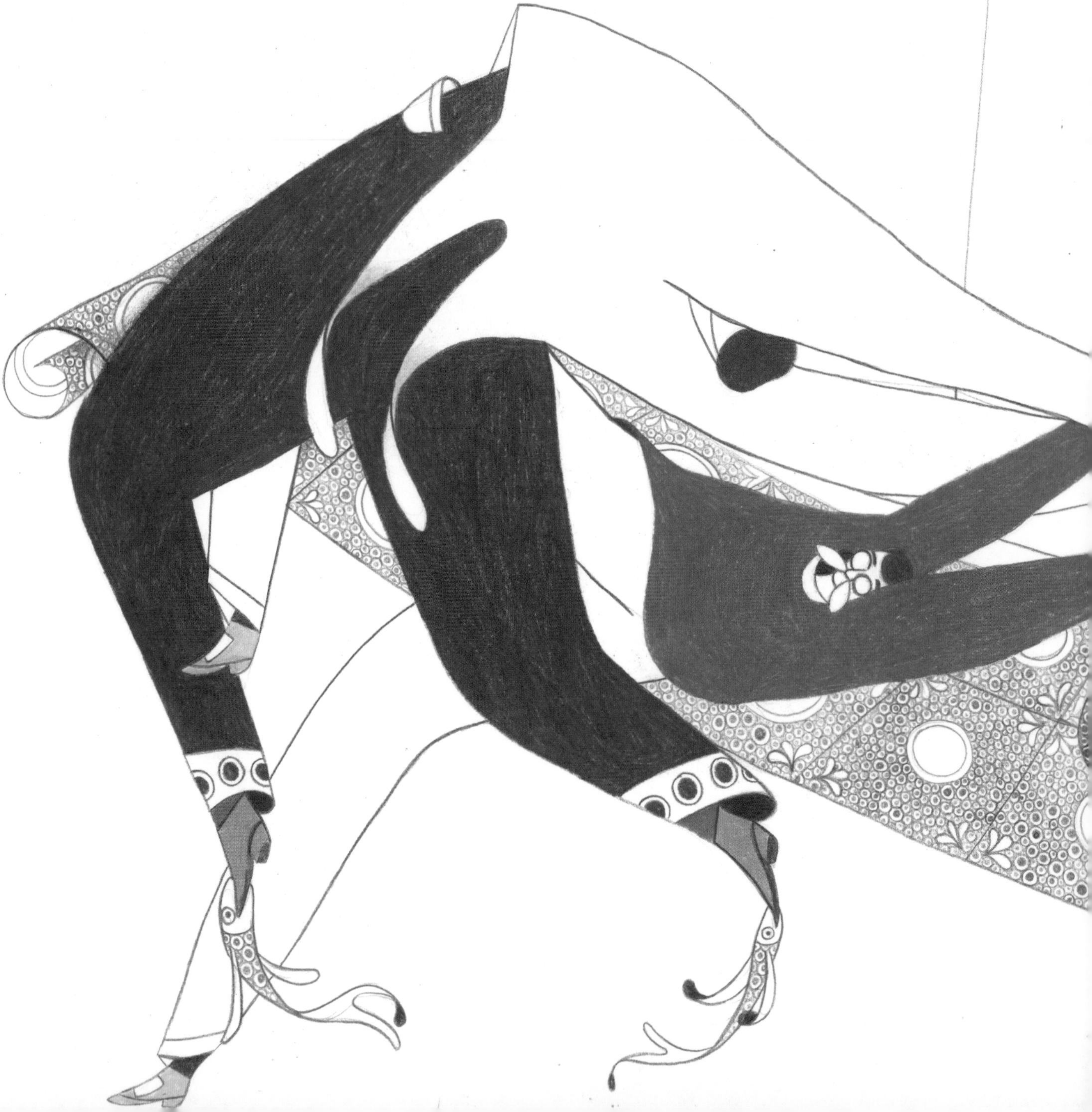

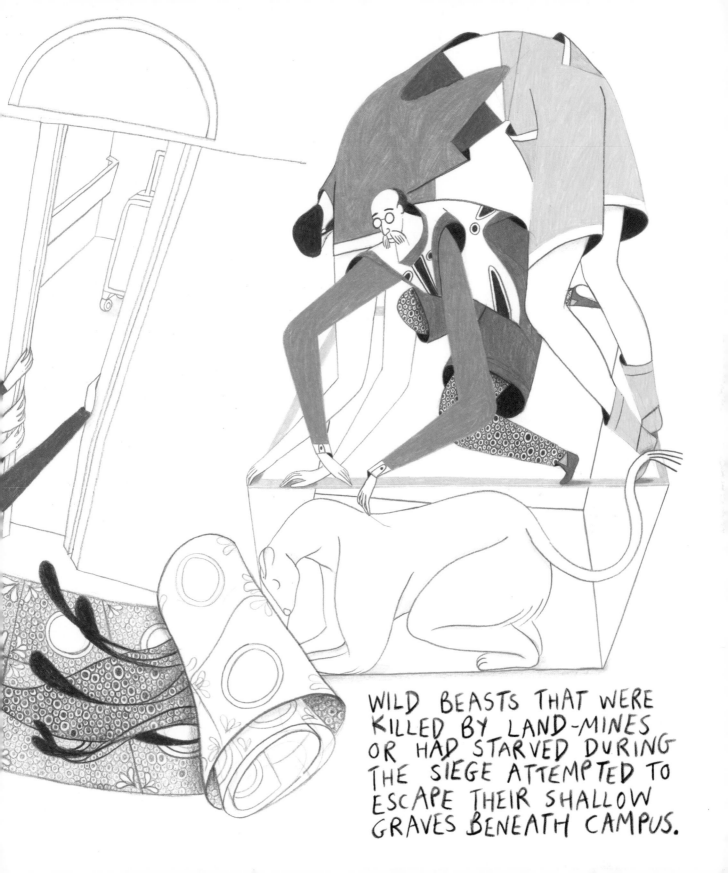

WILD BEASTS THAT WERE
KILLED BY LAND-MINES
OR HAD STARVED DURING
THE SIEGE ATTEMPTED TO
ESCAPE THEIR SHALLOW
GRAVES BENEATH CAMPUS.

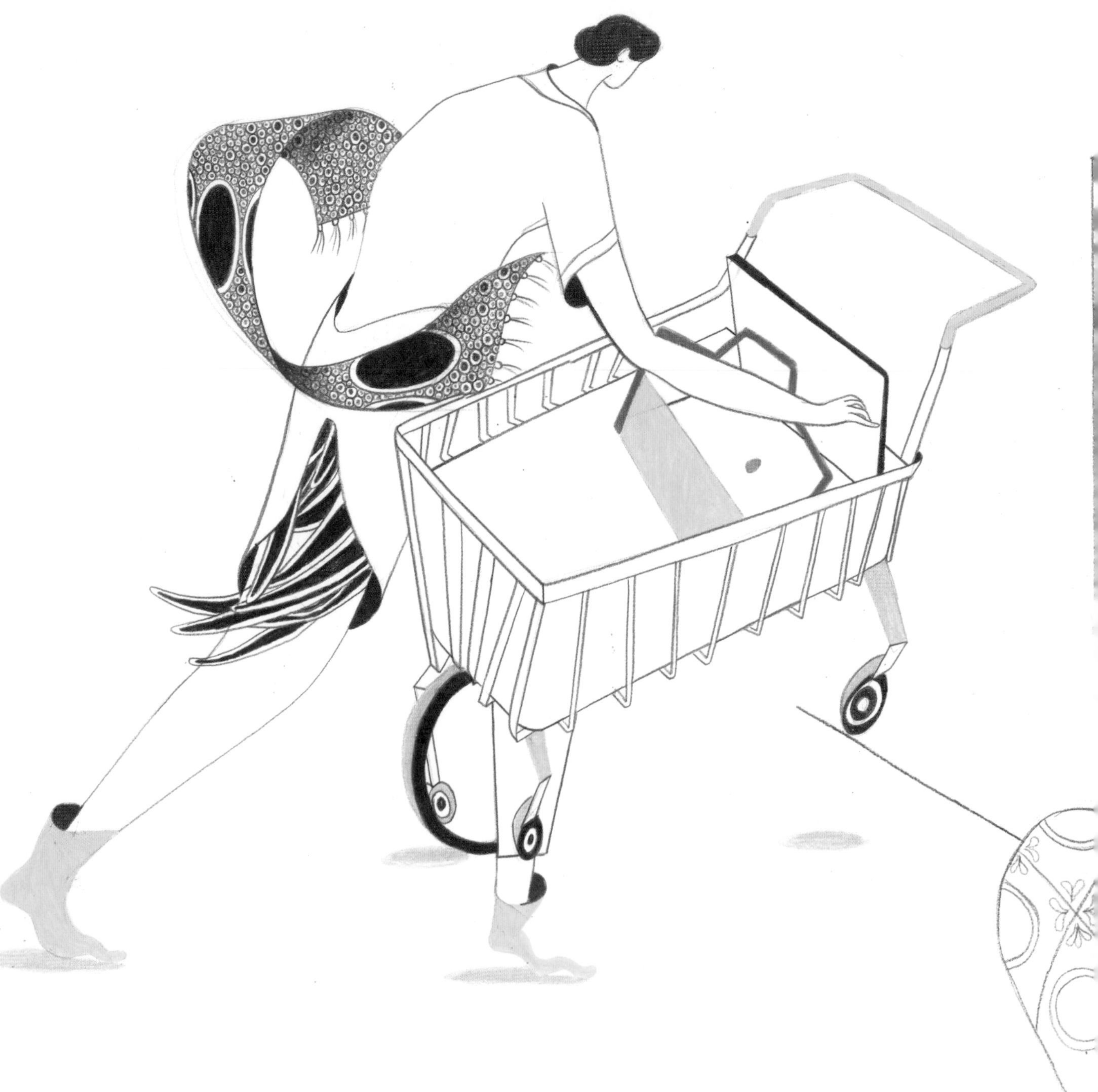

RIVI PLACED A SINGLE GRAPE
IN A DESERTED SHOPPING CART.

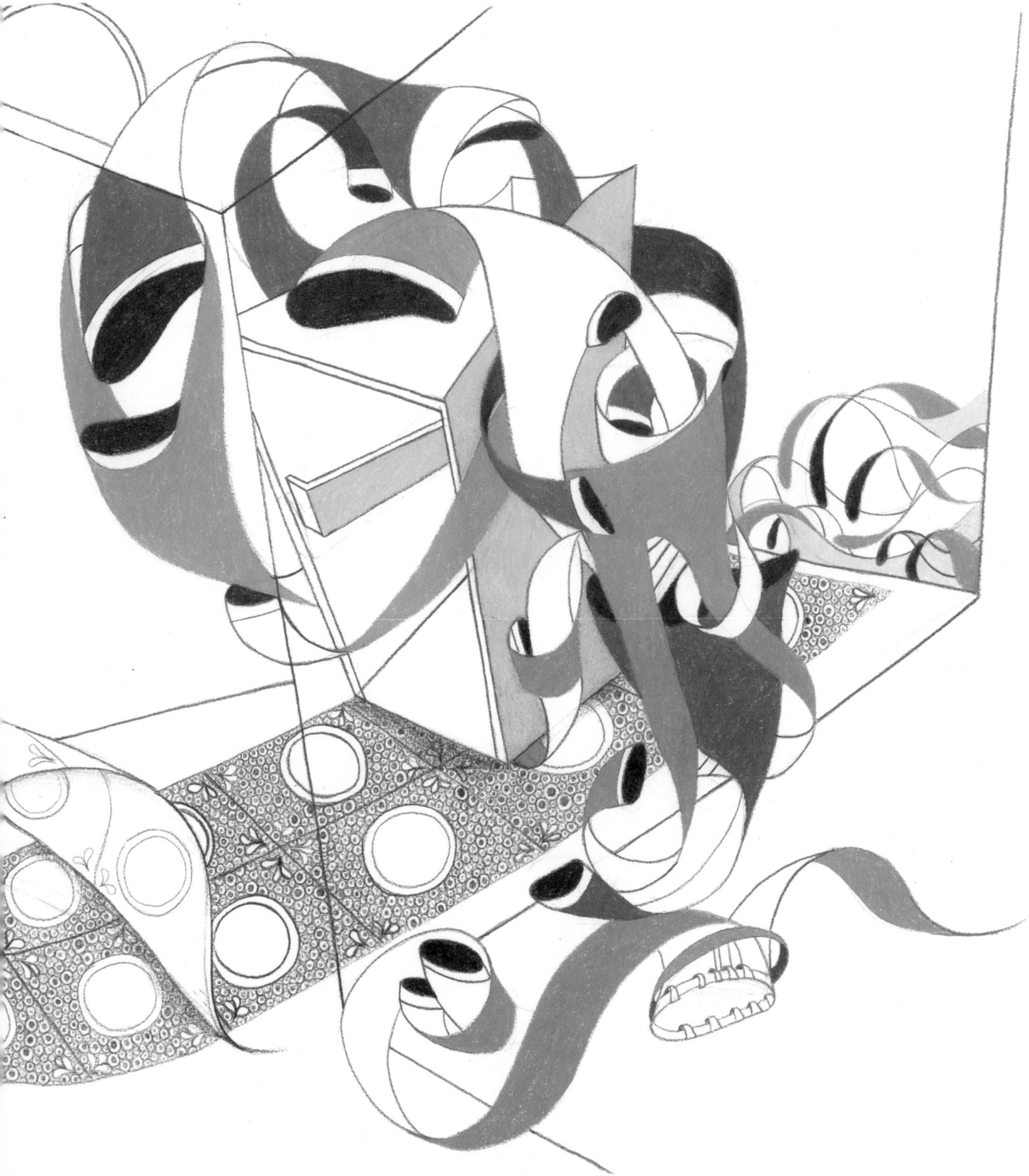

HER FATHER HADN'T NOTICED HER DISAPPEAR BEHIND HIM.

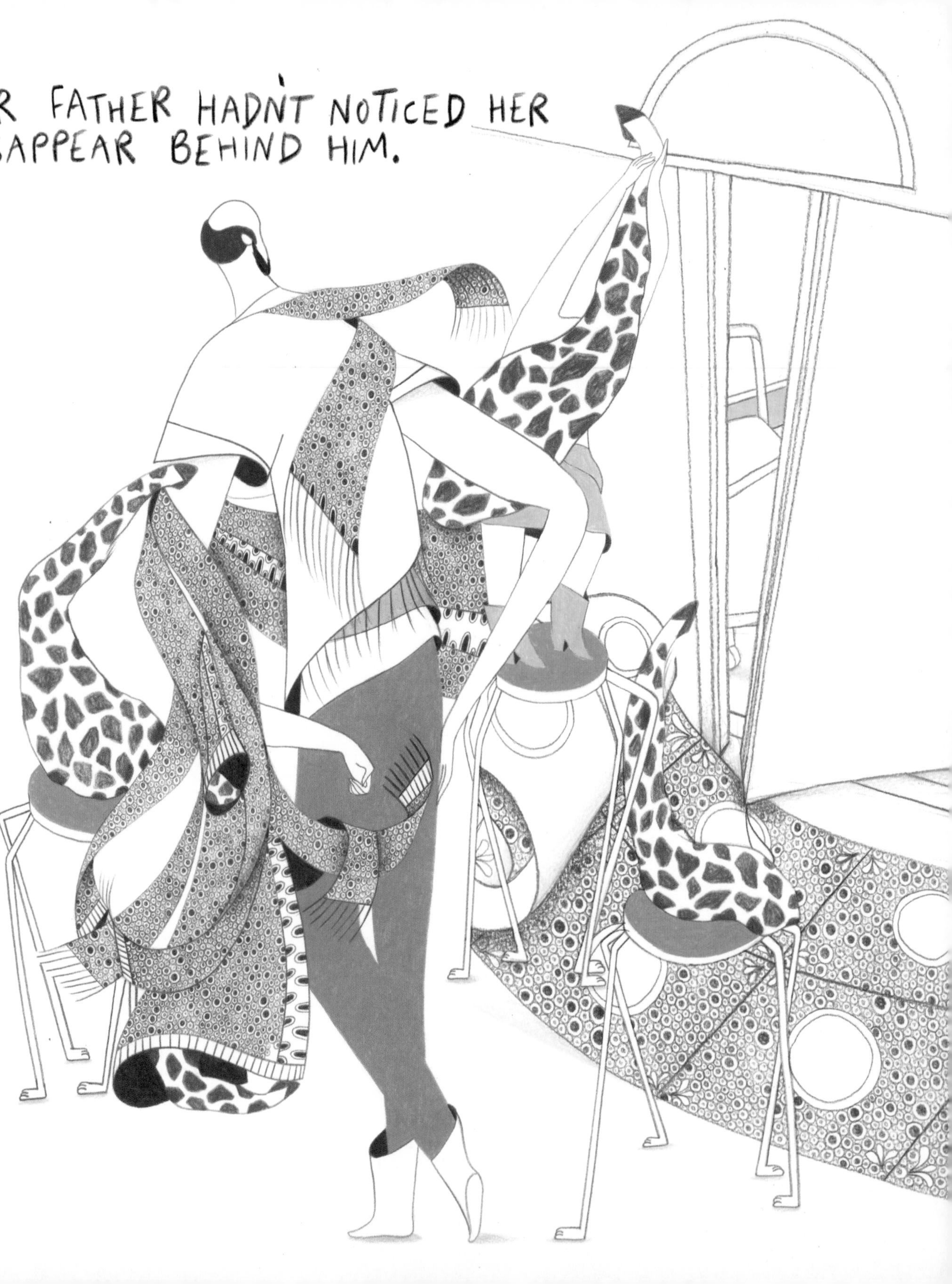

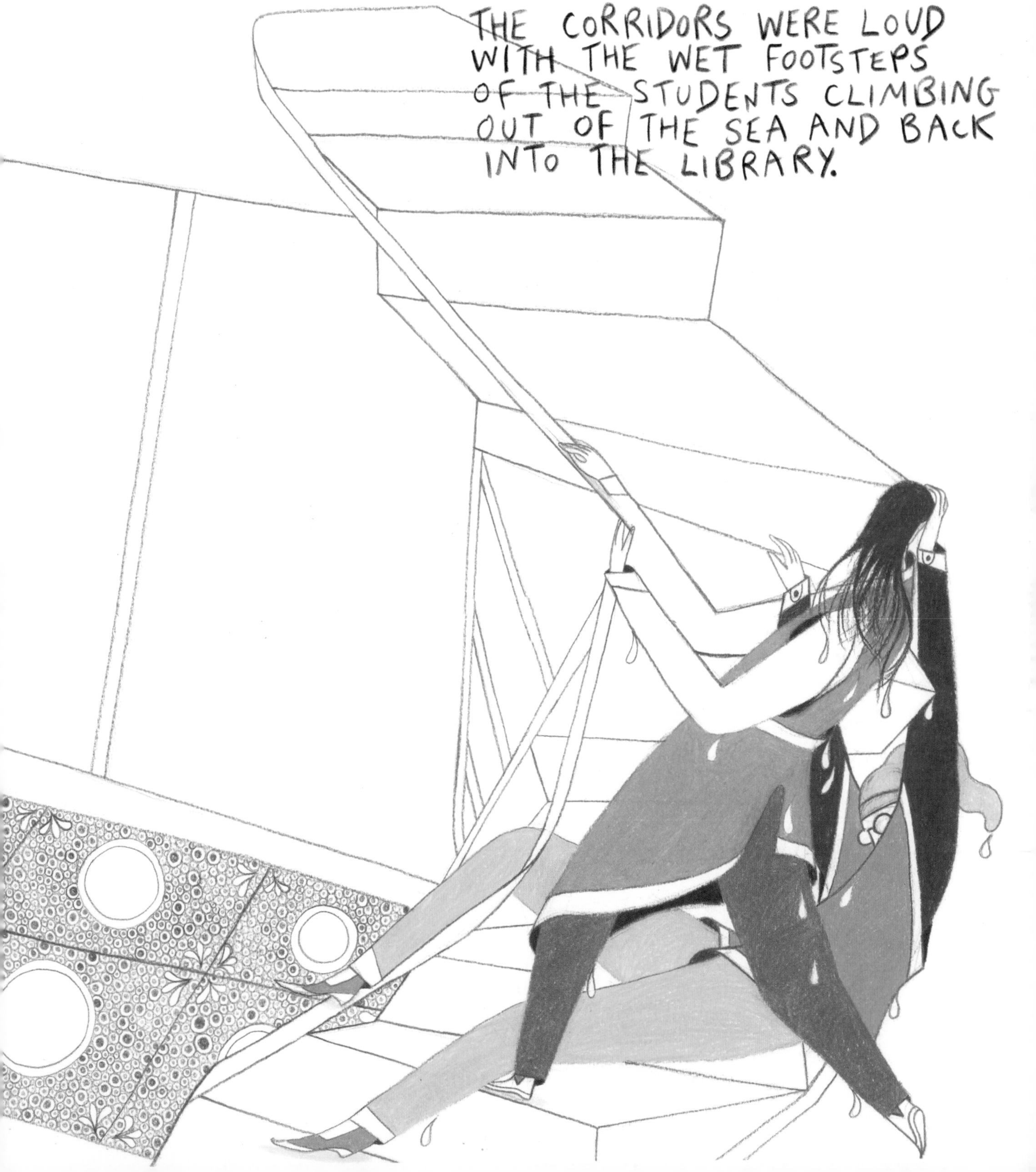
THE CORRIDORS WERE LOUD WITH THE WET FOOTSTEPS OF THE STUDENTS CLIMBING OUT OF THE SEA AND BACK INTO THE LIBRARY.

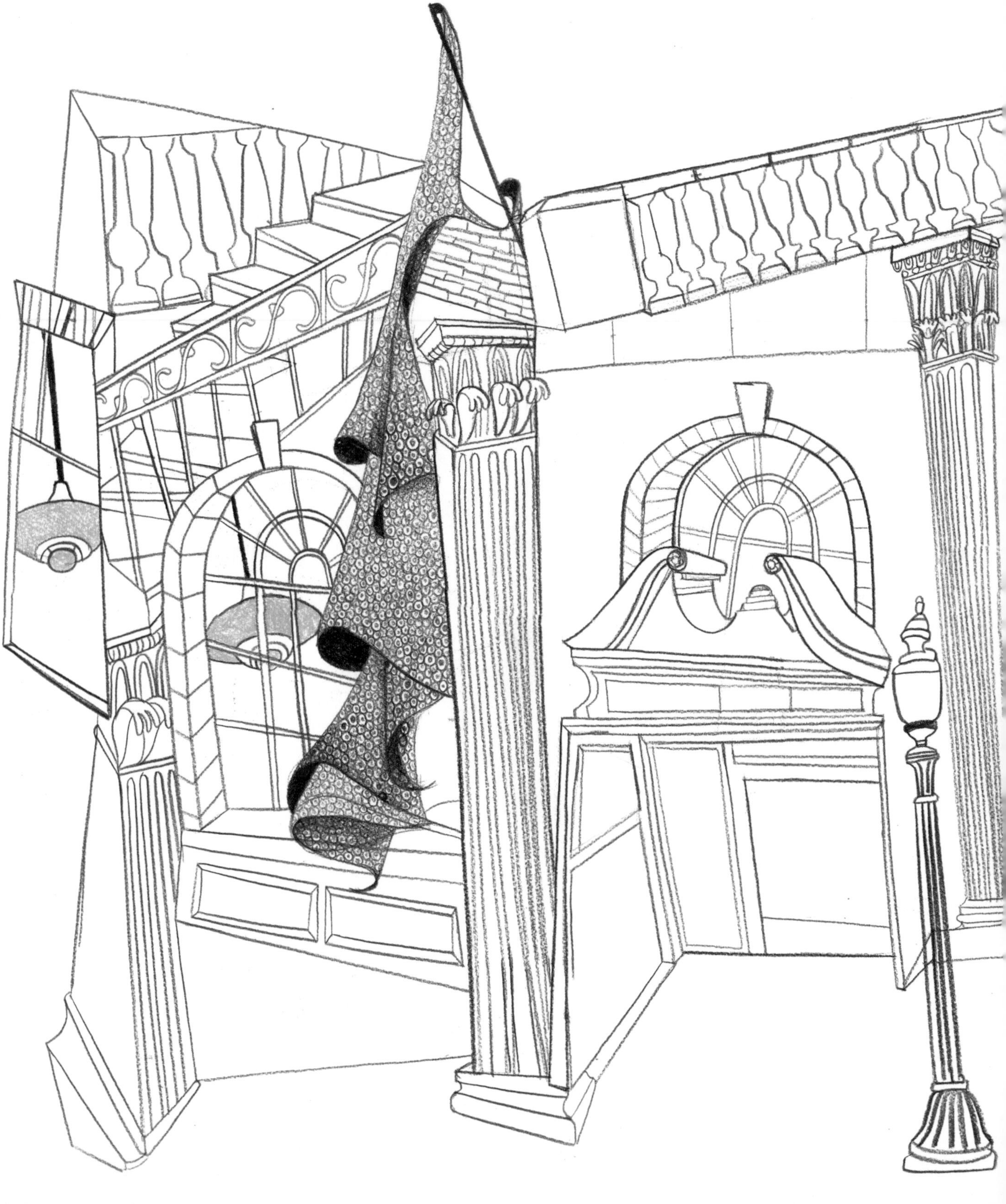

chapter 5:

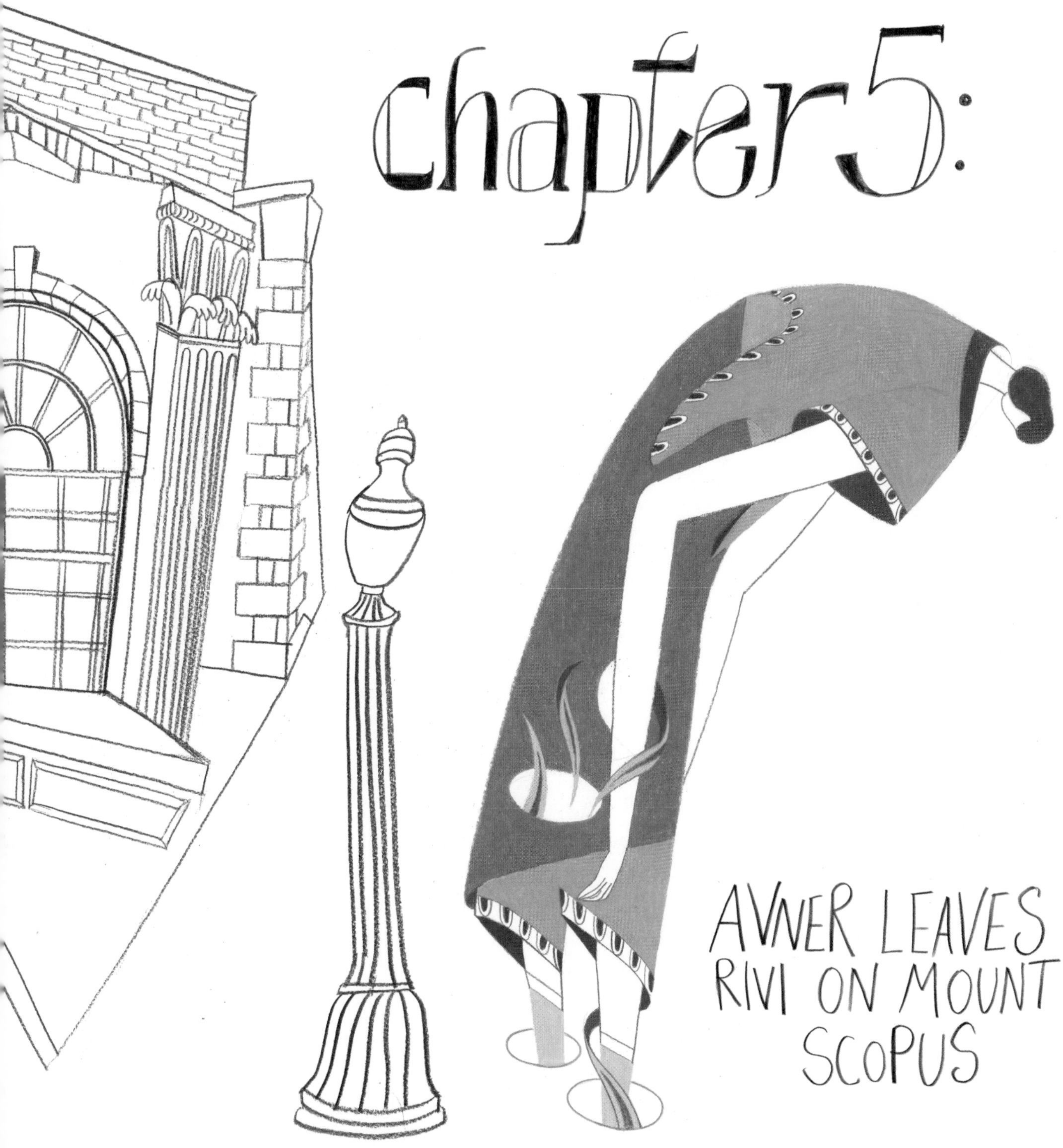

AVNER LEAVES RIVI ON MOUNT SCOPUS

THE NIGHT BEFORE SCHOOL COMMENCES, RIVI'S FATHER LEAVES HIS DAUGHTER AND WISHES HER A GOOD YEAR.

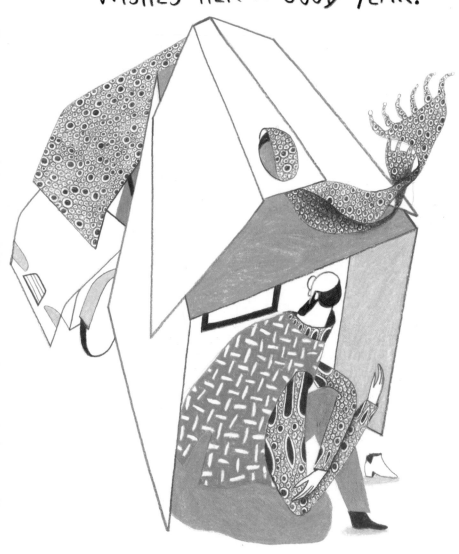

HE IS CONCERNED.

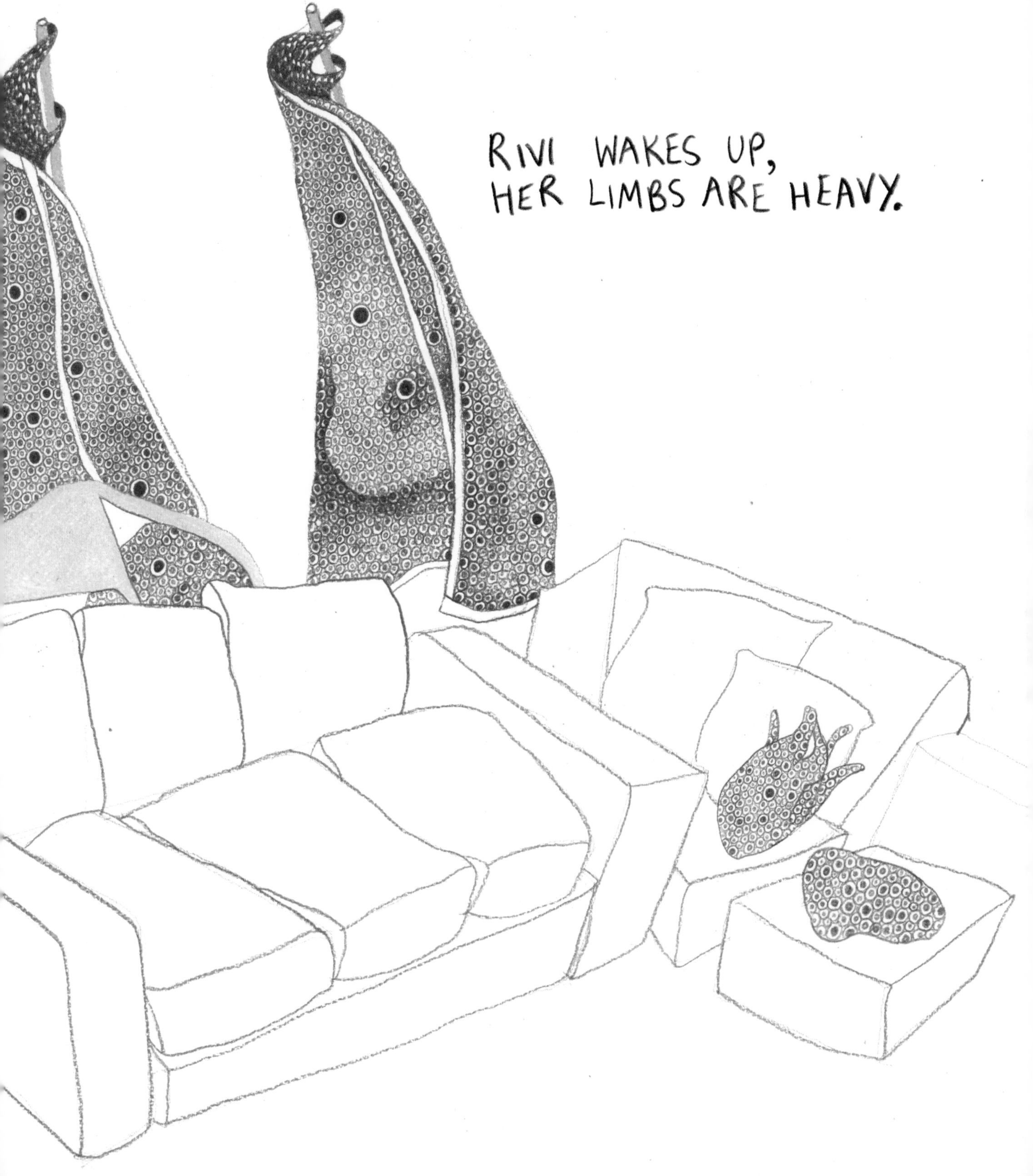
RIVI WAKES UP,
HER LIMBS ARE HEAVY.

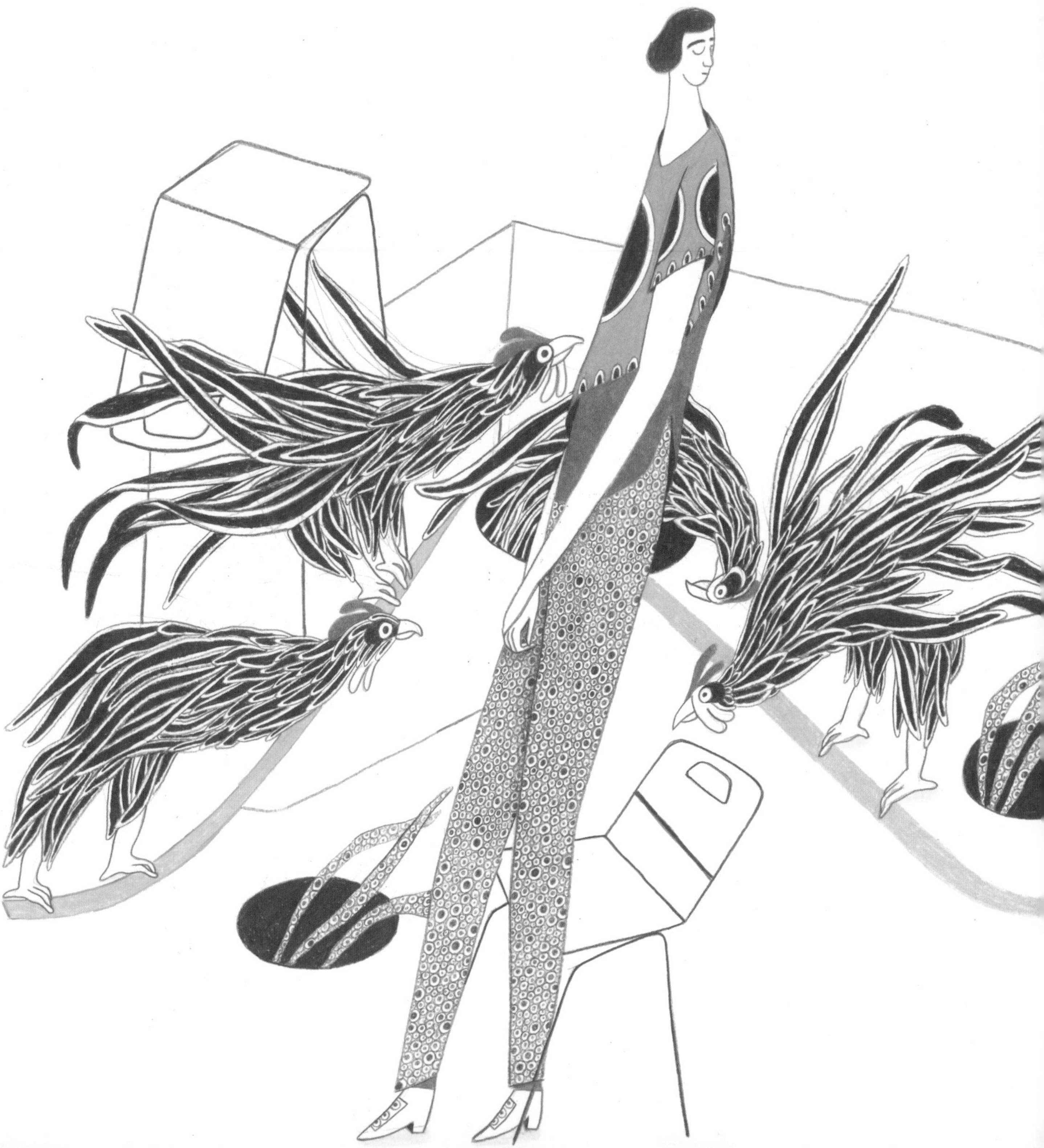

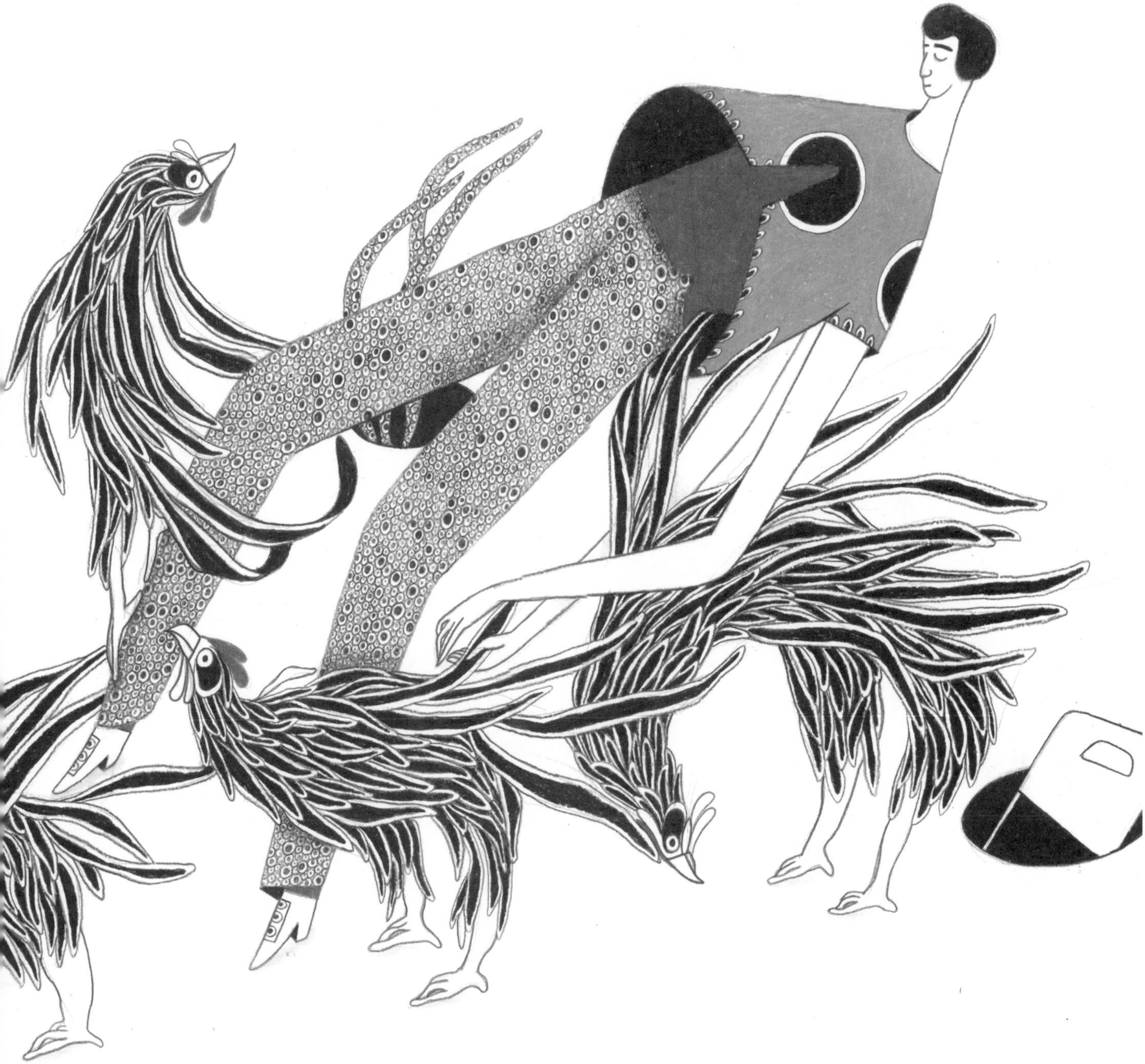

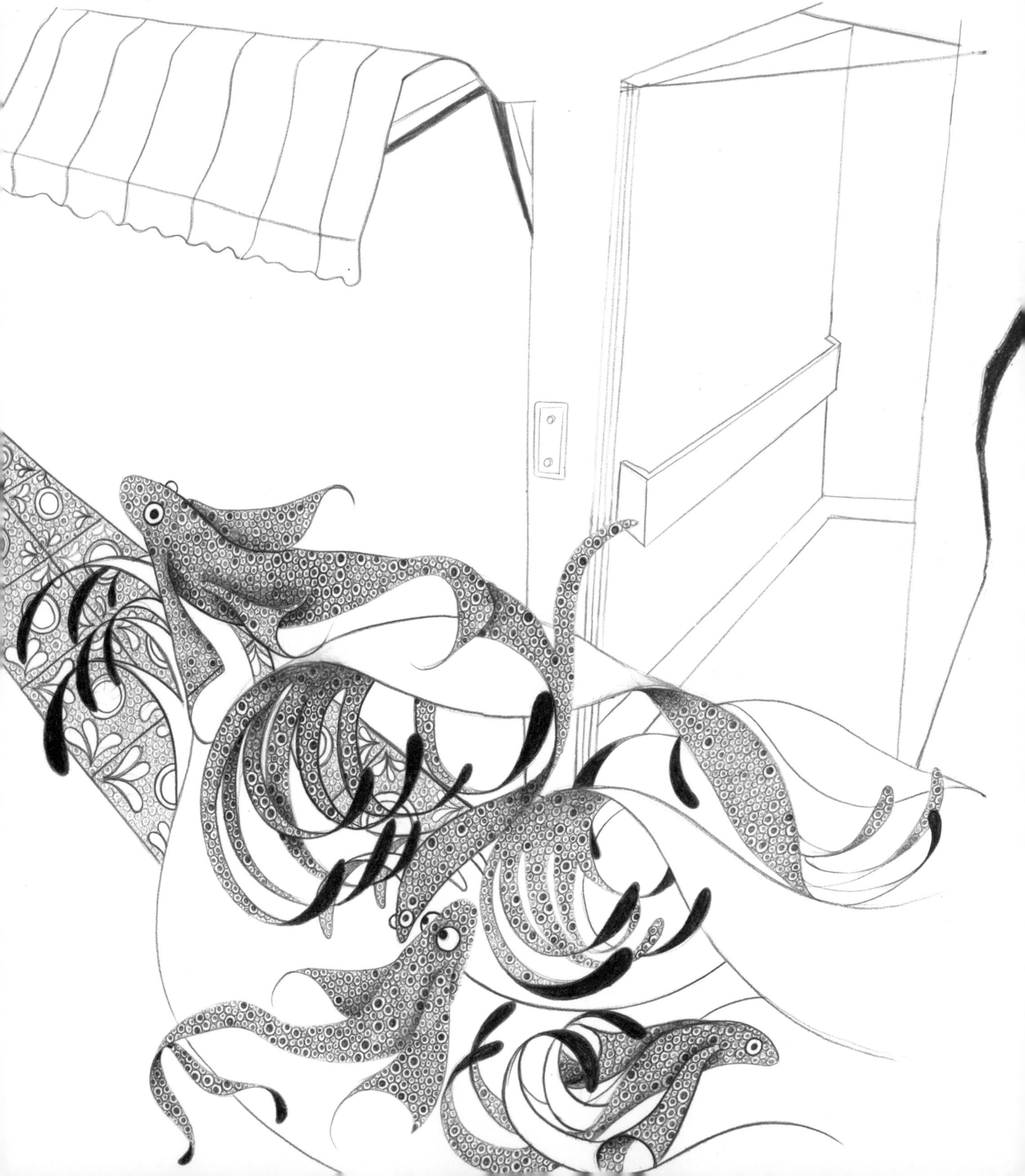

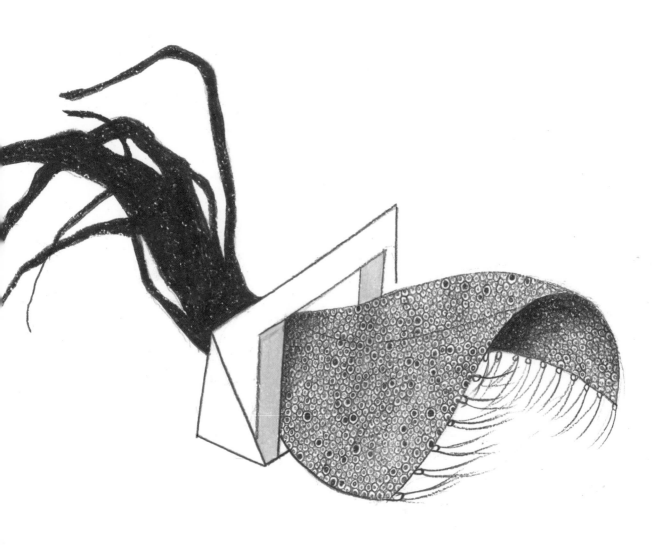

NOVAK HAS POSTPONED THE
RECORDING OF THE SHOW DUE
TO THE INCESSANT WINDS
HOWLING AT THEIR WINDOW.

A VENDOR SETS UP A SMALL KIOSK OUTSIDE THEIR DORMS.

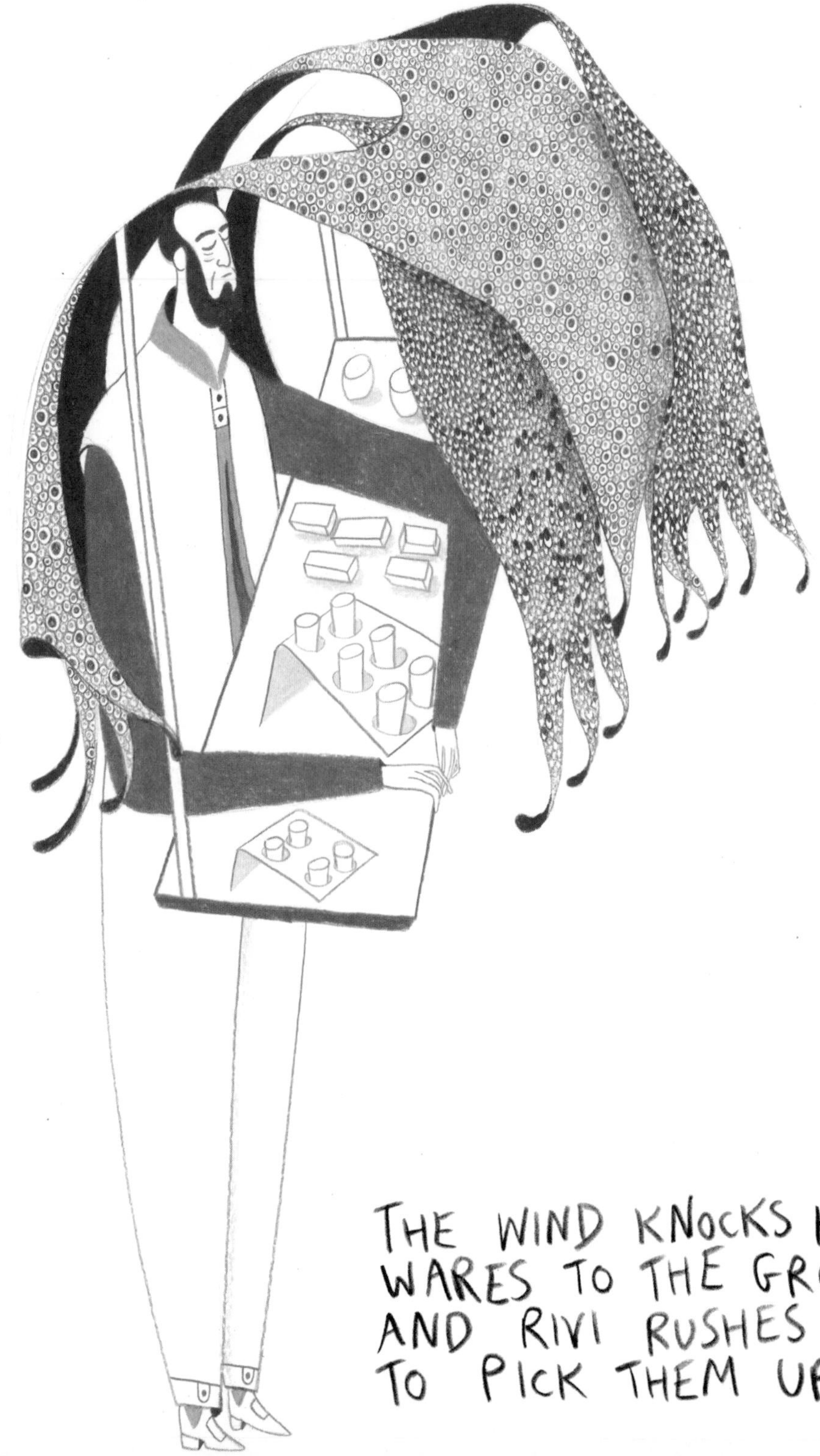

THE WIND KNOCKS HIS WARES TO THE GROUND AND RIVI RUSHES DOWNSTAIRS TO PICK THEM UP.

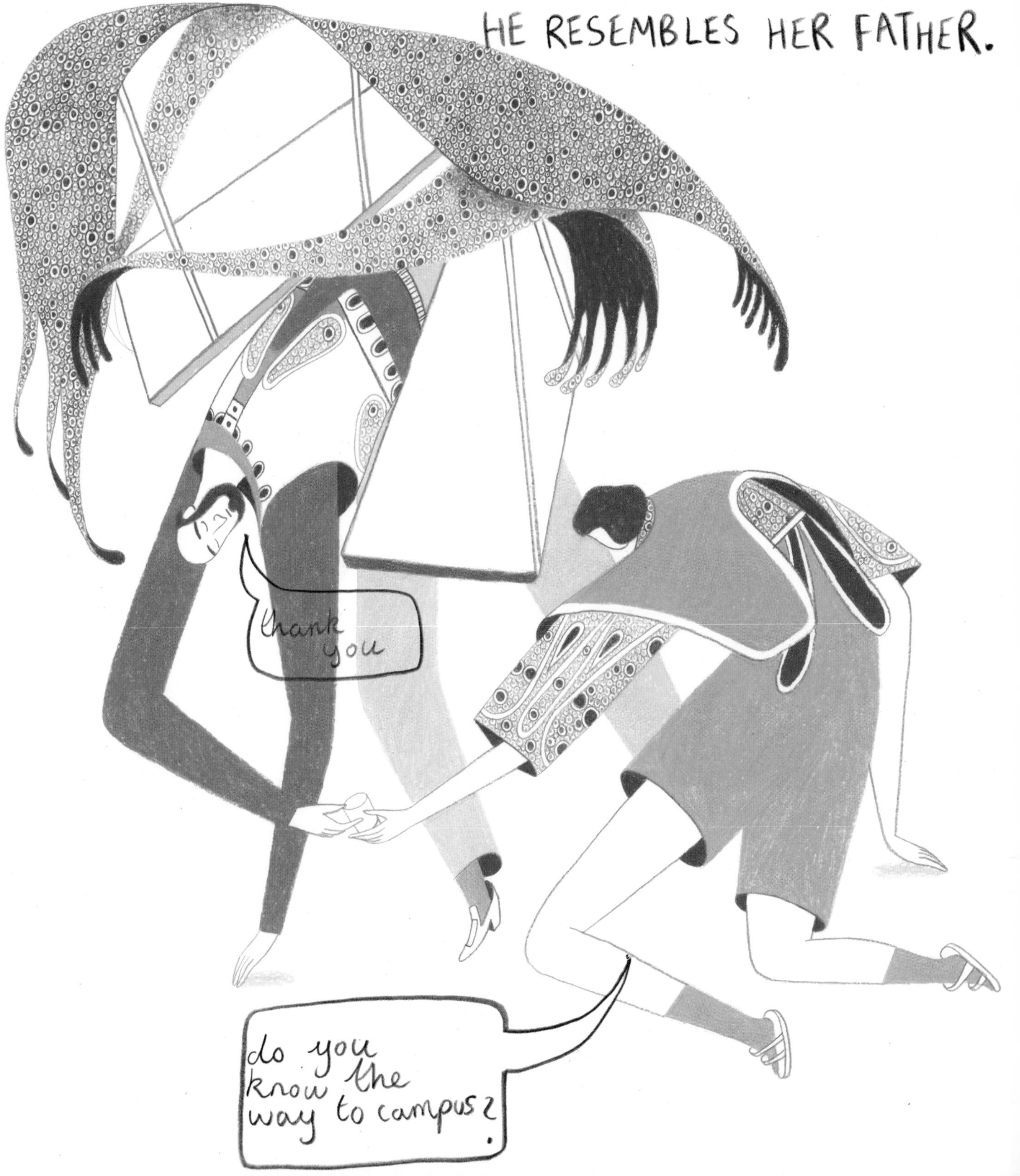
HE RESEMBLES HER FATHER.
thank you
do you know the way to campus?

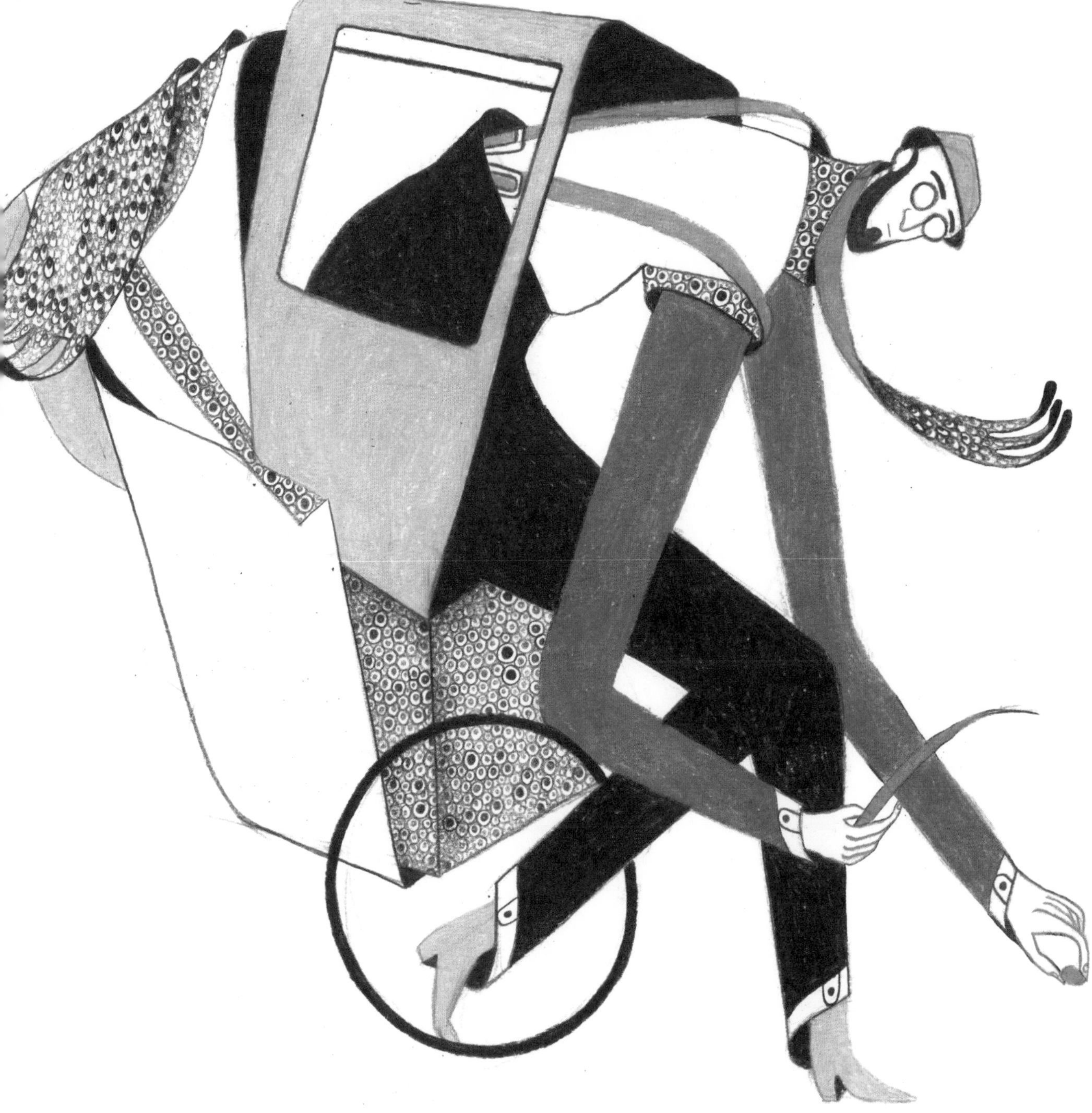

RIVI STOPS BY THE KIOSK EACH MORNING TO ASK HIM THE SAME QUESTION.

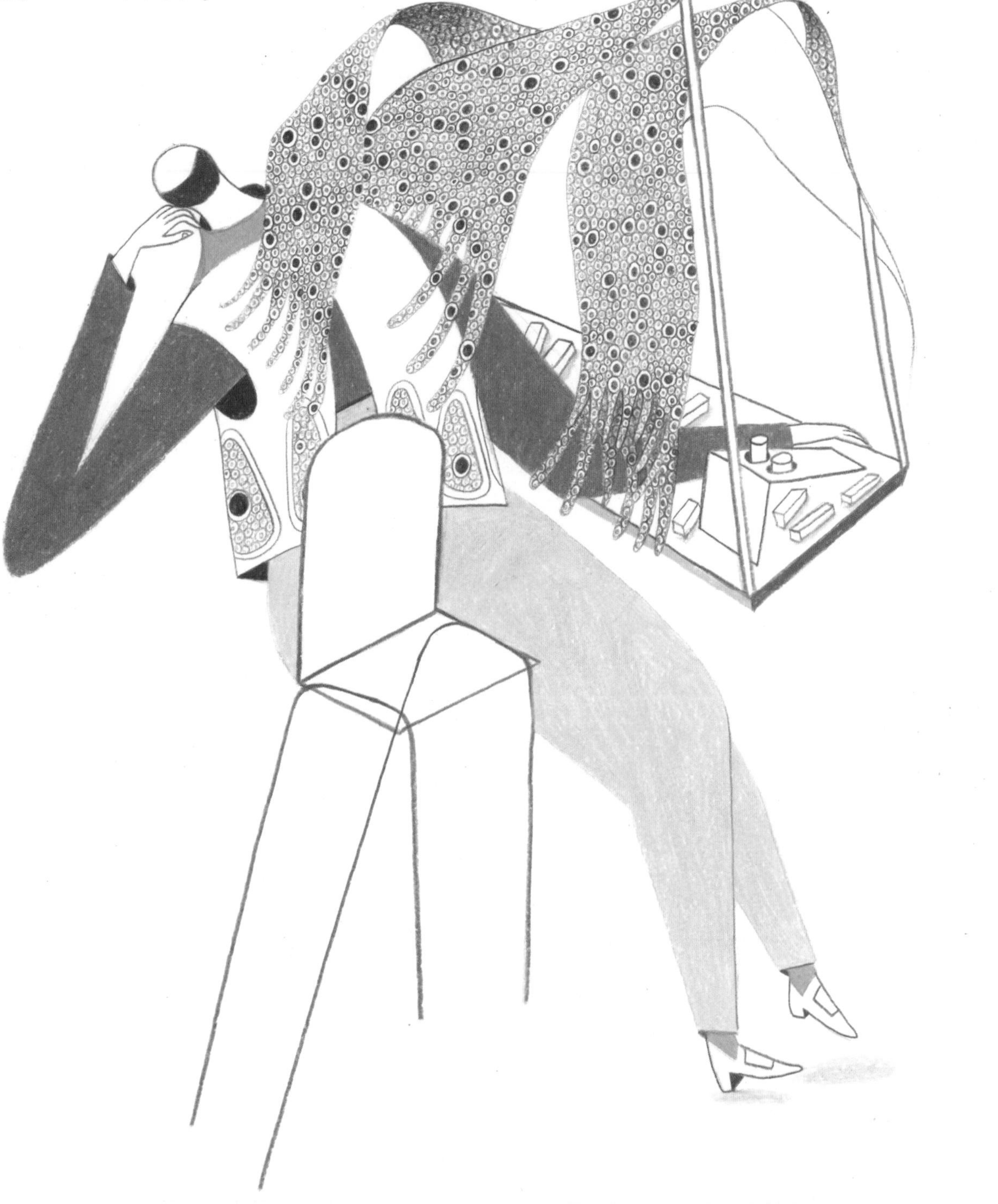

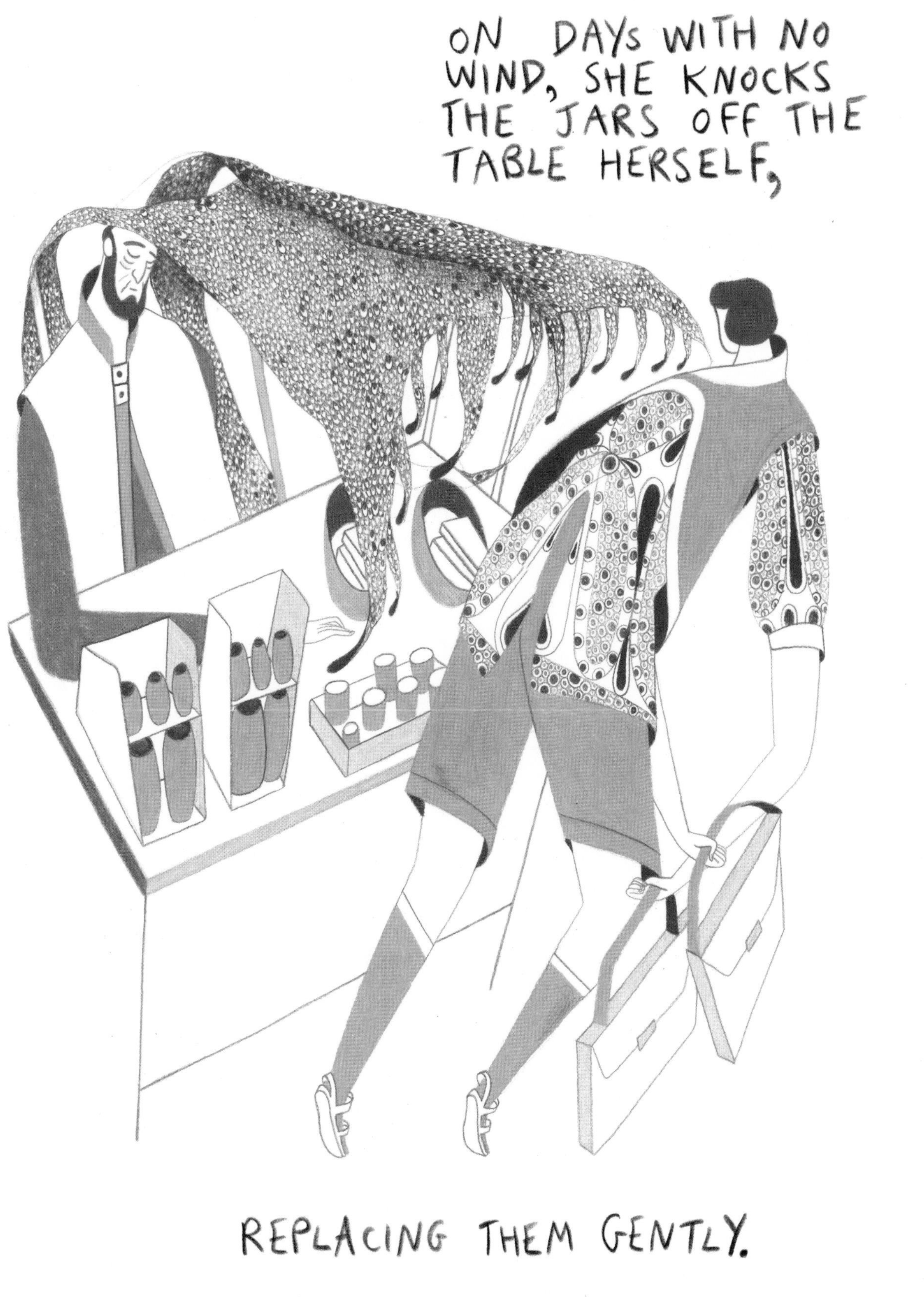
ON DAYS WITH NO WIND, SHE KNOCKS THE JARS OFF THE TABLE HERSELF,
REPLACING THEM GENTLY.

ON THE MORNING
A HUNDRED GRAPES
HAVE BEEN FOUND,
CONSUMED AND REPORTED,
YAKOV WAITS BY THE
ENTRANCE TO THE DORM.

HE NOTICES RIVI PICKING
UP THE JAR. HER MOVEMENT
IS FAMILIAR.

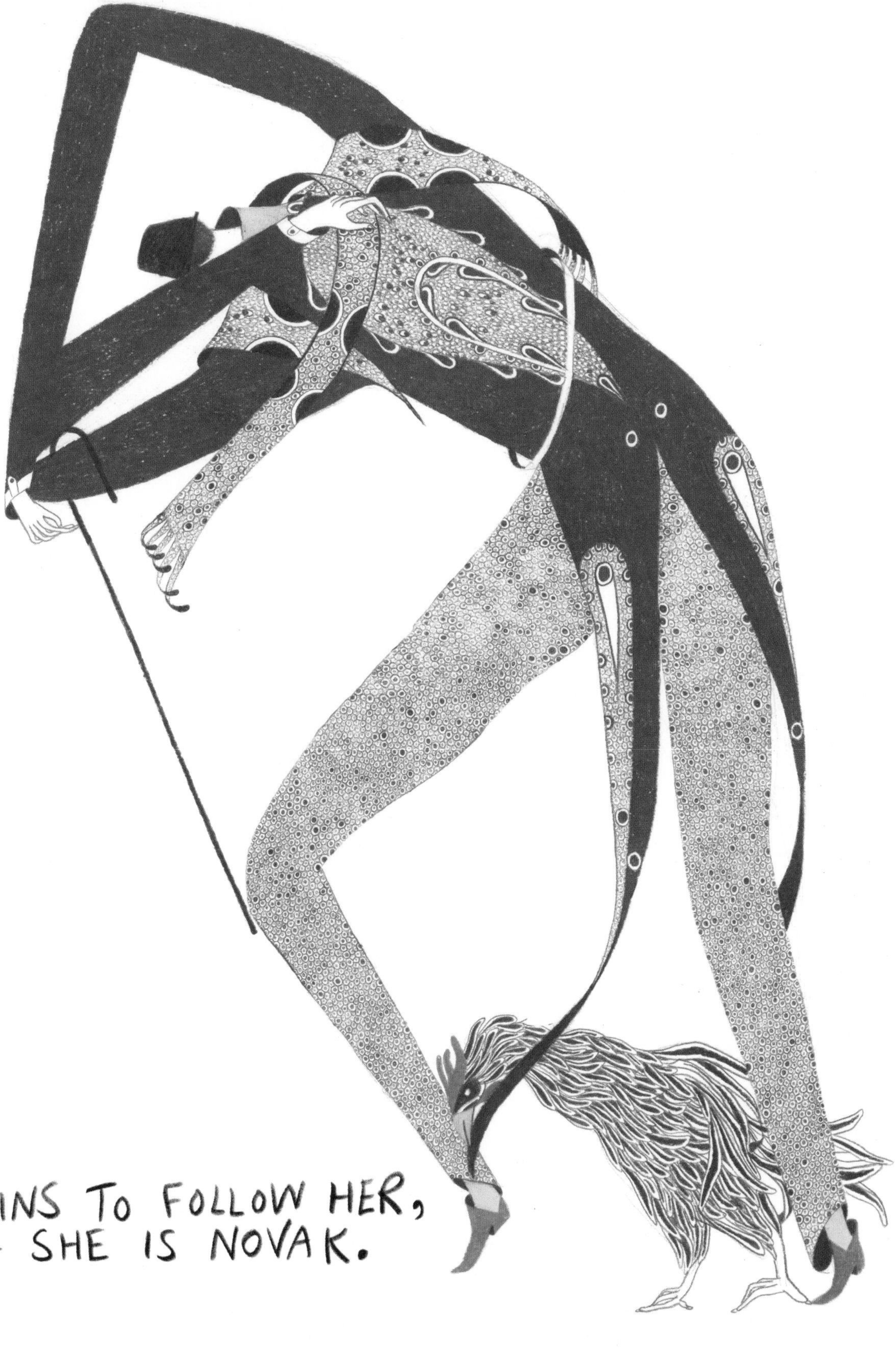

HE BEGINS TO FOLLOW HER,
THINKING SHE IS NOVAK.

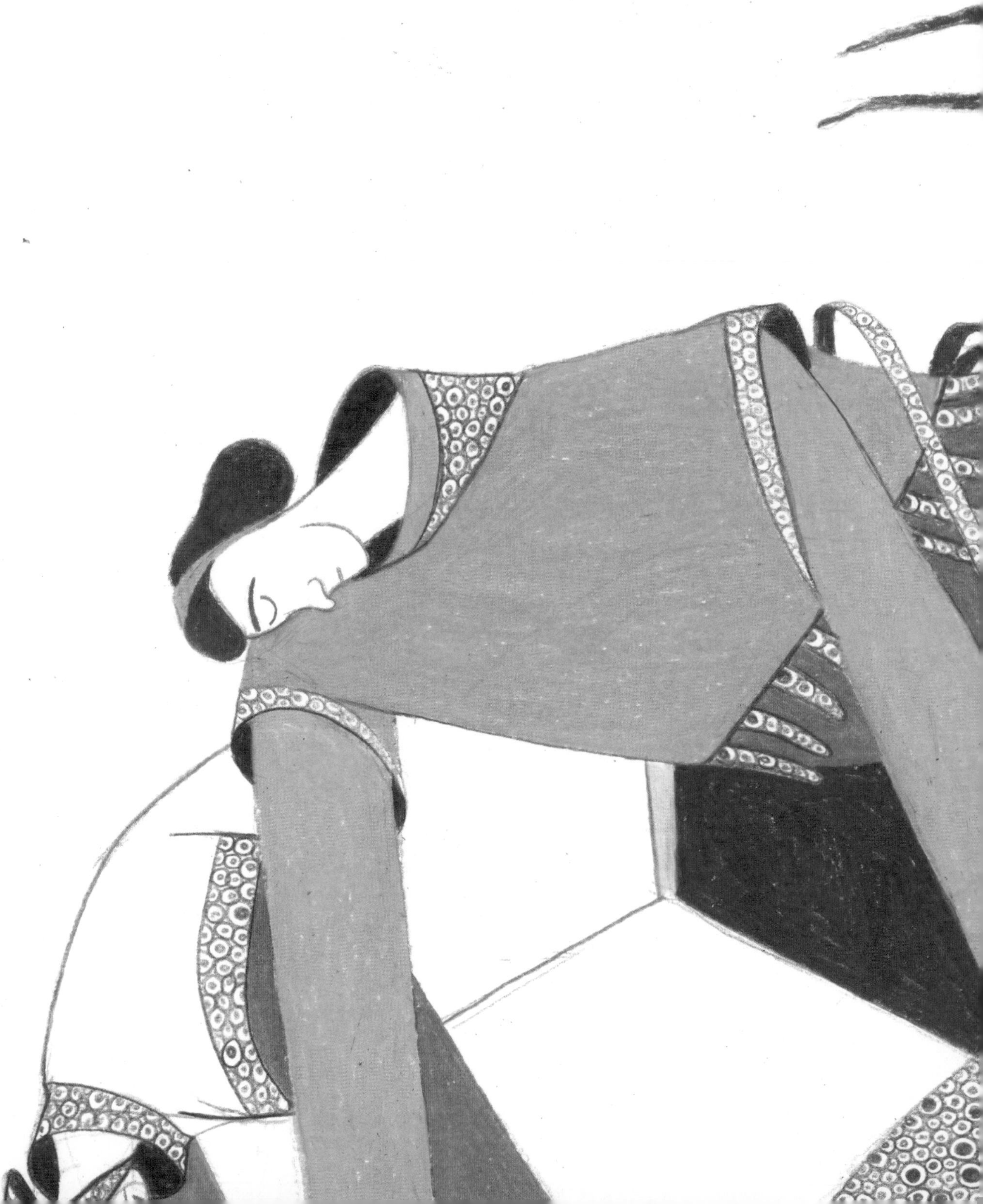

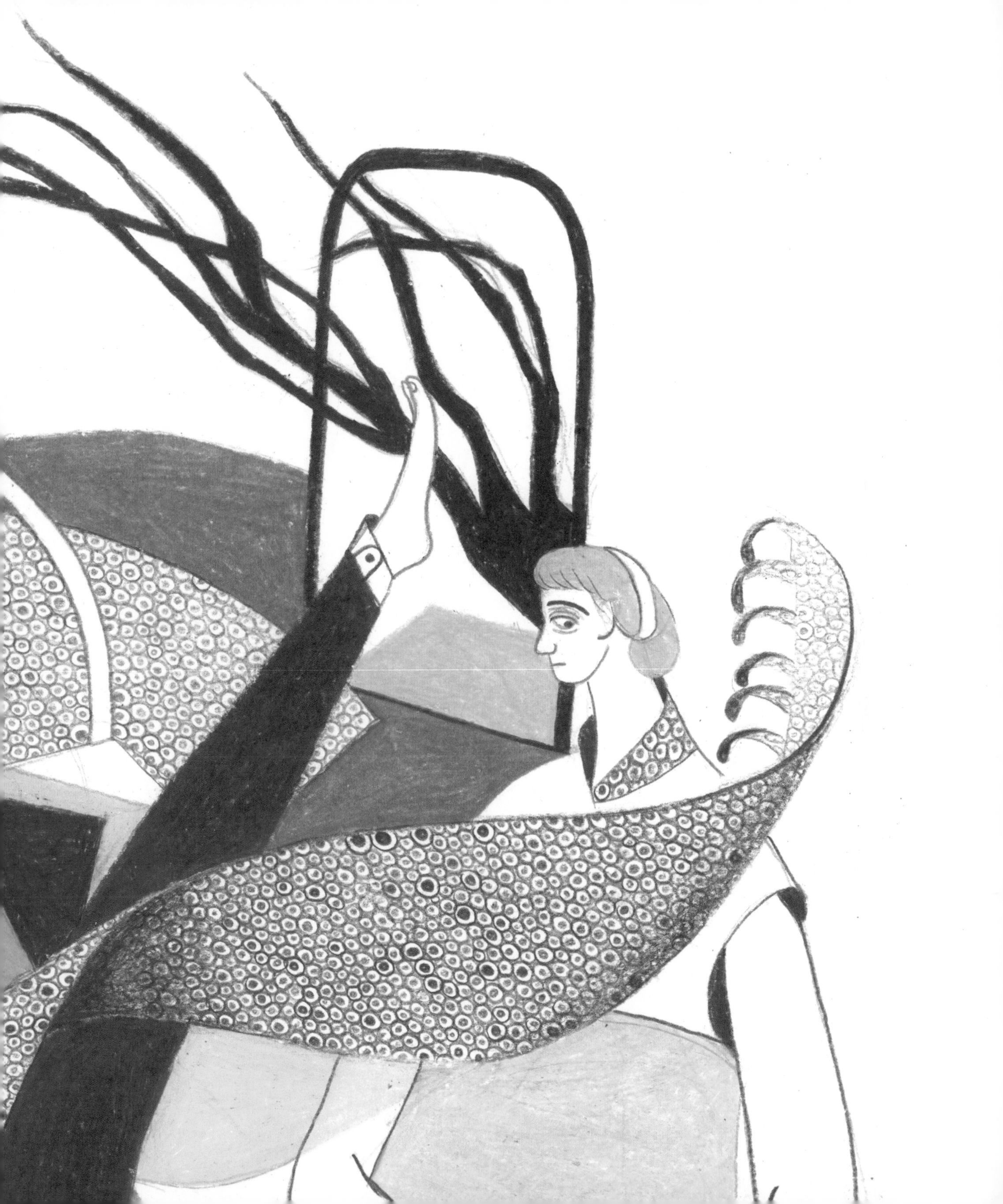

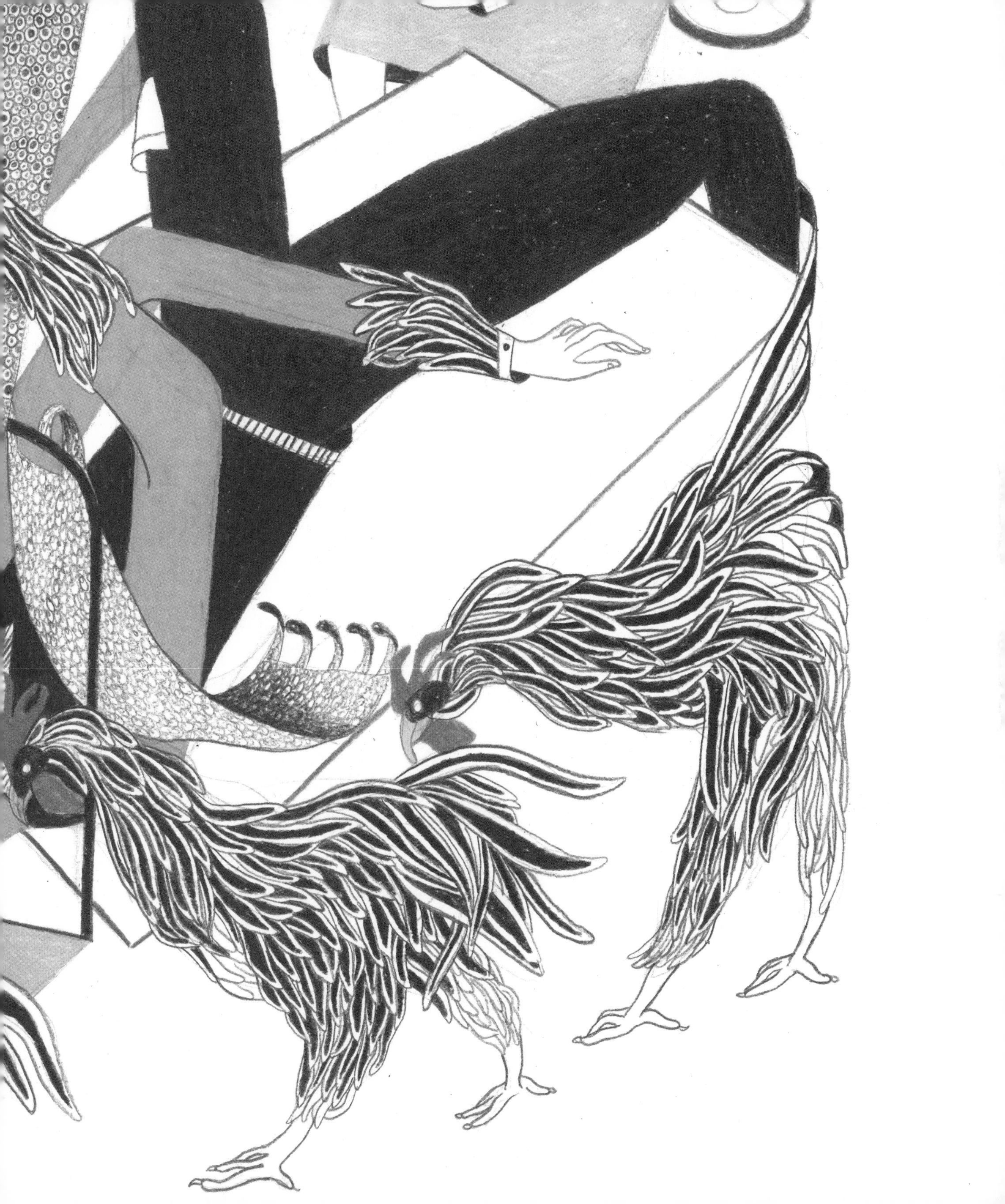

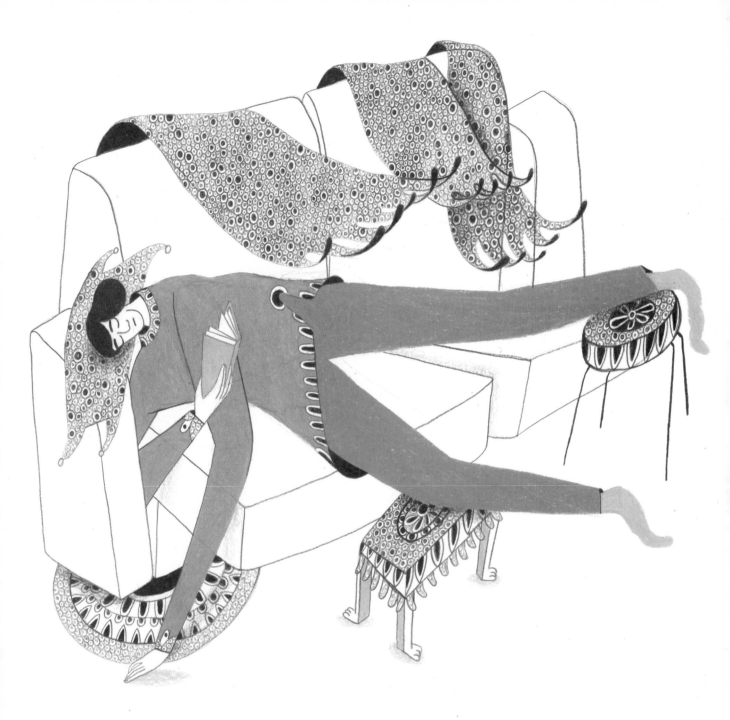

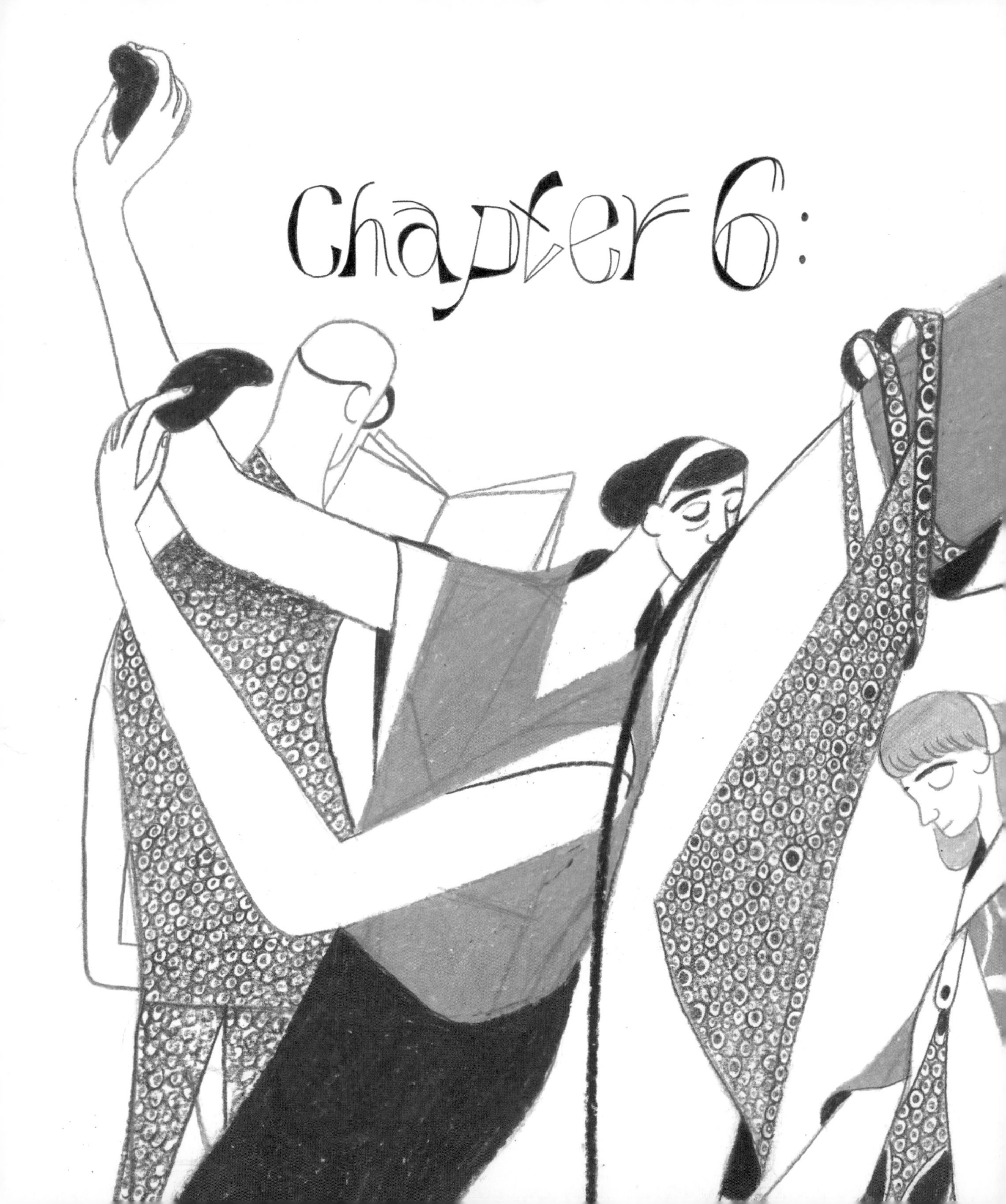
Chapter 6:

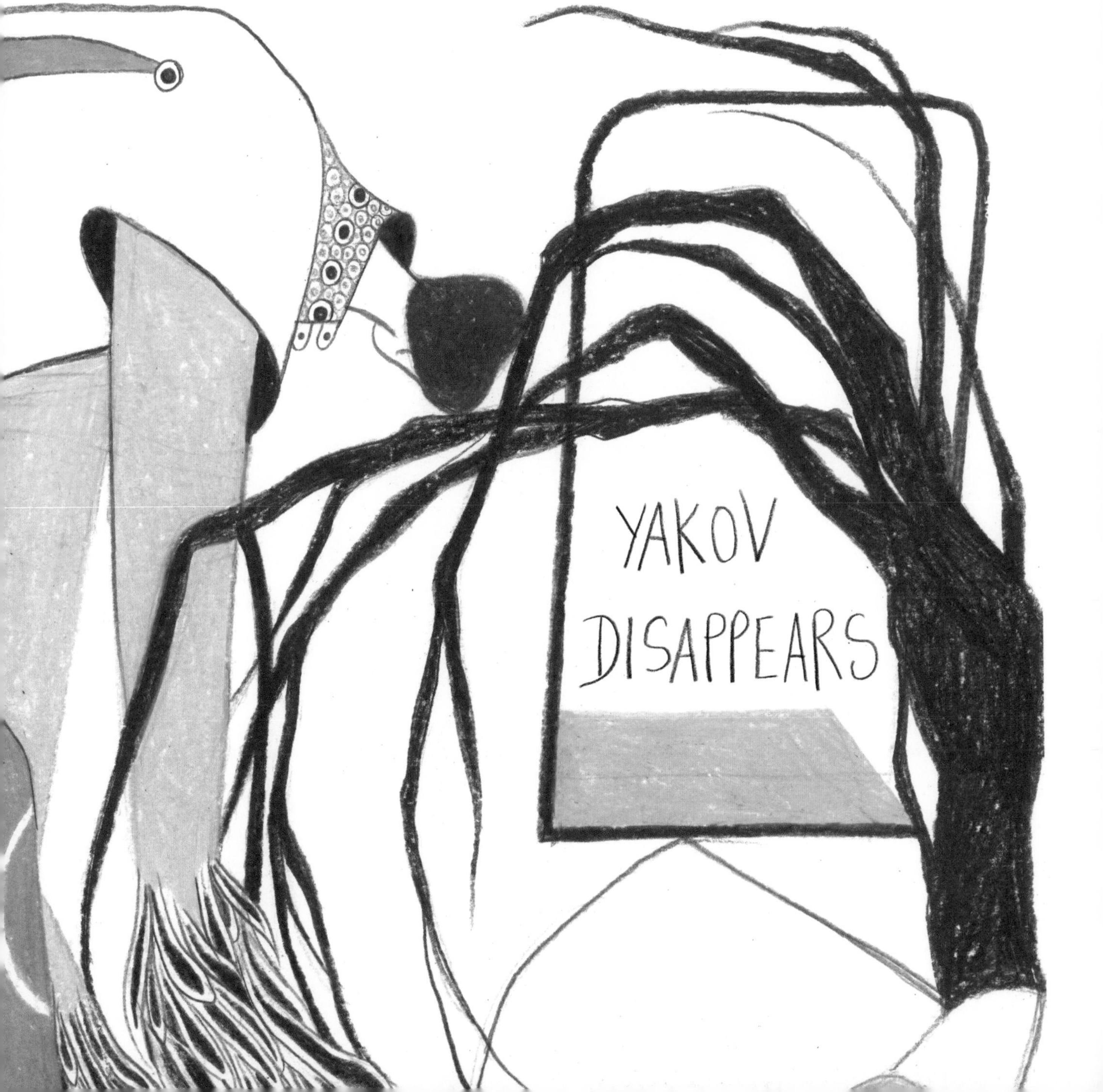
YAKOV
DISAPPEARS

Dad, I need your
help to look for
someone who disappeared,

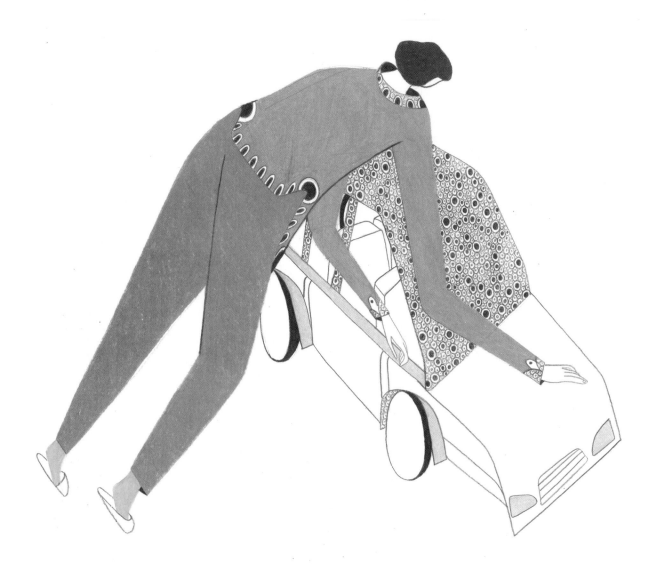

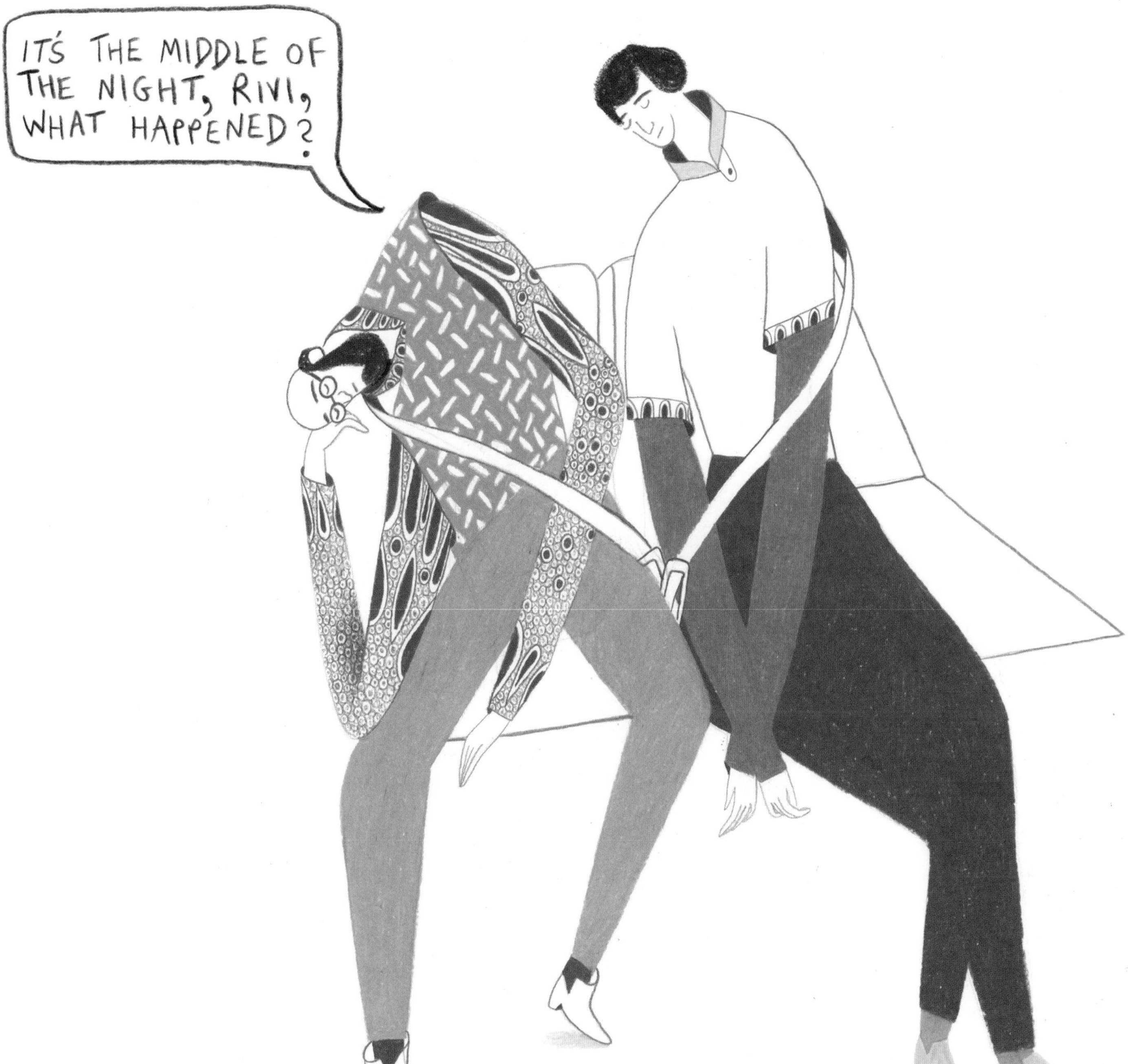
ITS THE MIDDLE OF THE NIGHT, RIVI, WHAT HAPPENED?

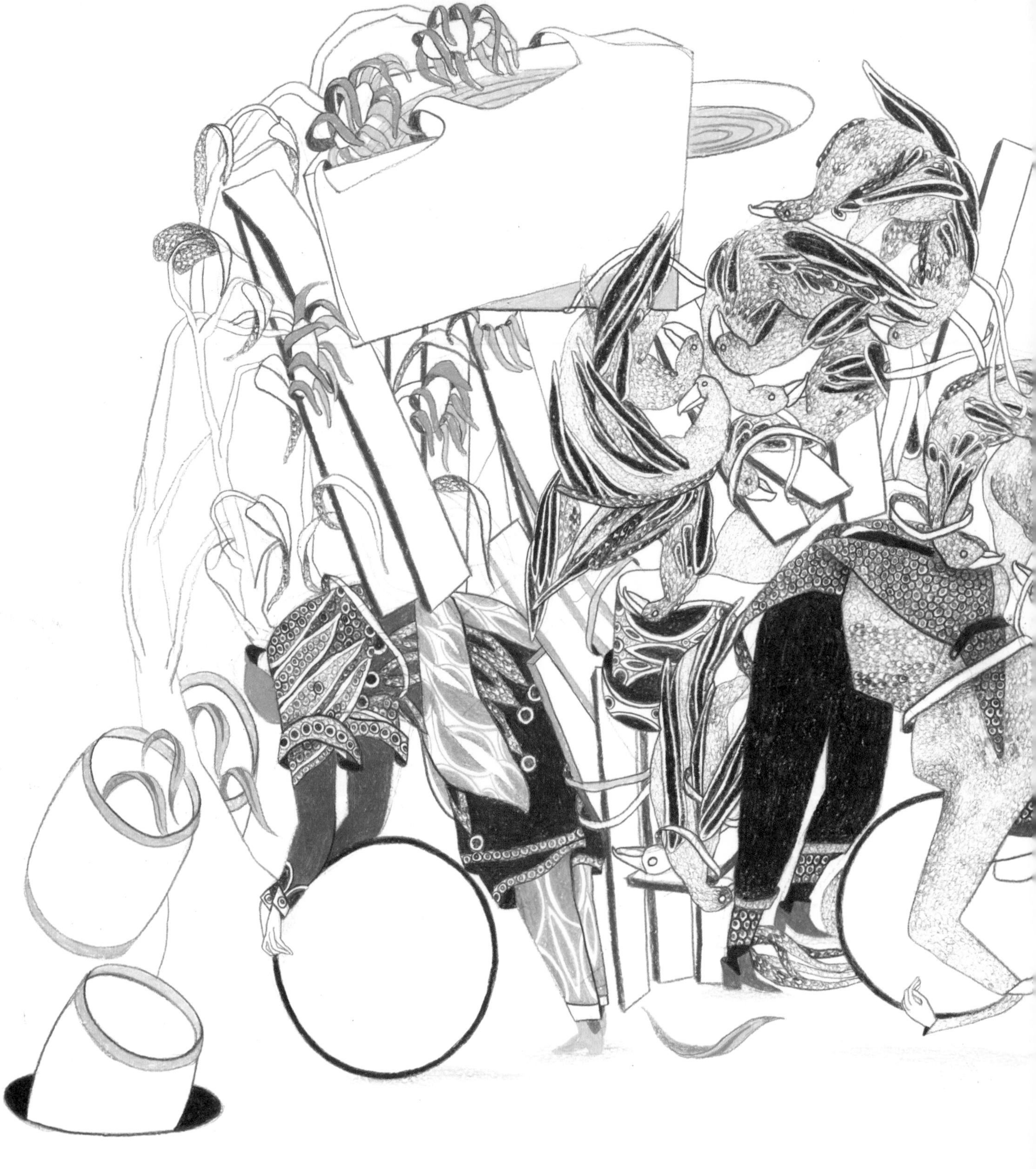

Someone I love, I havent seen him around campus in two weeks and I'm worried sick that something happened to him.

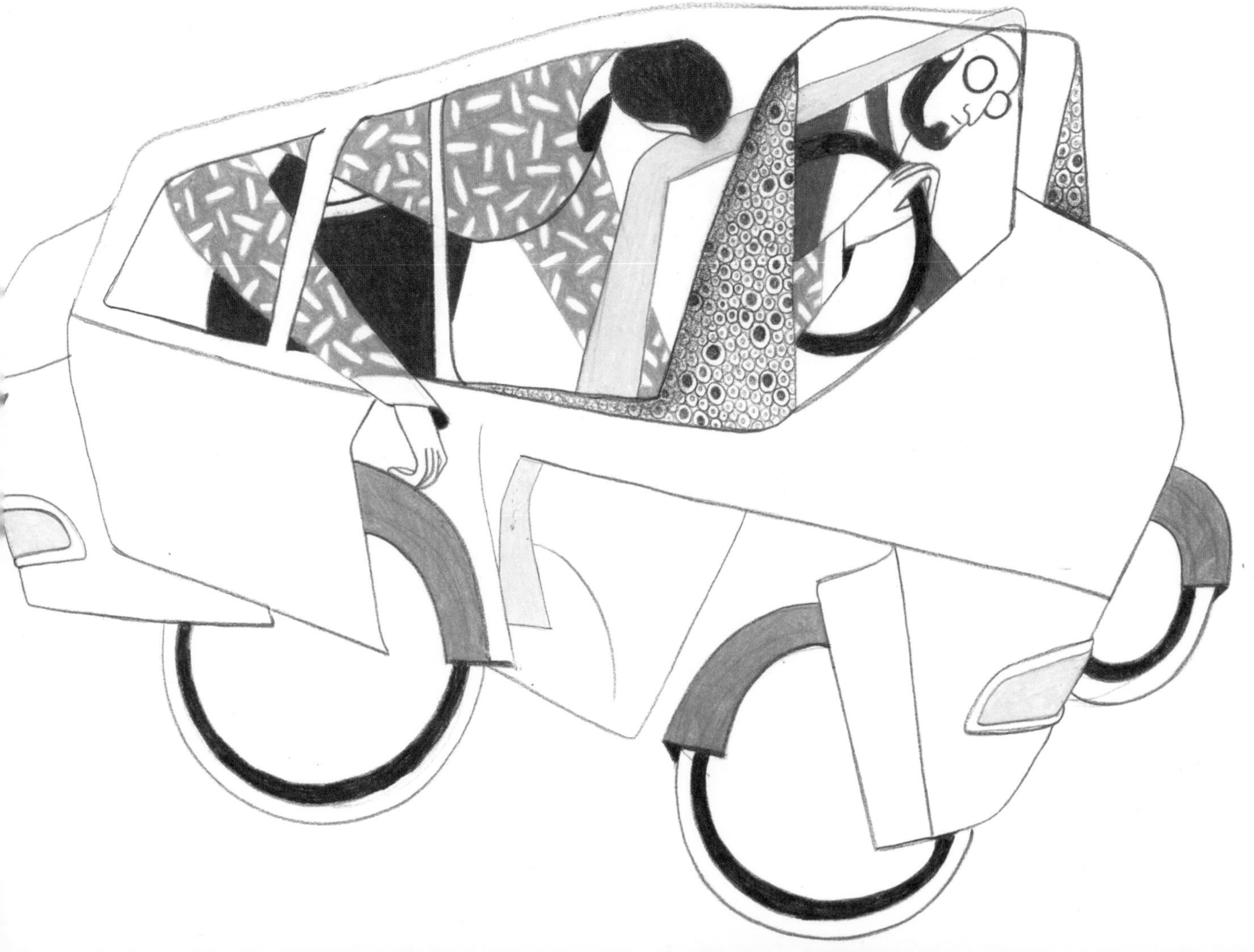

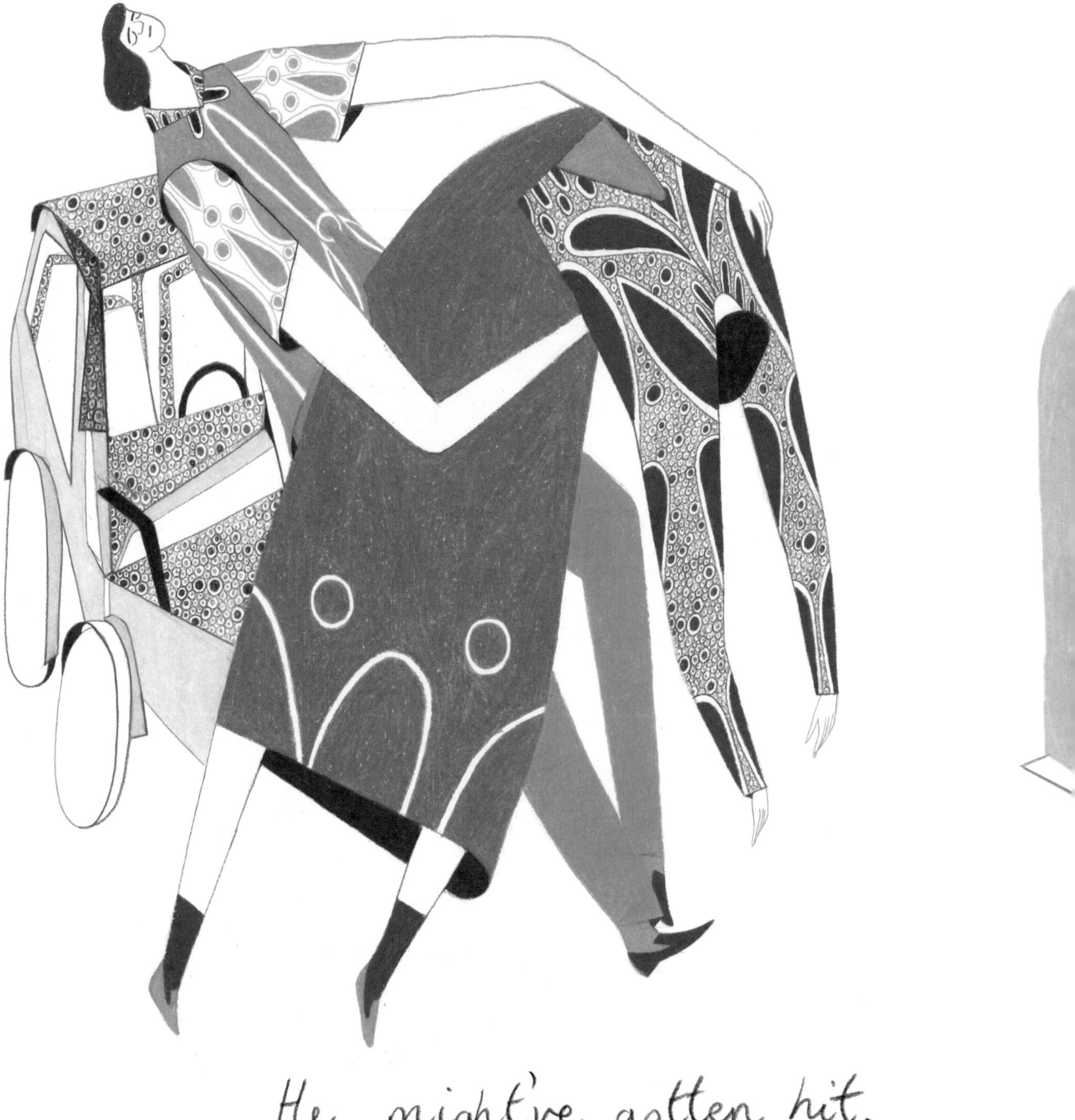

He might've gotten hit,

or have fallen off
the mountain,

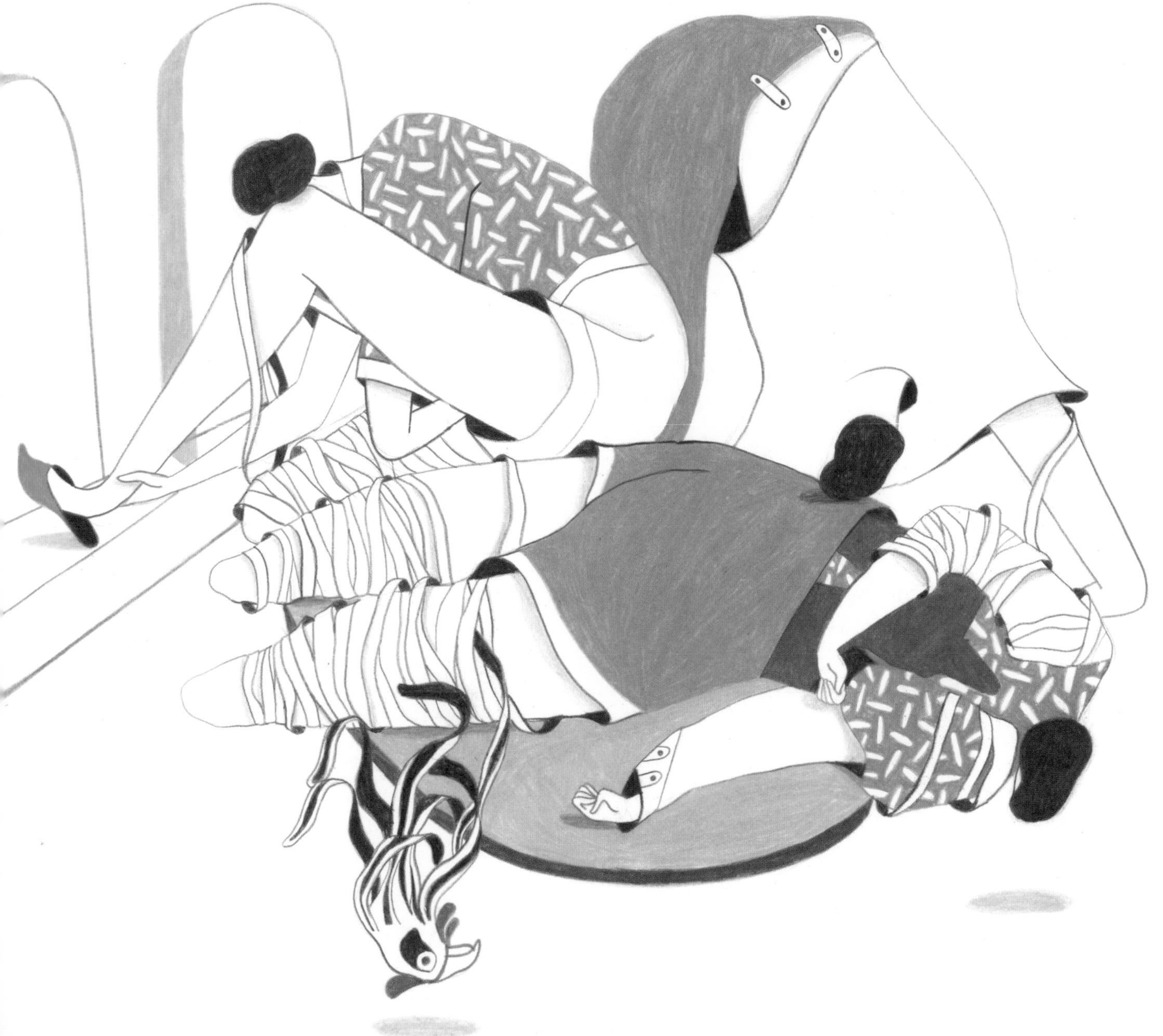

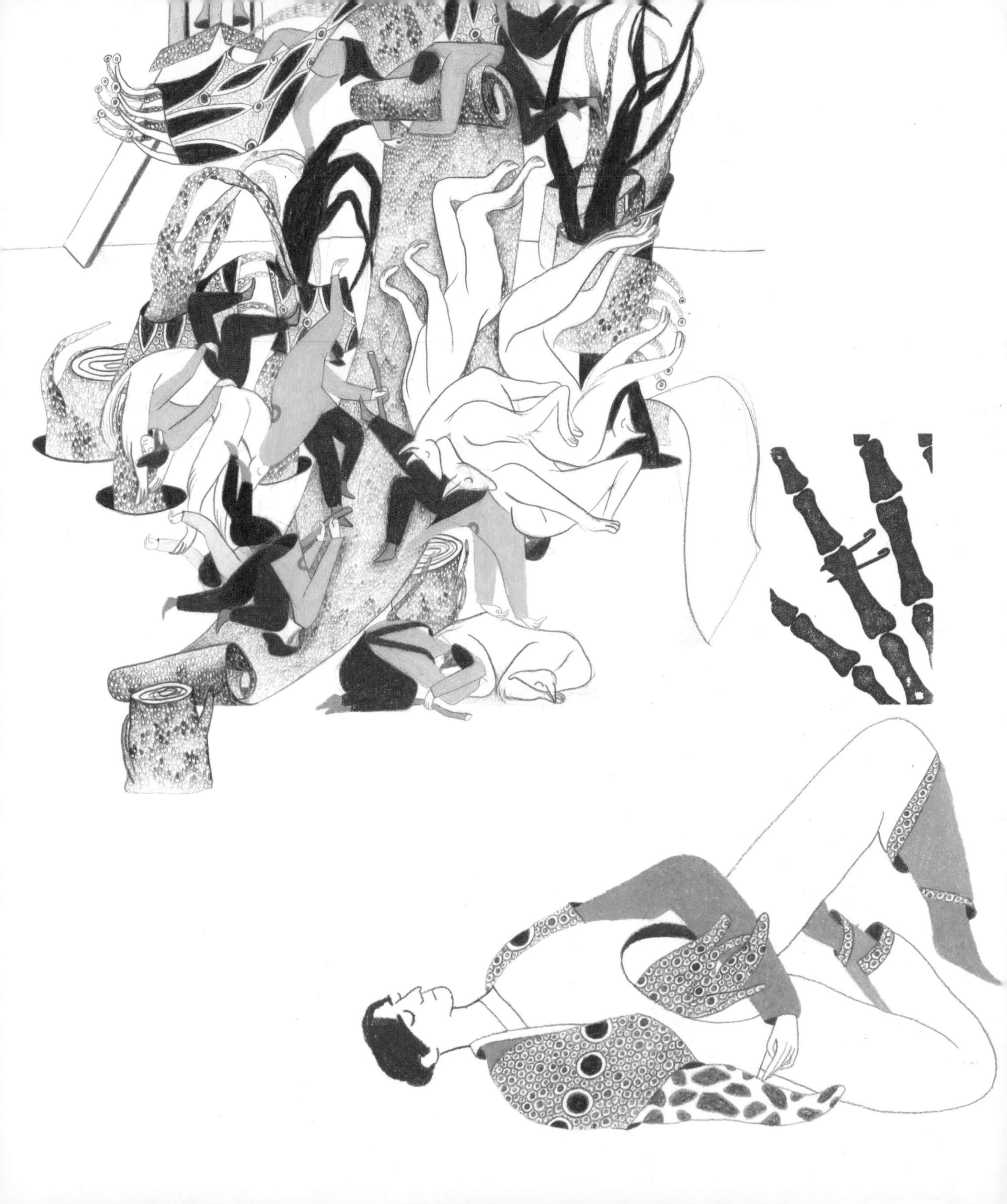

and now he cannot
open the door to leave his room.

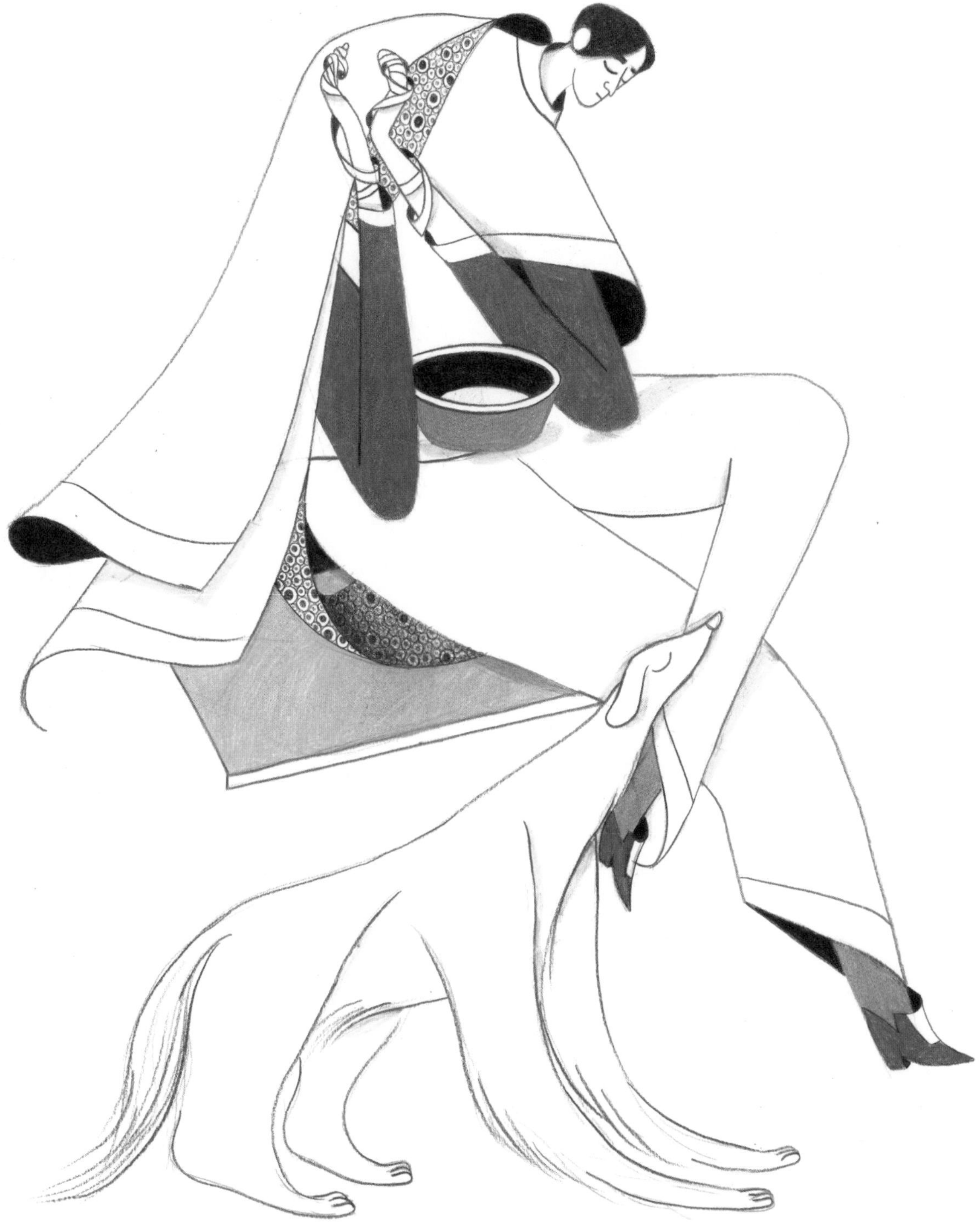

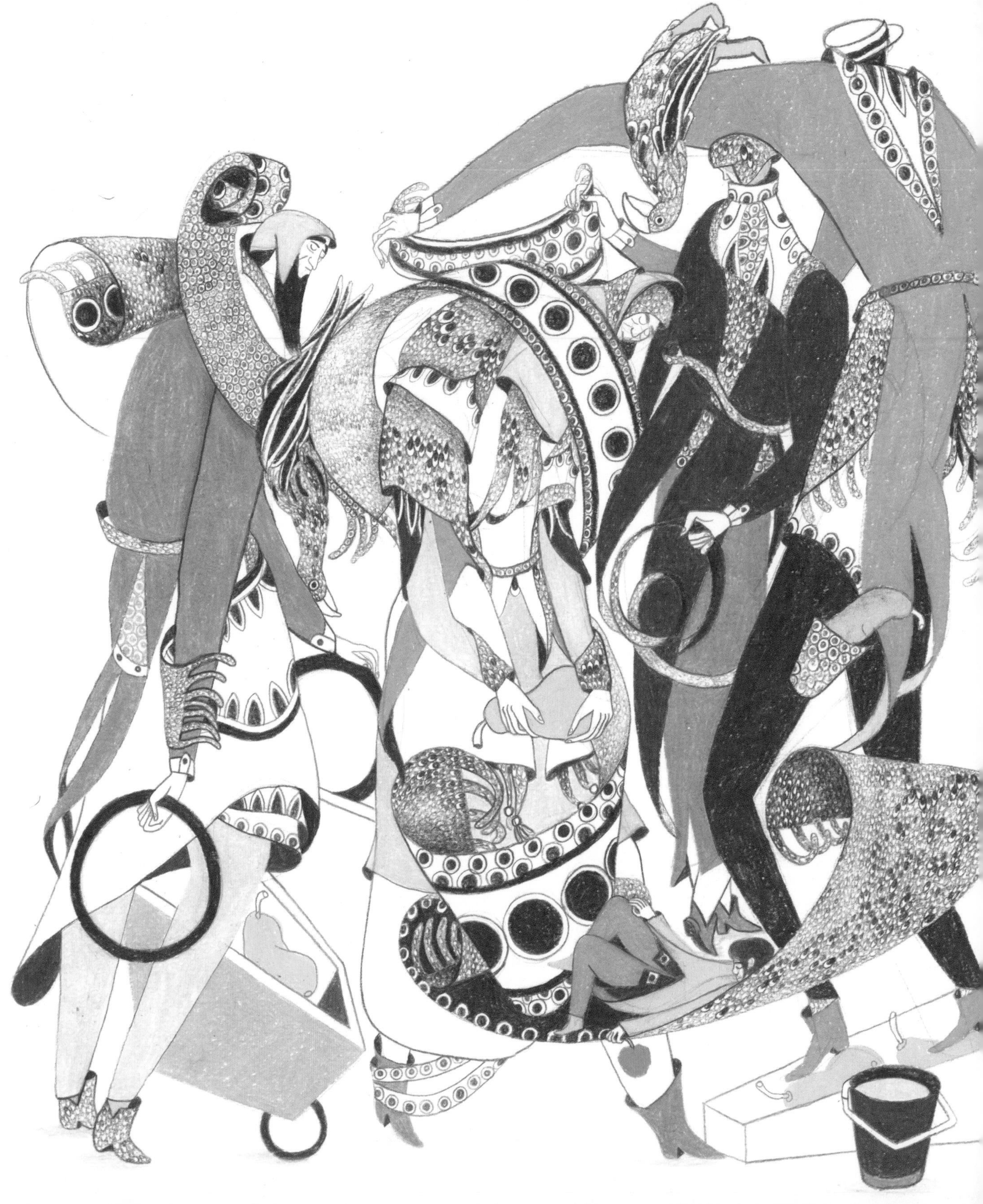

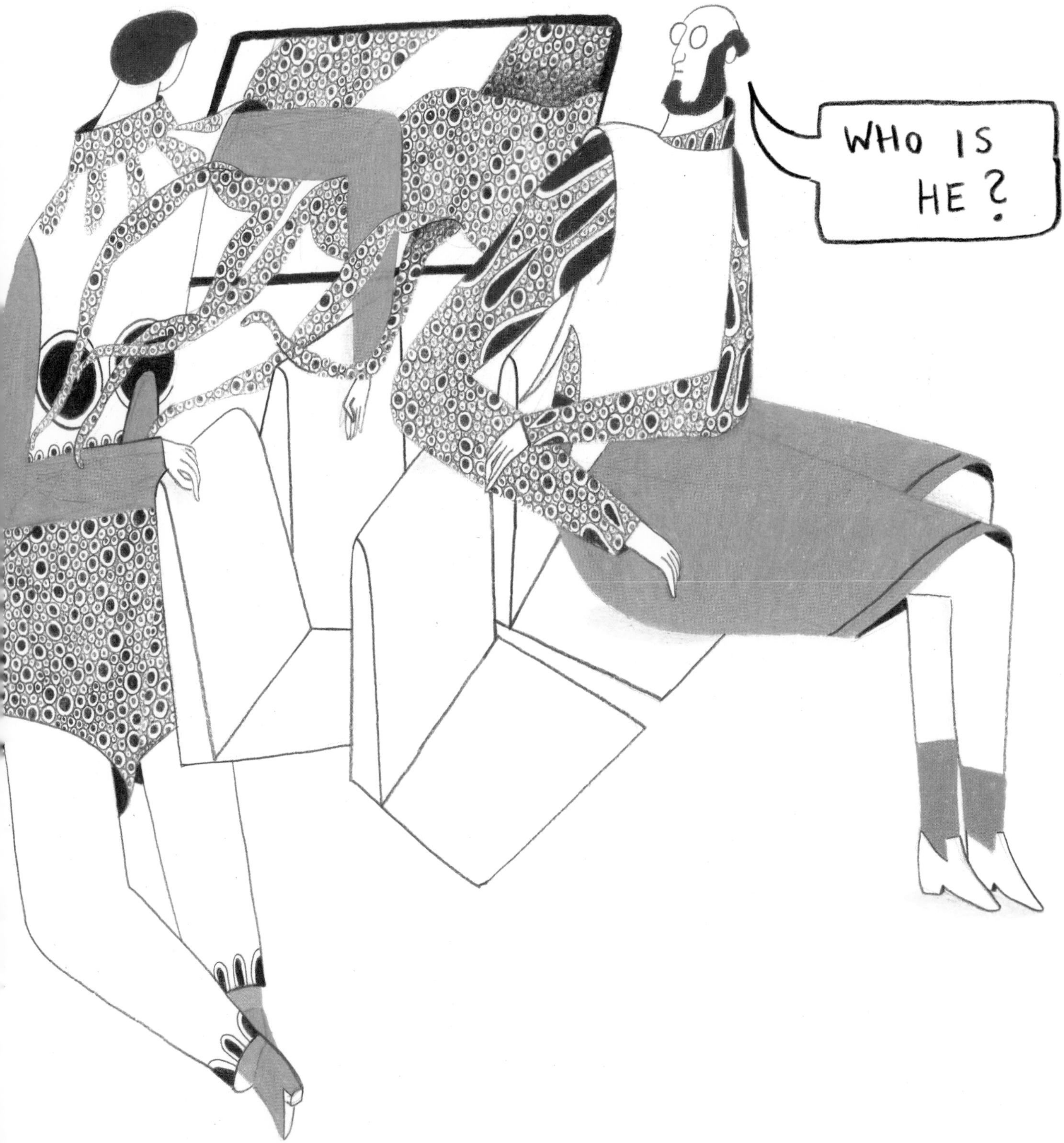
WHO IS HE ?

I don't know his name,
I posted fliers all over
campus asking for him,

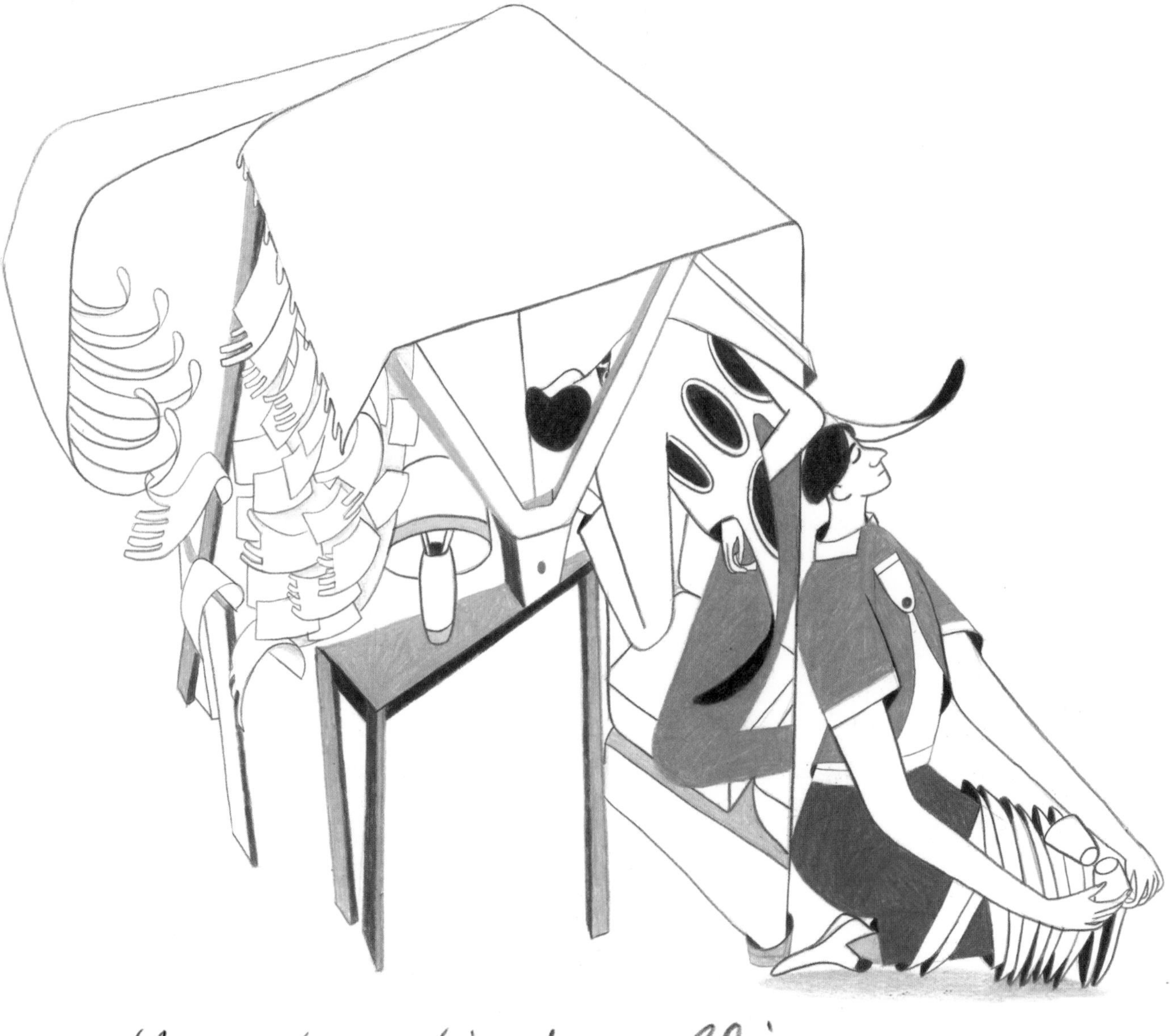

then I noticed a flier
calling for volunteers who
like to dance,

I went there because I didn't know what else to do. The experiment was held in the basement lab. I wore my red shoes,

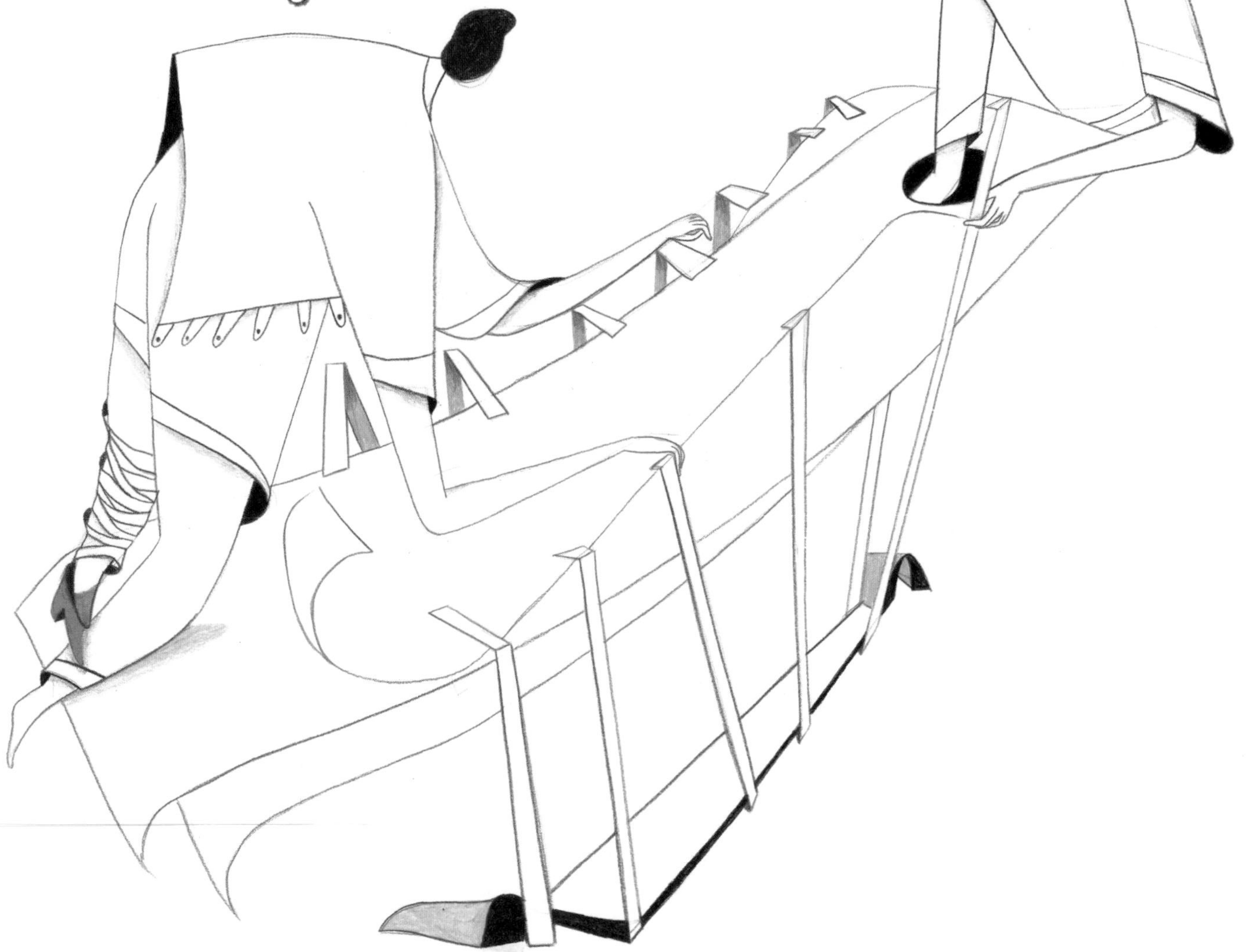

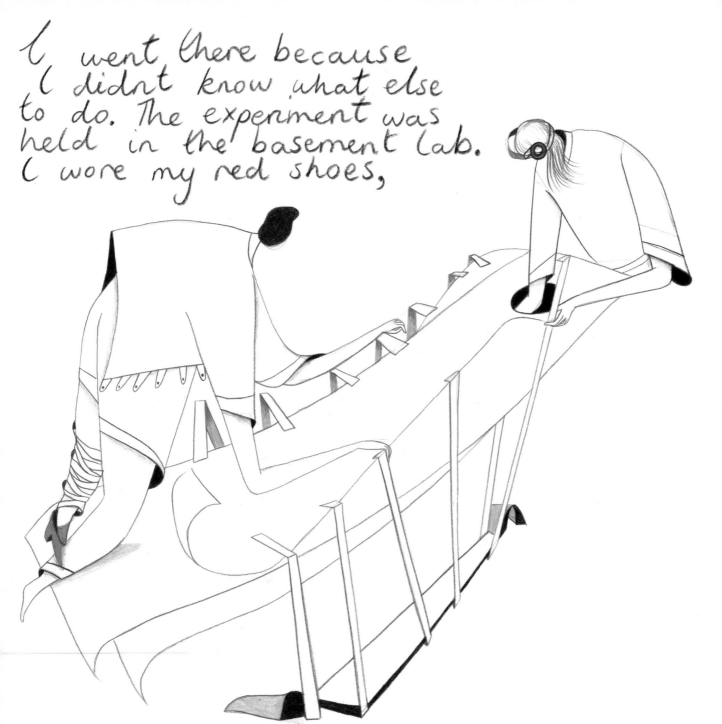

but the dancing turned out to be a hoax designed to grab the attention of the students.

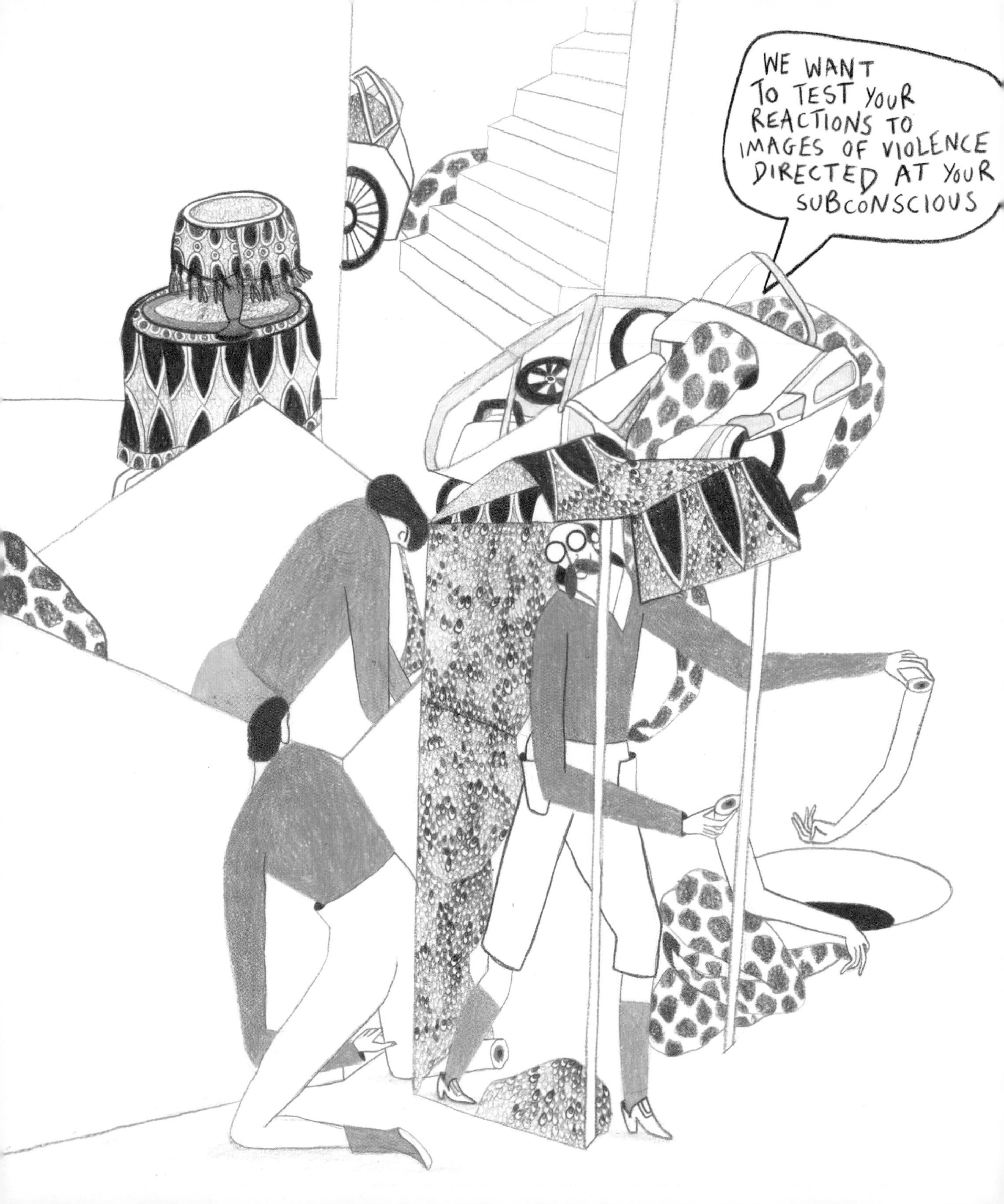
WE WANT TO TEST YOUR REACTIONS TO IMAGES OF VIOLENCE DIRECTED AT YOUR SUBCONSCIOUS

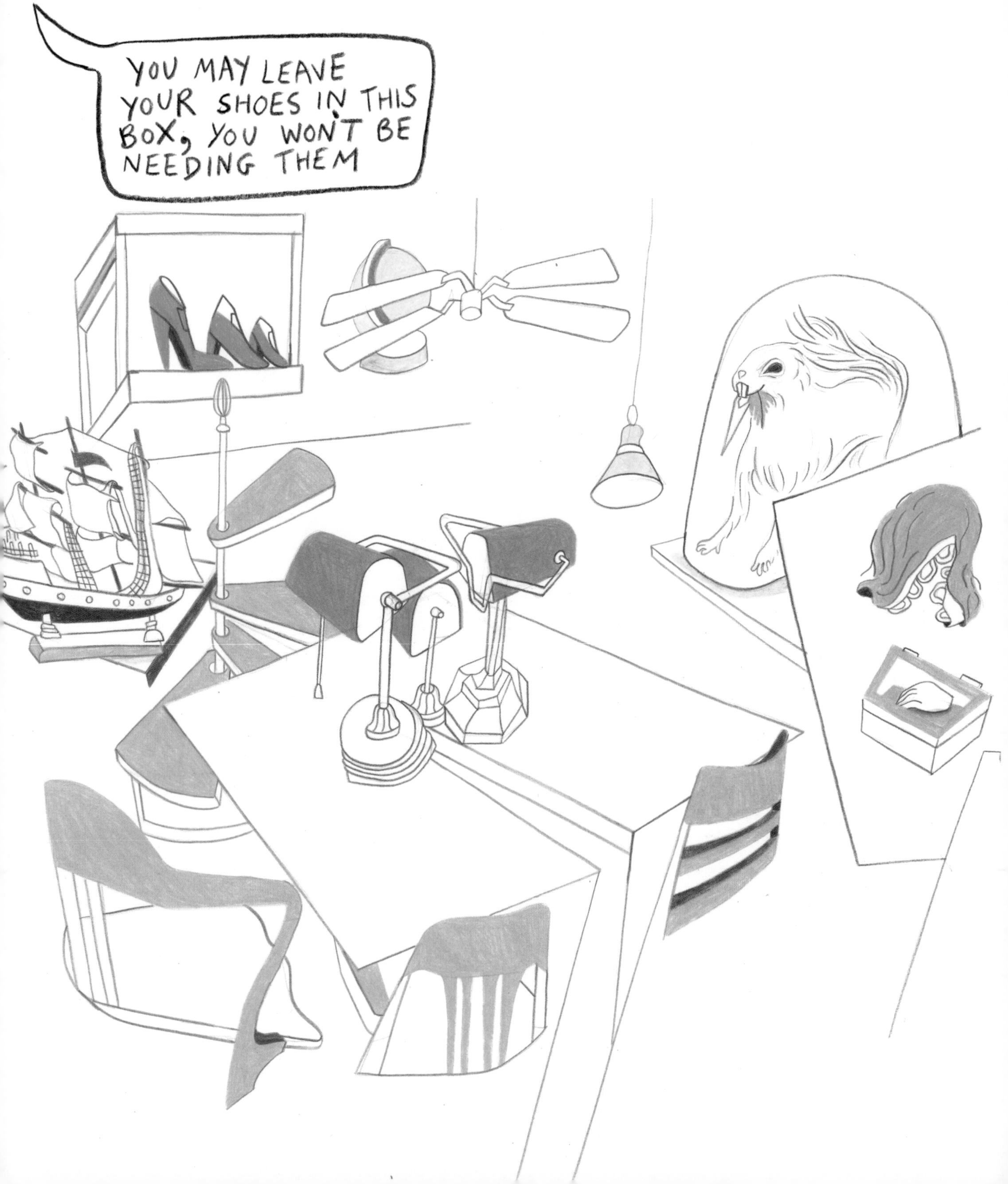
YOU MAY LEAVE YOUR SHOES IN THIS BOX, YOU WON'T BE NEEDING THEM

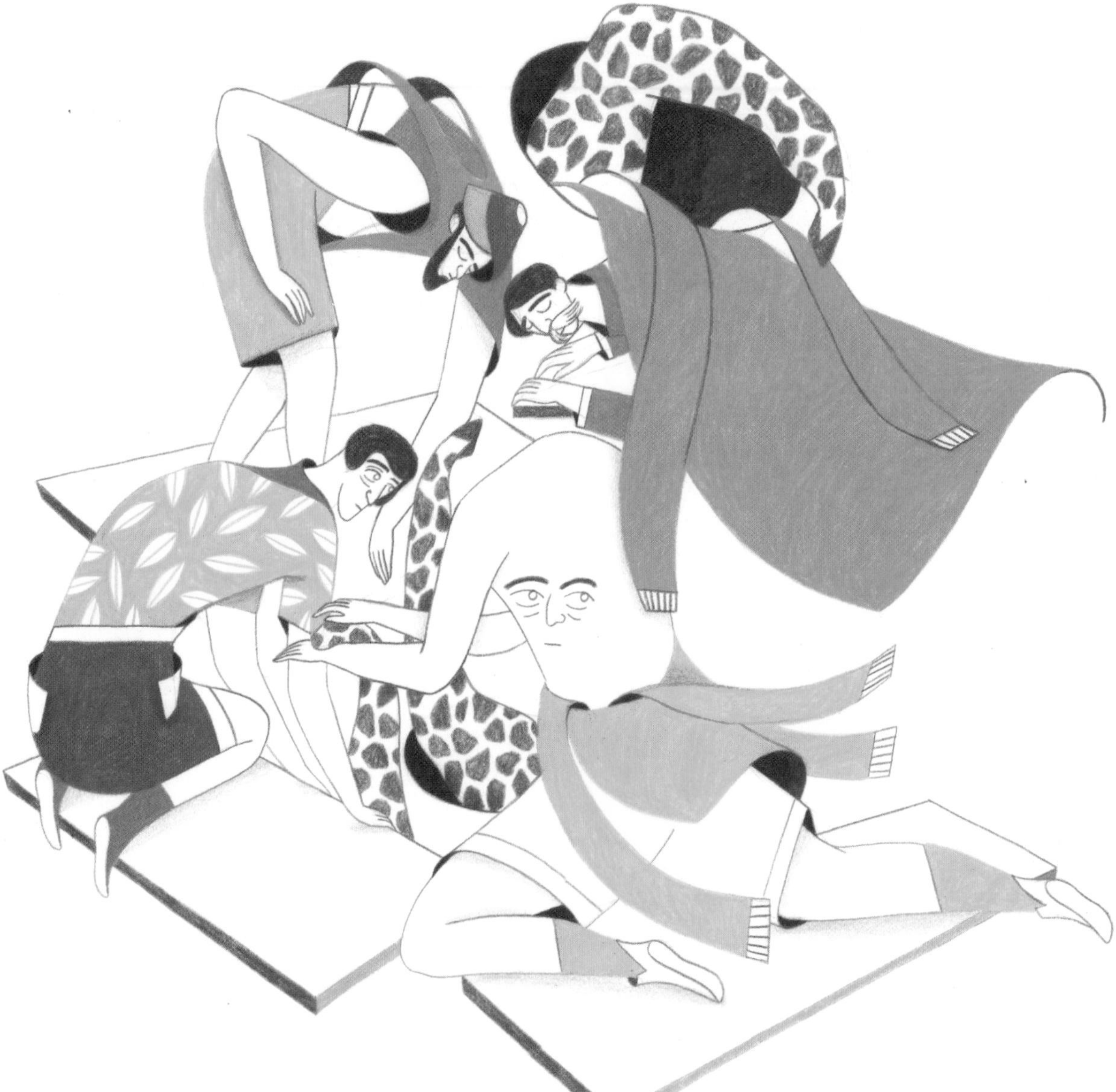

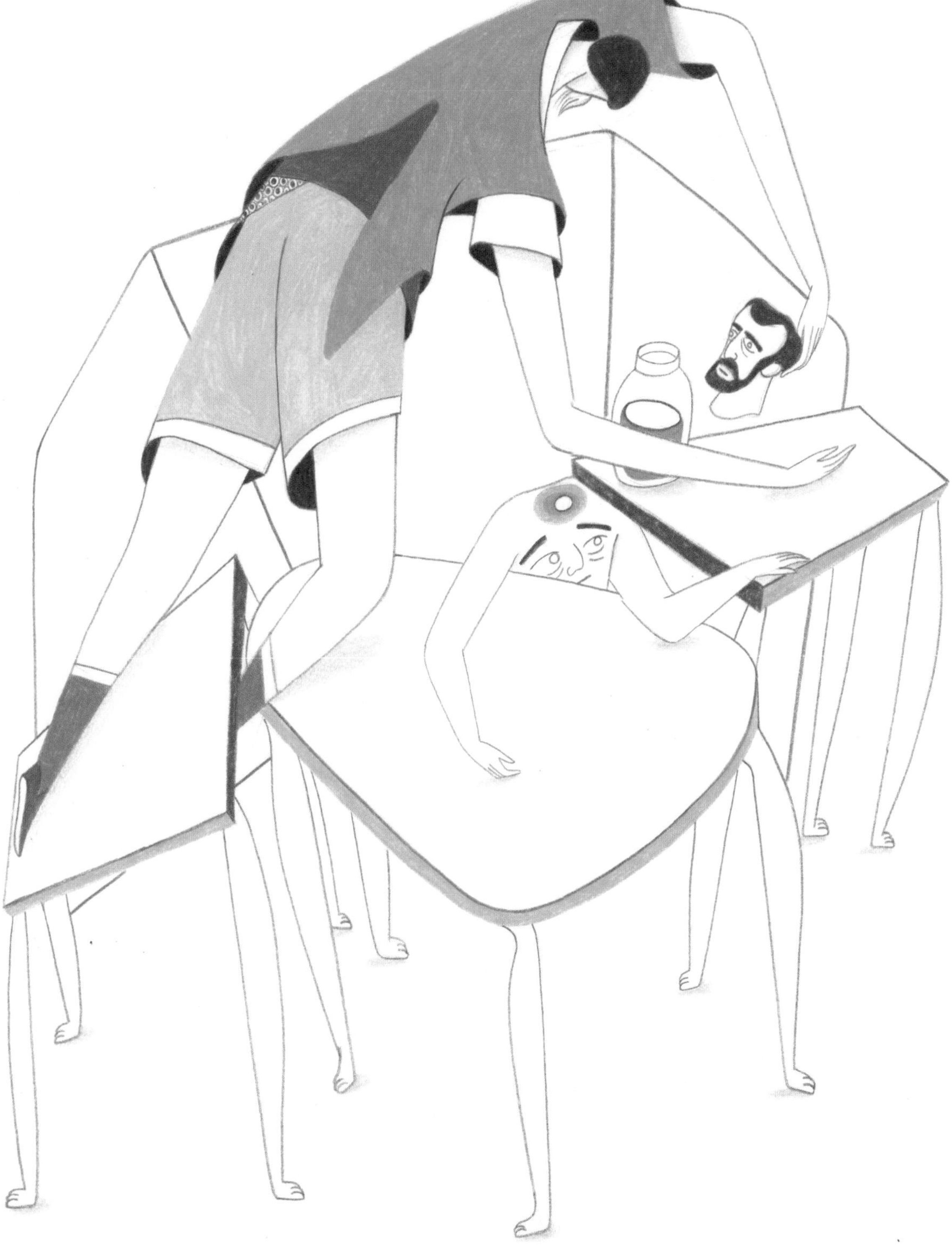

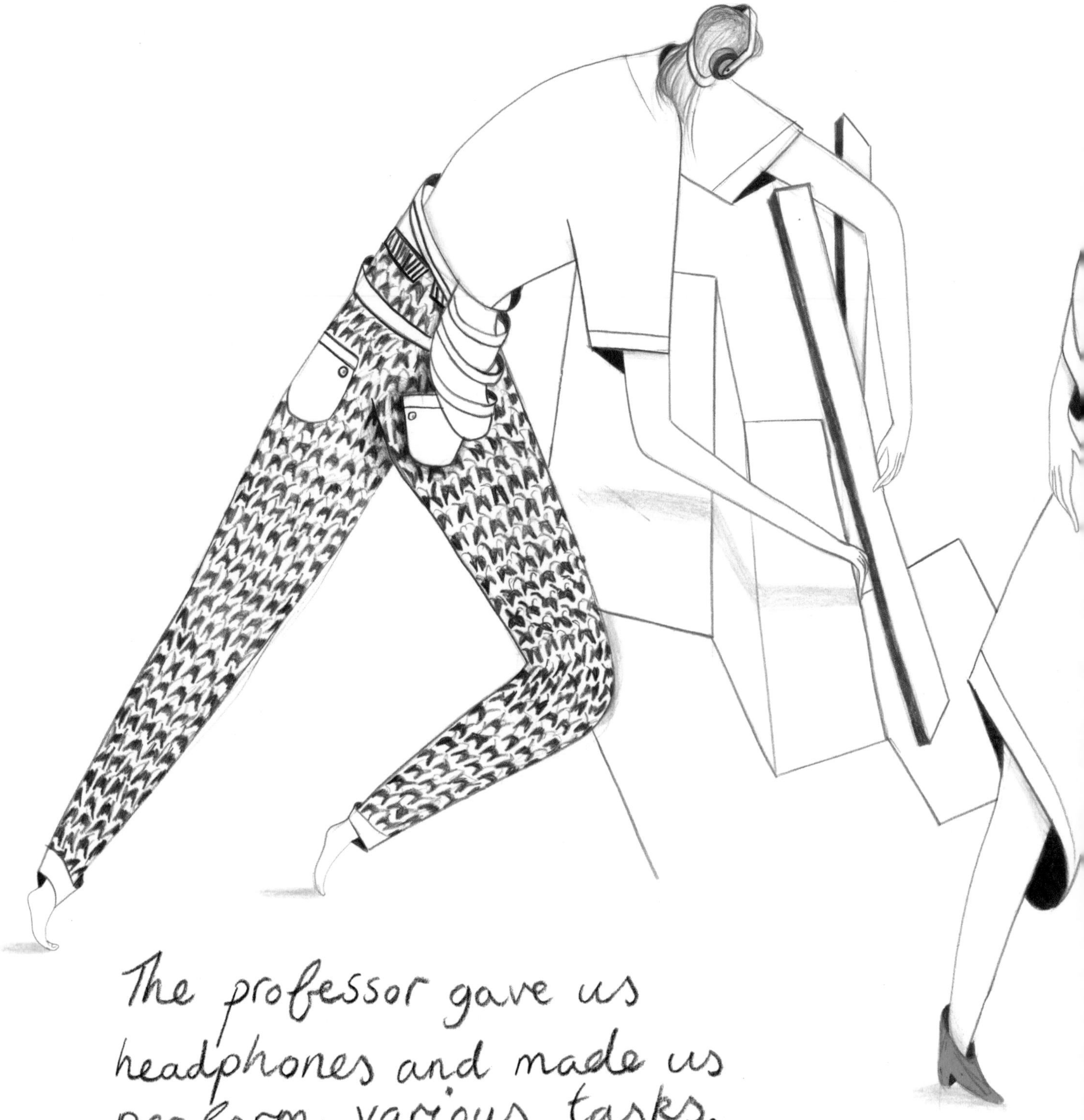

The professor gave us
headphones and made us
perform various tasks.

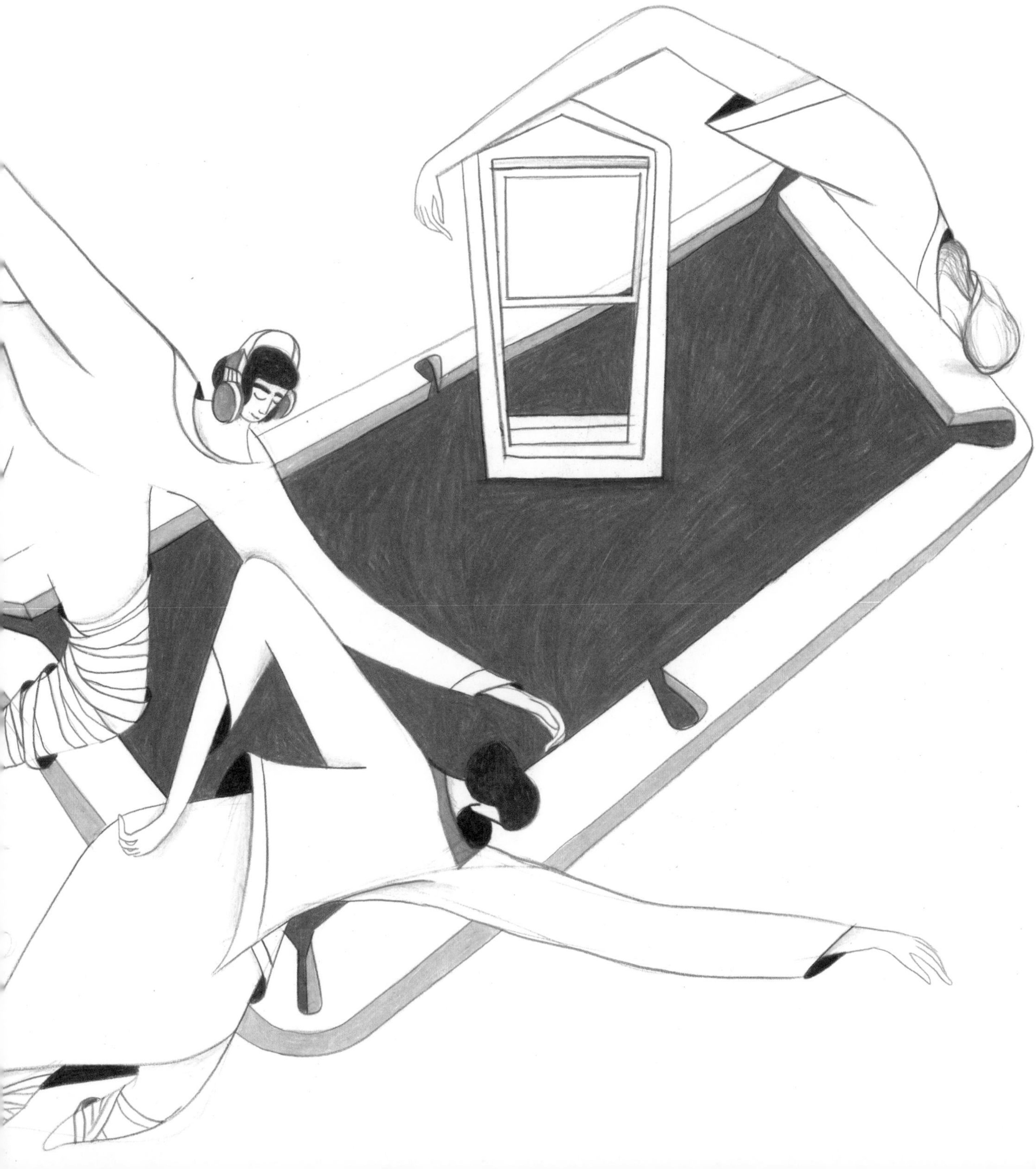

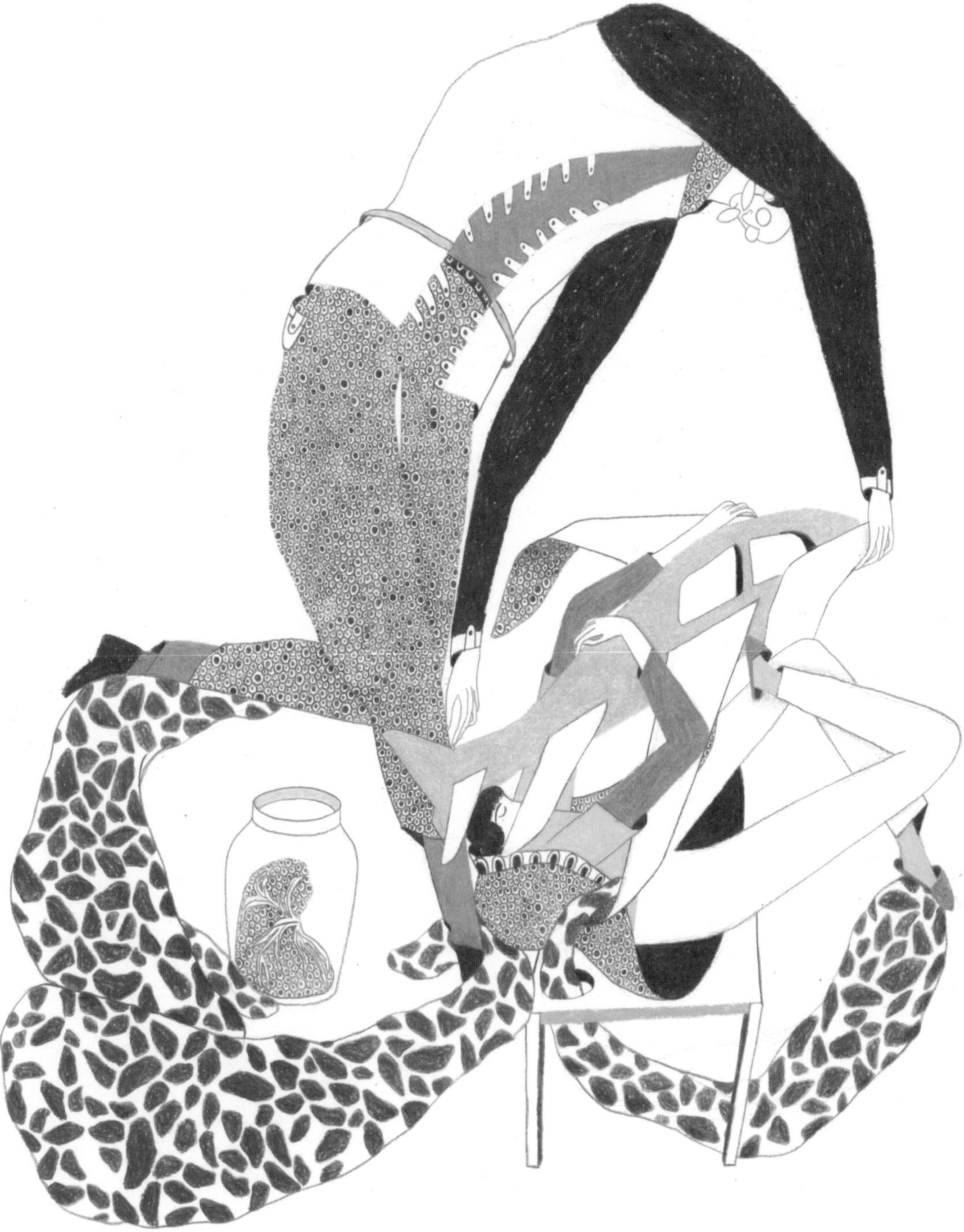

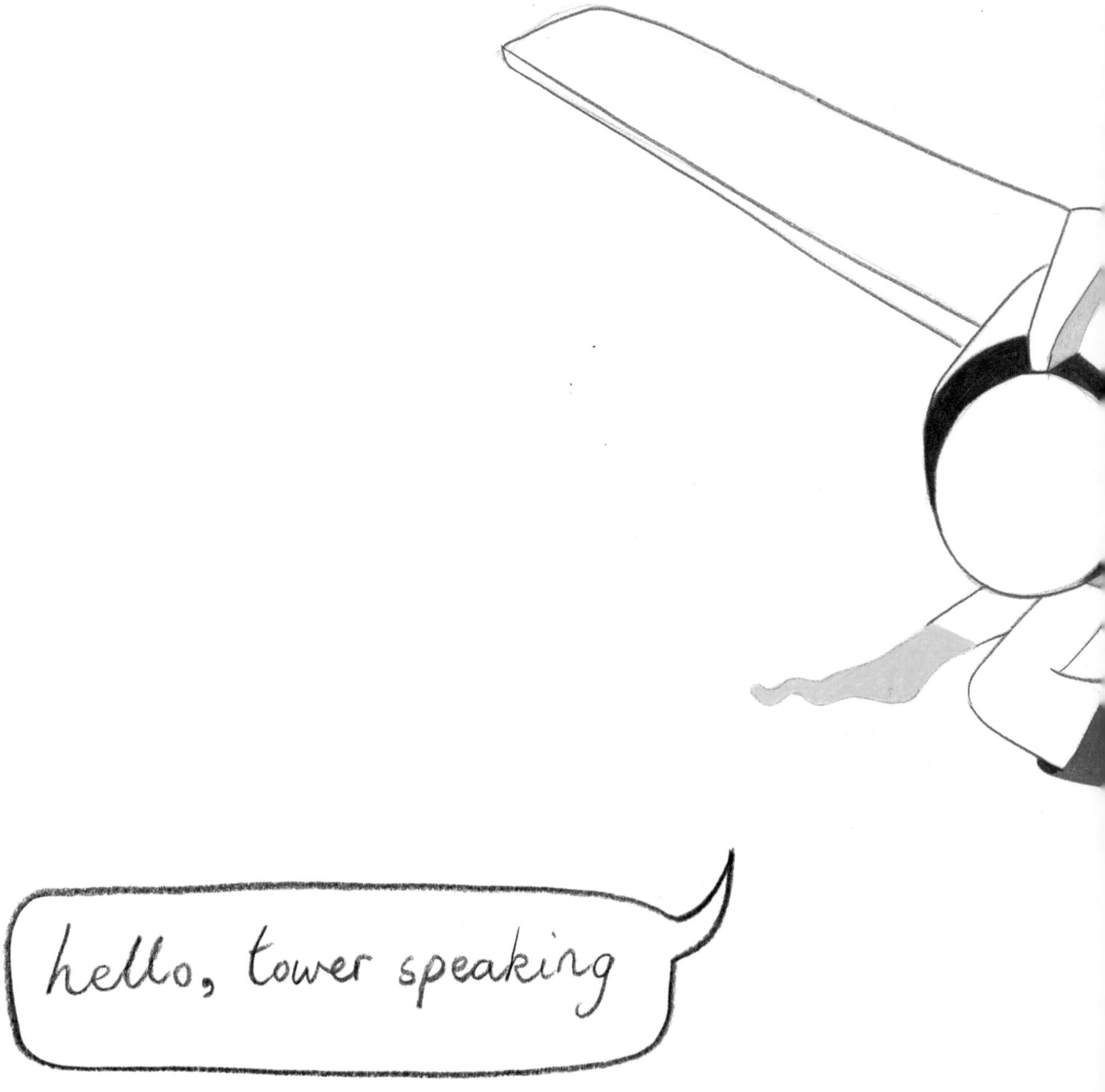
hello, tower speaking

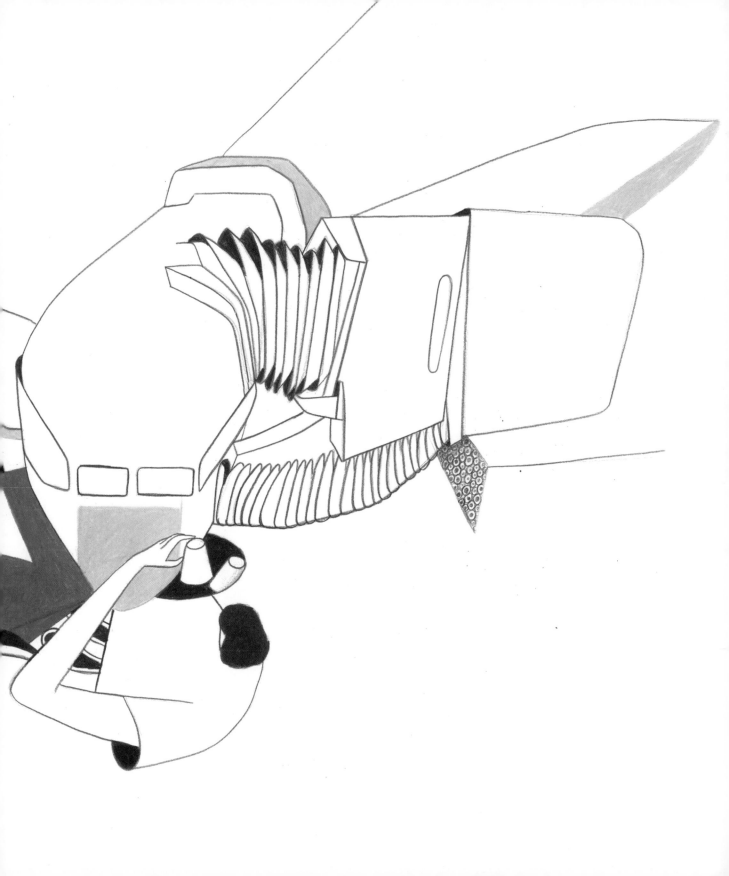

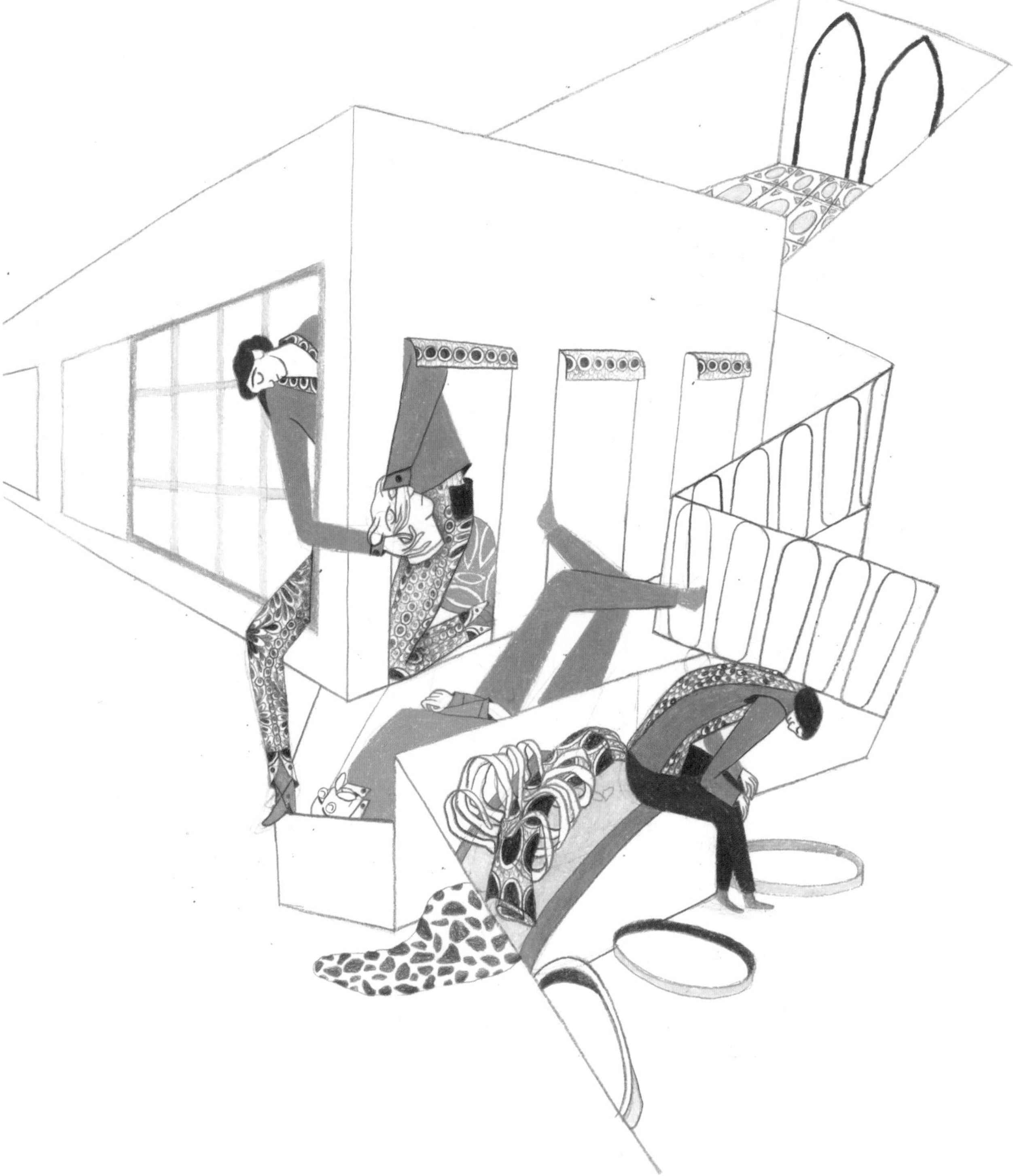

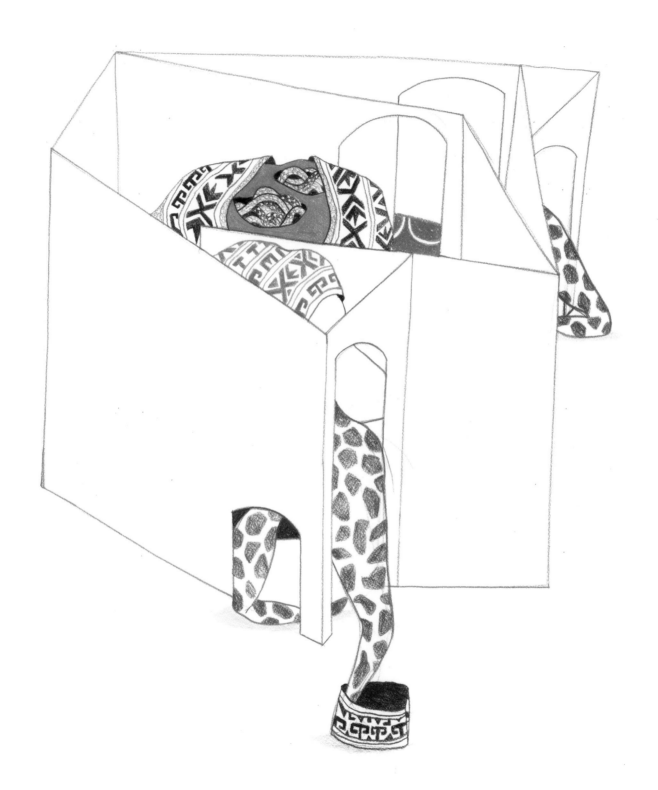

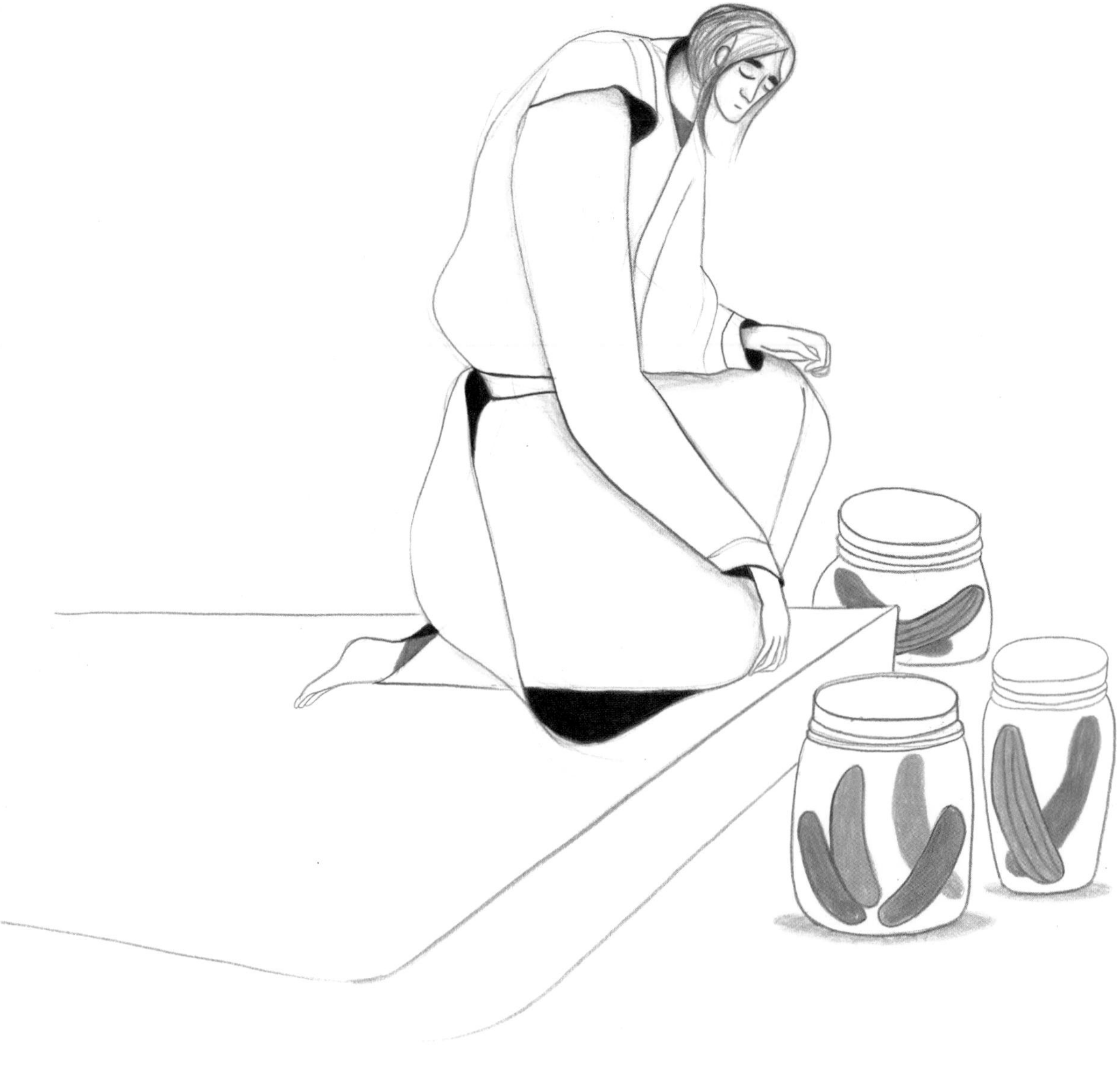

When the testing ended,
none of us remembered
seeing anything violent.

All we could think about was that time was passing and we were not dancing.

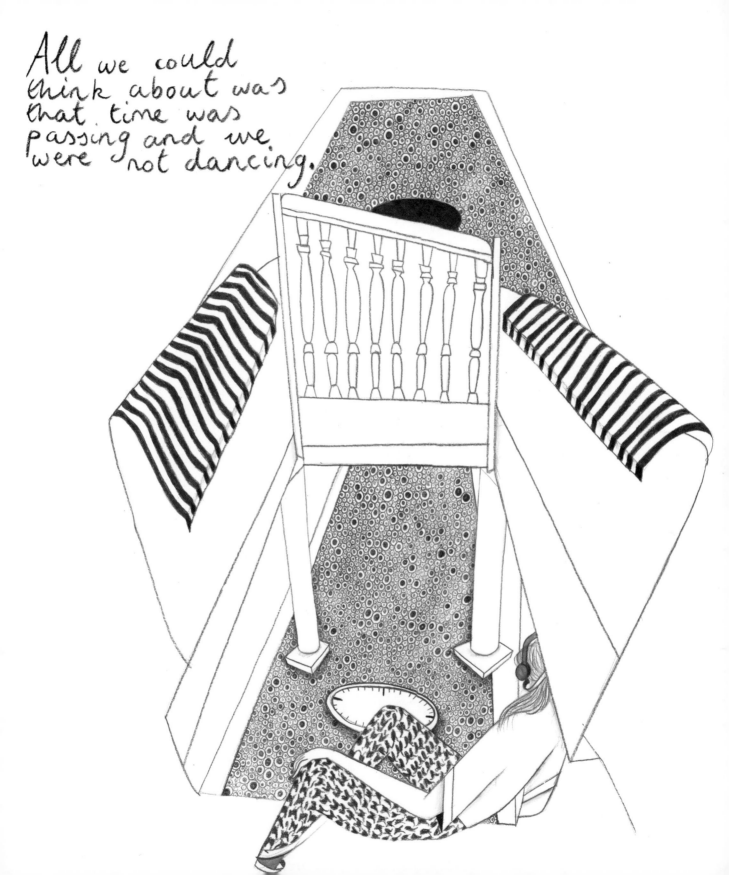

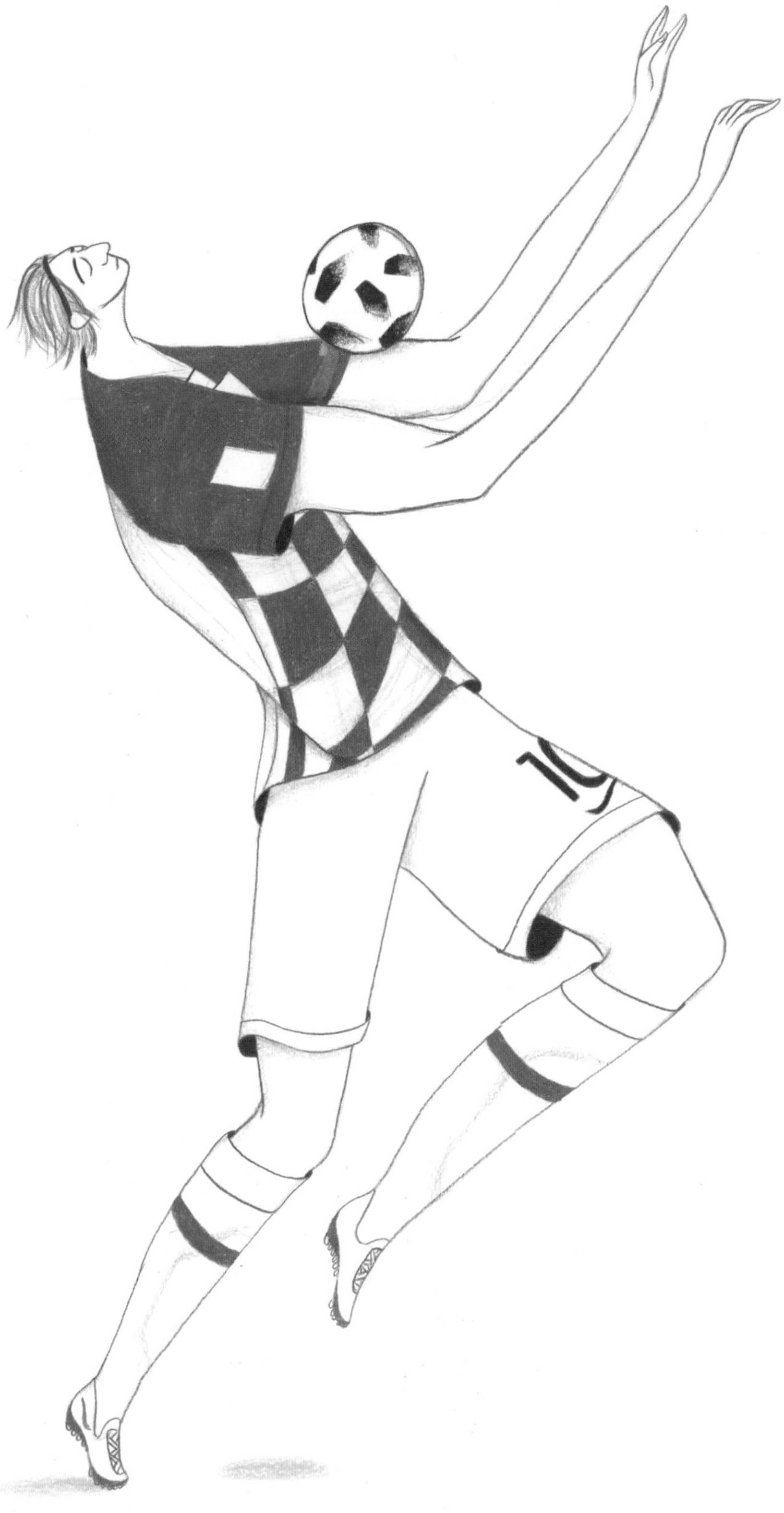
10

When I glanced at the professor's charts he had recorded only one moment in the experiment.

It was the moment I thought of you, in your chair, unable to move.

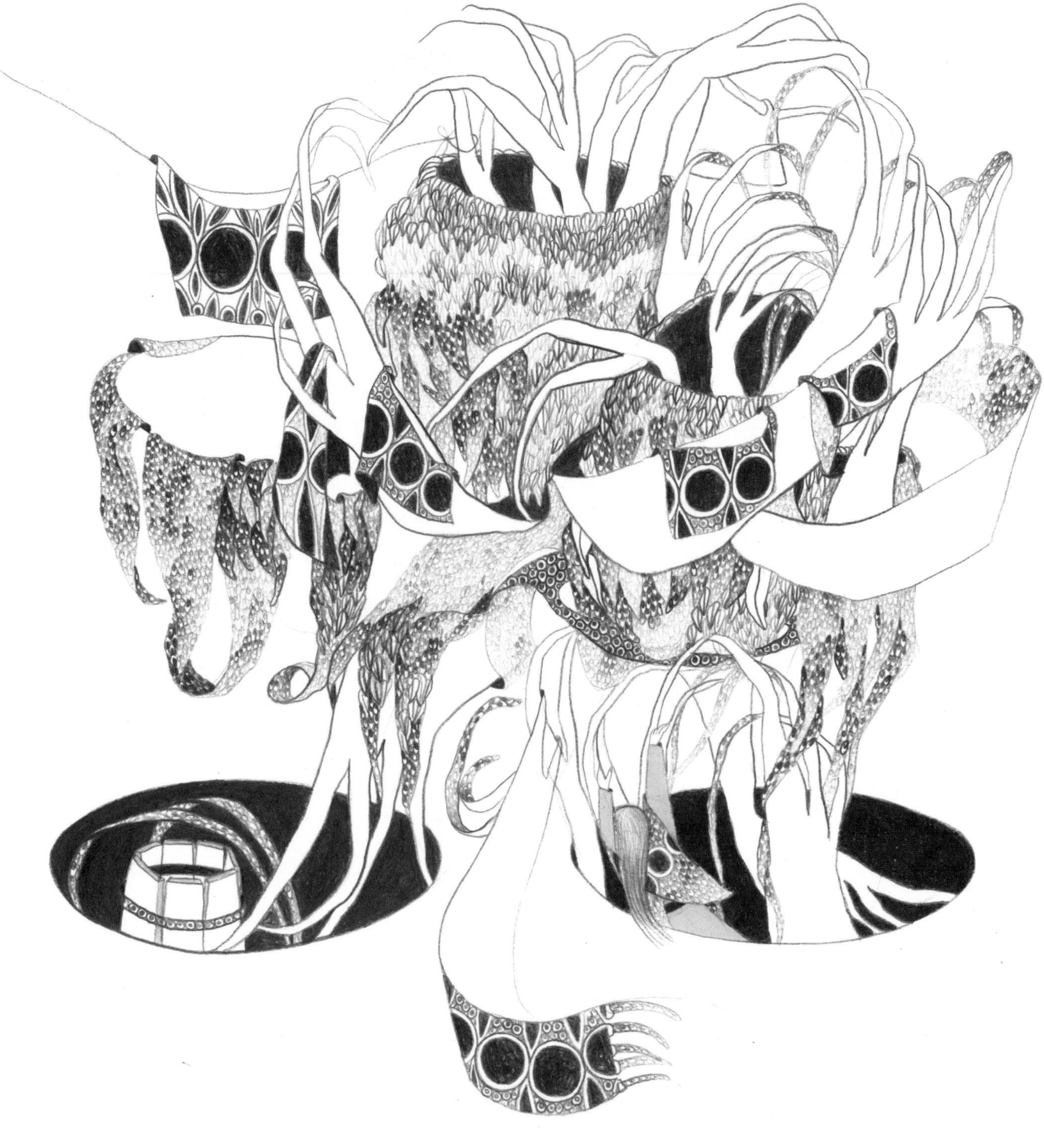

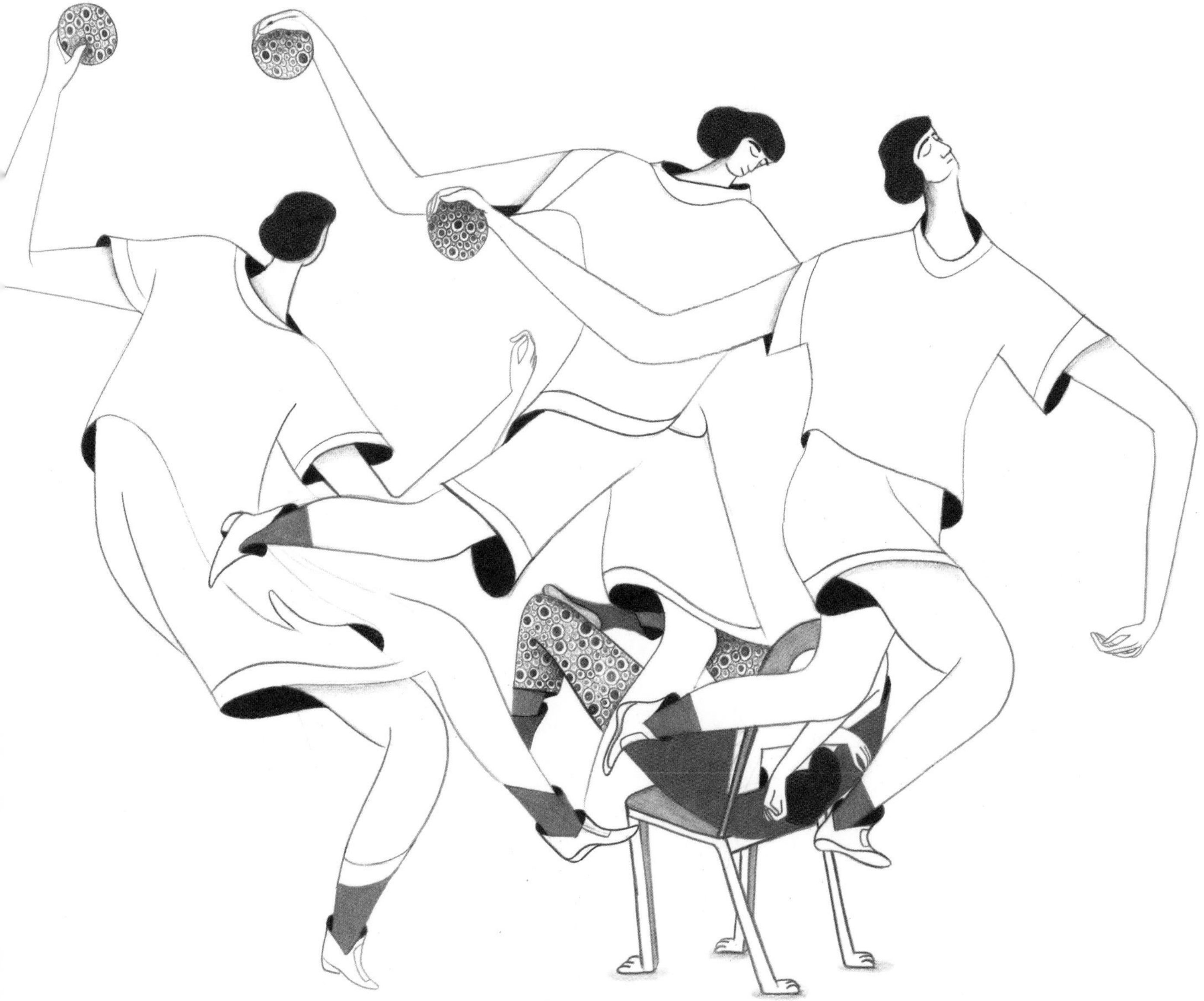

when I was little I watched
you getting kicked and punched
on the handball court but
I'm much more frightened now,
when the only thing that I have
known about you, is gone.

I walk in circles around
the relics of your travels
and the words burried in
them and forgotten because
you came home and we
were sleeping.

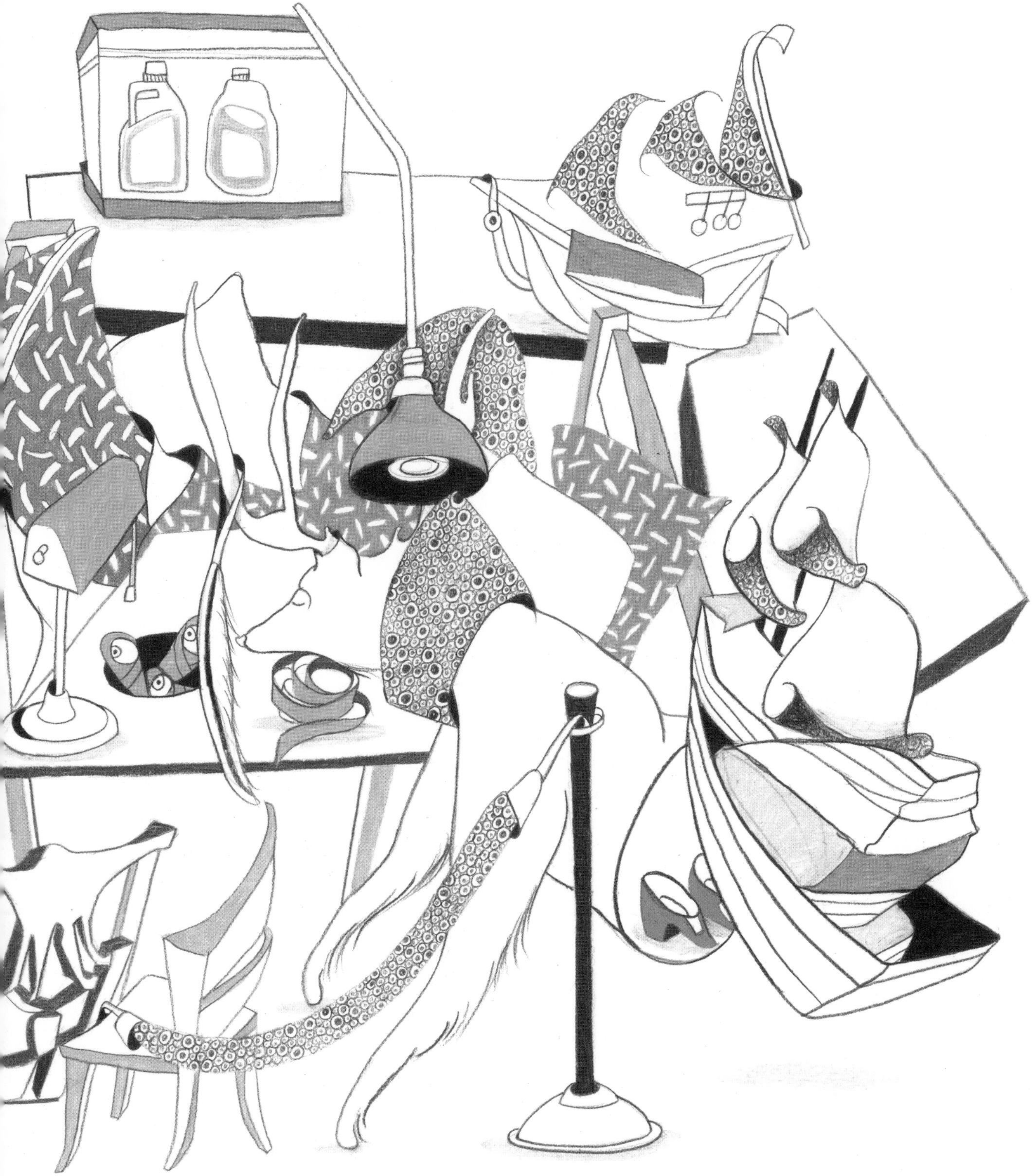

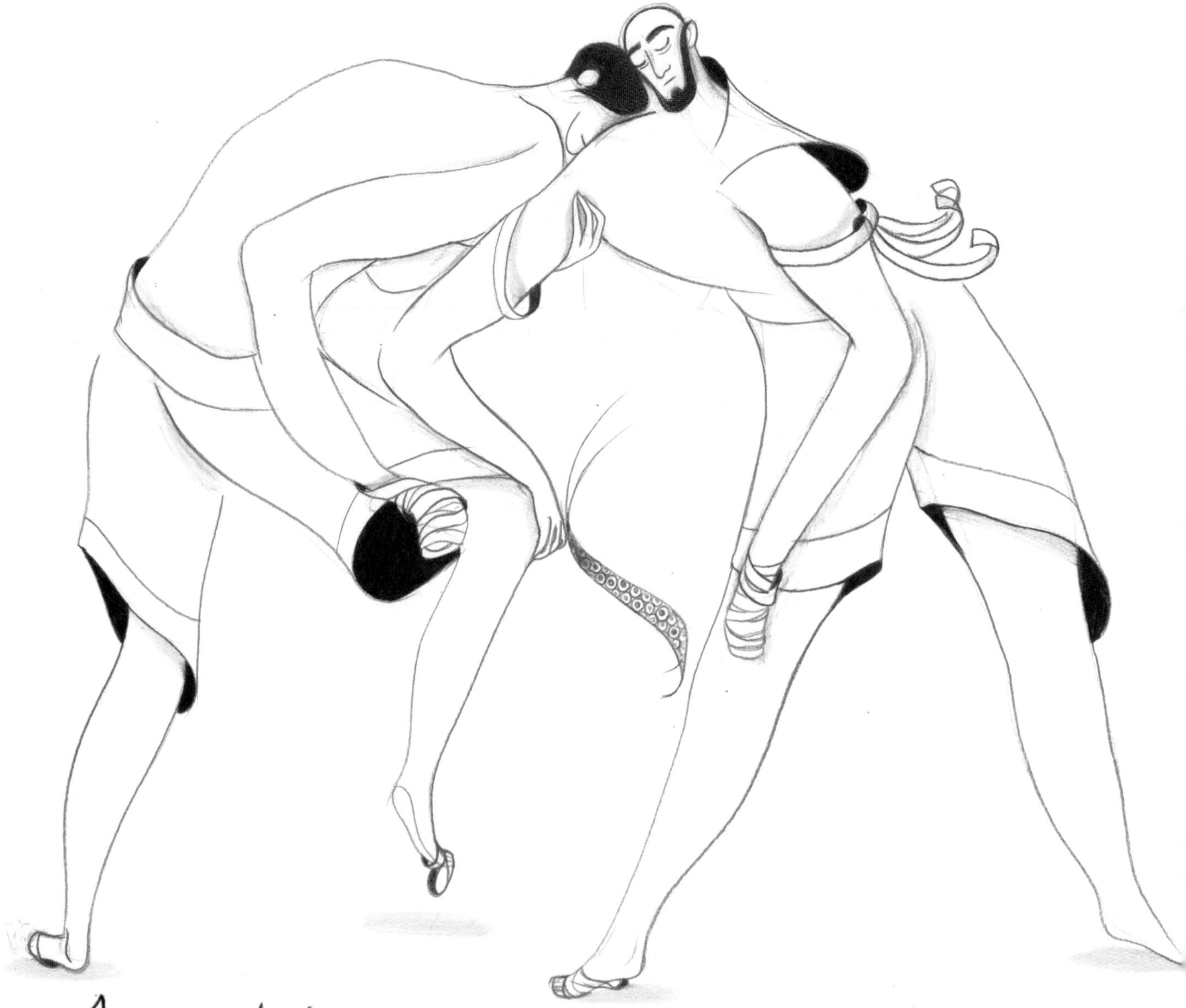

I want to
force us both into free
fall to disconnect us
from the silence that has
settled between us over the
years.

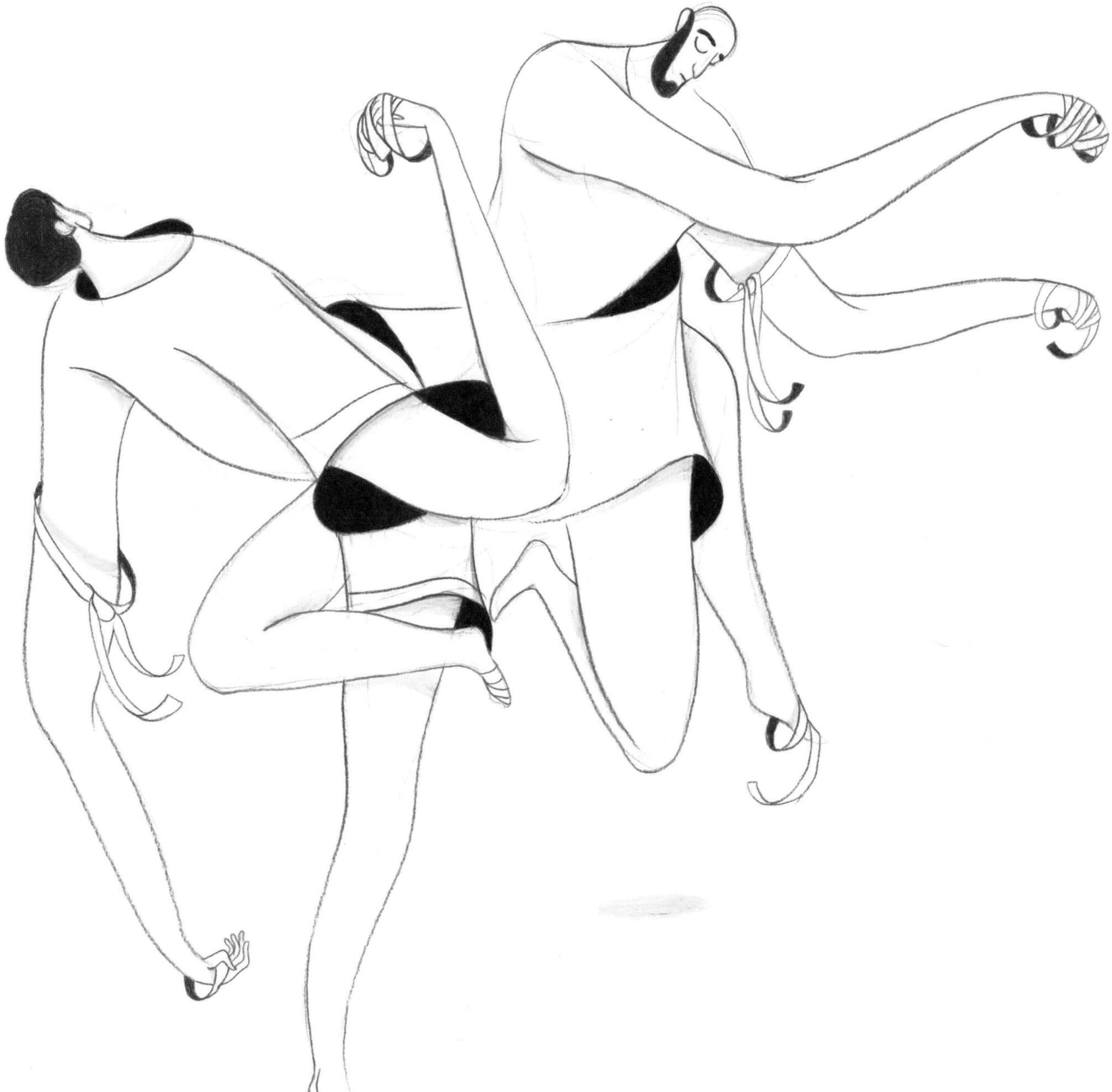

It was shortly after the experiment that the man who followed me disappeared. I'm afraid my movements changed somehow and he cannot recognize me anymore.

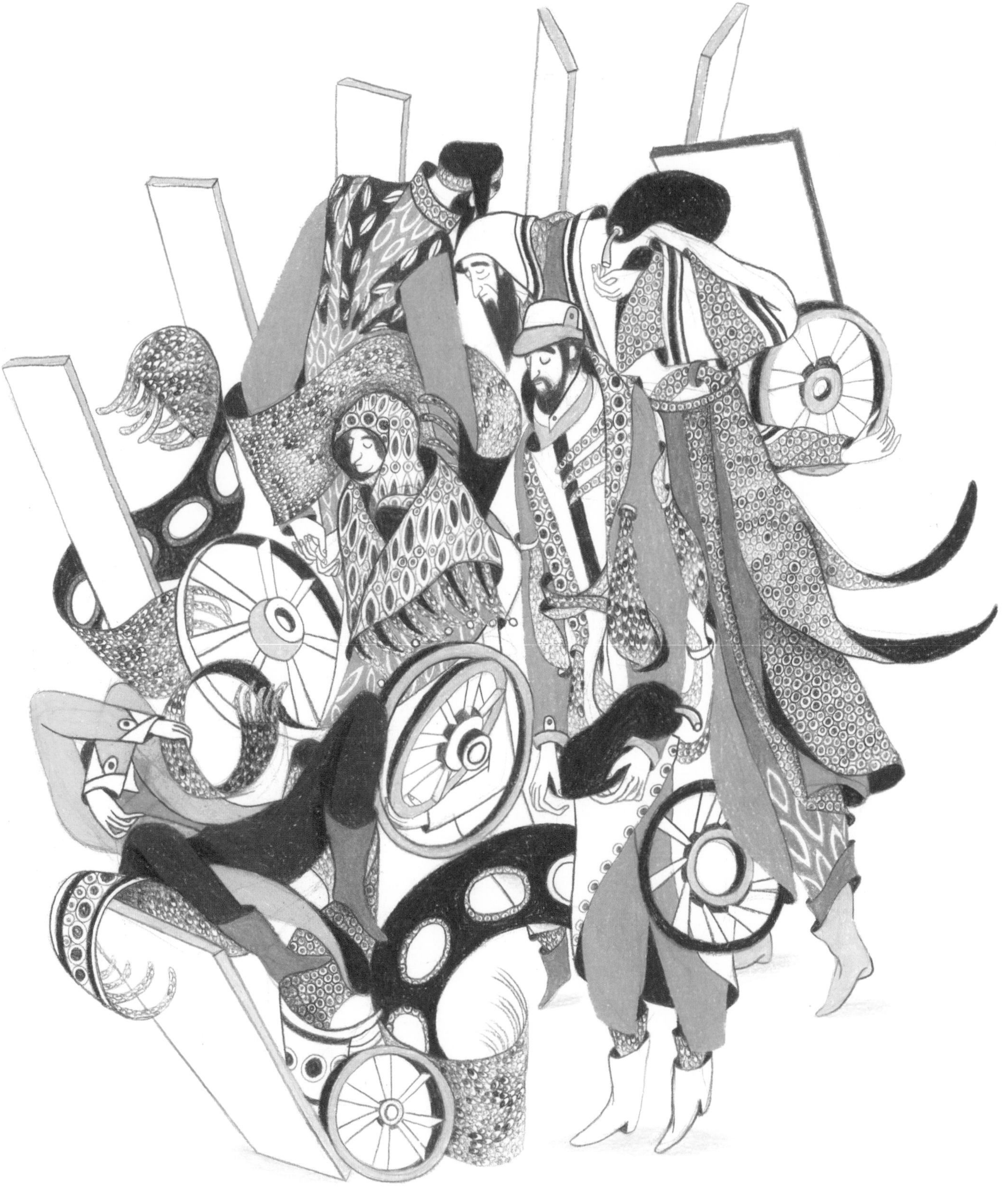

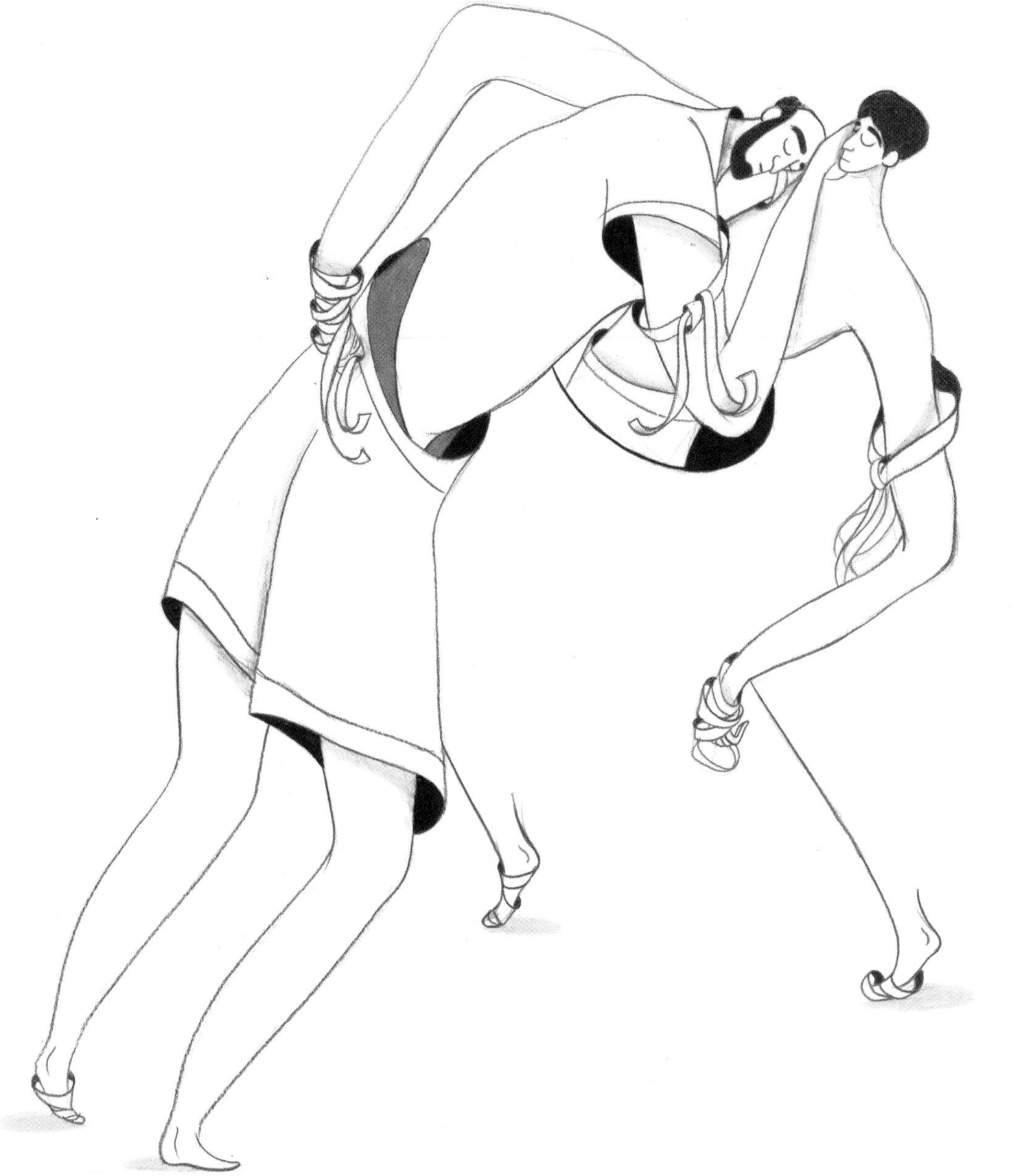

I have stopped eating
so that at least one
of us can move backwards
in time.

I have become smaller,
cut my hair short, shaped
myself as an injured man.

I hate you for
breaking your back.

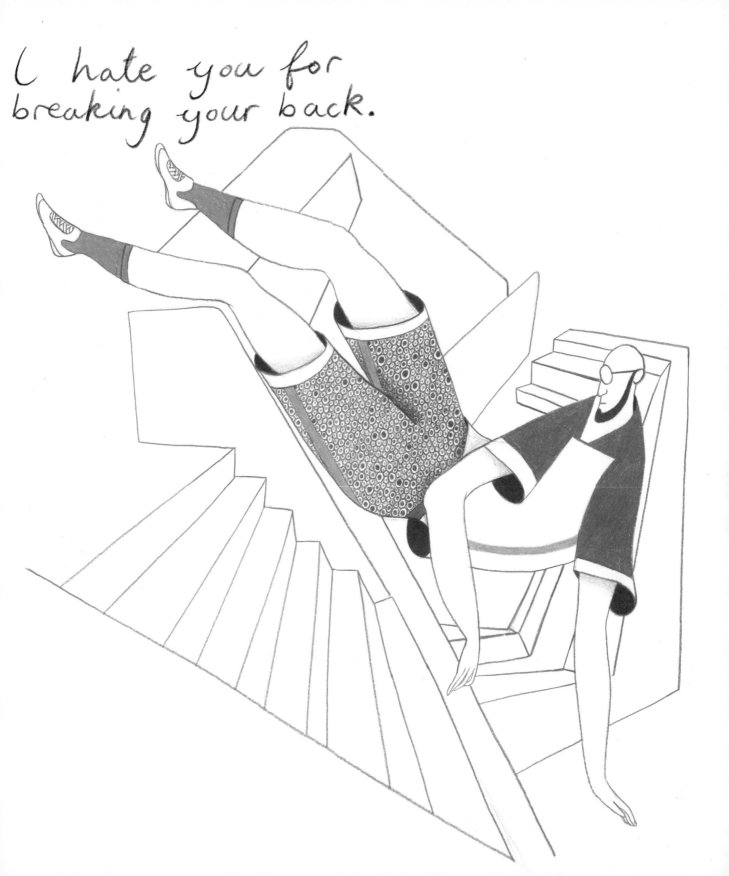

Chapter 7:
NOVAK DISAPPEARS

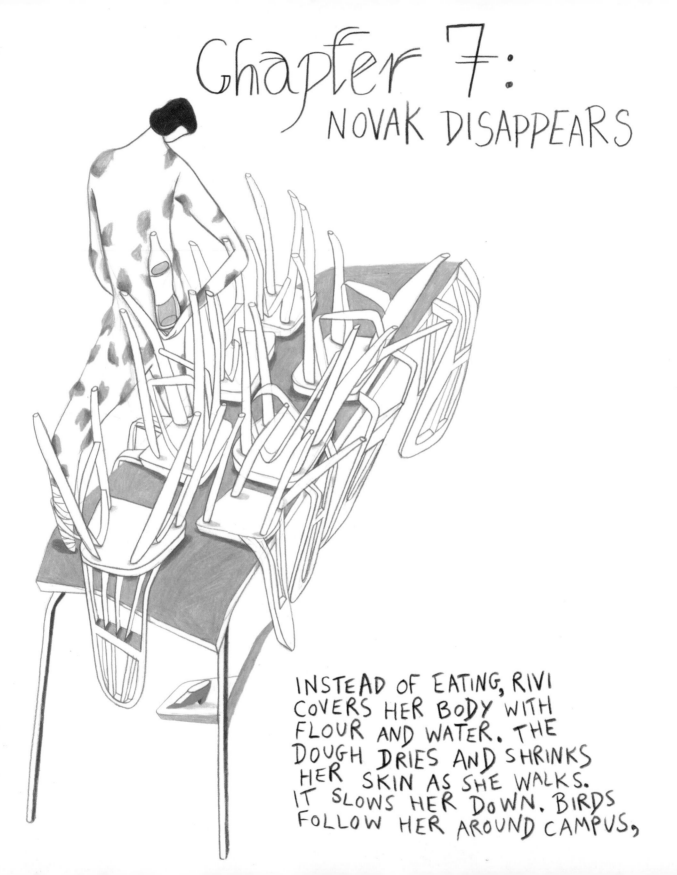

INSTEAD OF EATING, RIVI
COVERS HER BODY WITH
FLOUR AND WATER. THE
DOUGH DRIES AND SHRINKS
HER SKIN AS SHE WALKS.
IT SLOWS HER DOWN. BIRDS
FOLLOW HER AROUND CAMPUS,

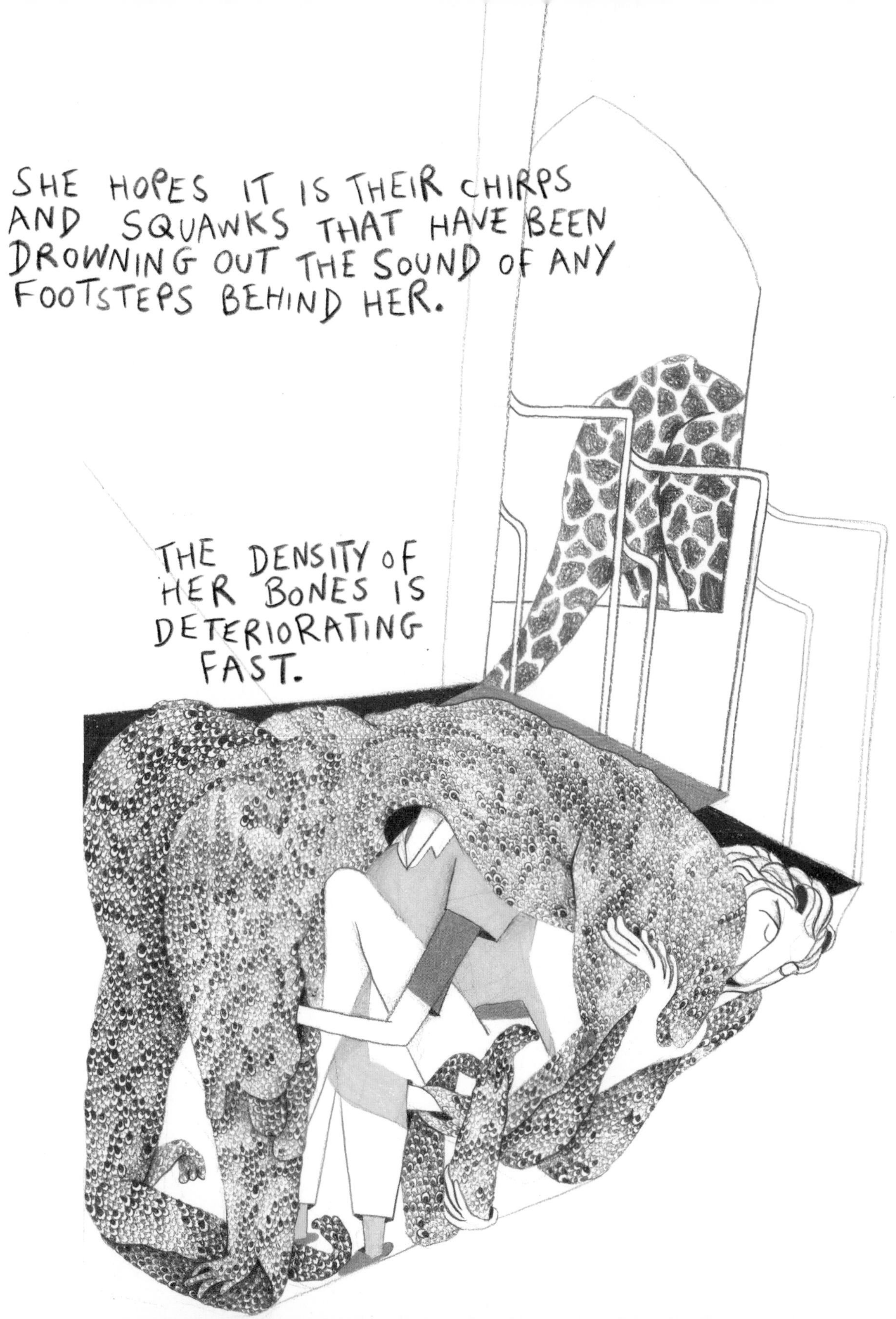
SHE HOPES IT IS THEIR CHIRPS AND SQUAWKS THAT HAVE BEEN DROWNING OUT THE SOUND OF ANY FOOTSTEPS BEHIND HER.
THE DENSITY OF HER BONES IS DETERIORATING FAST.

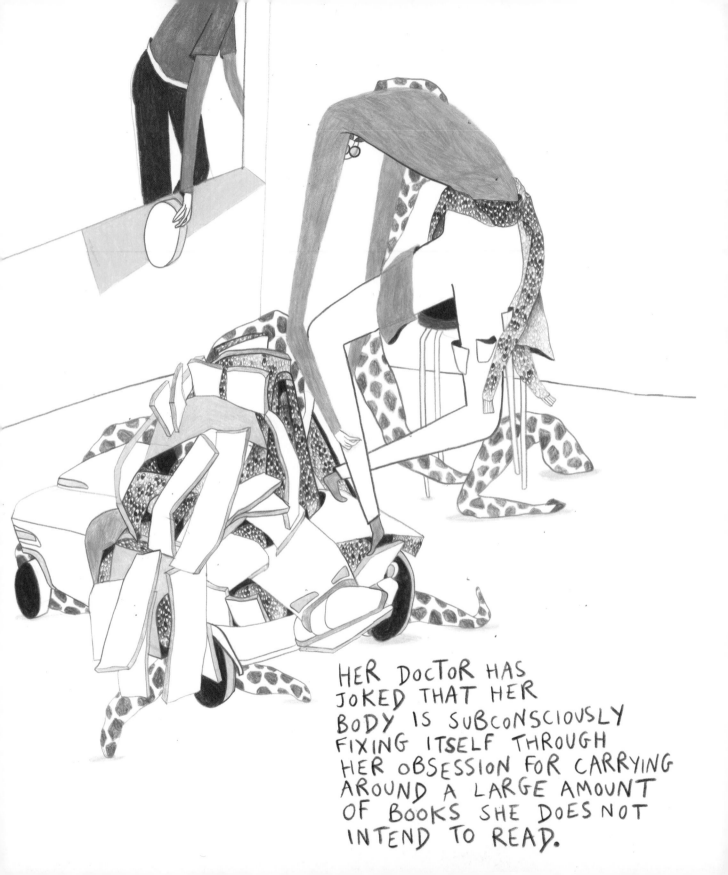

HER DOCTOR HAS
JOKED THAT HER
BODY IS SUBCONSCIOUSLY
FIXING ITSELF THROUGH
HER OBSESSION FOR CARRYING
AROUND A LARGE AMOUNT
OF BOOKS SHE DOES NOT
INTEND TO READ.

RIVI FALLS ASLEEP, THE BOOKS WEIGH HER CHEST DOWN. IN THE NEXT ROOM NOVAK'S SHOW IS PLAYING OUT.

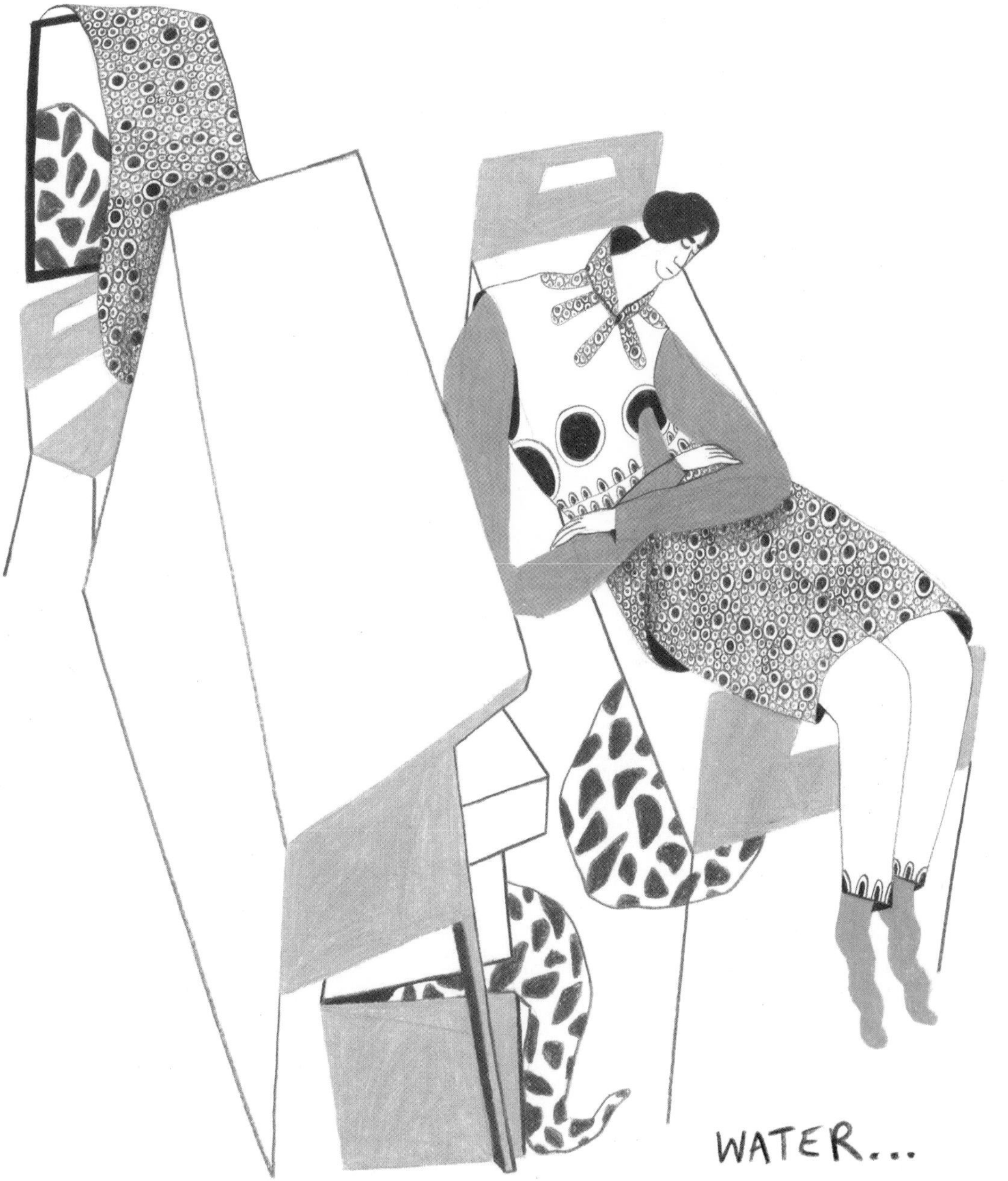
WATER...

SUDDENLY, RIVI SITS UP IN HER CHAIR. NOVAK MENTIONED YAKOV'S NAME.

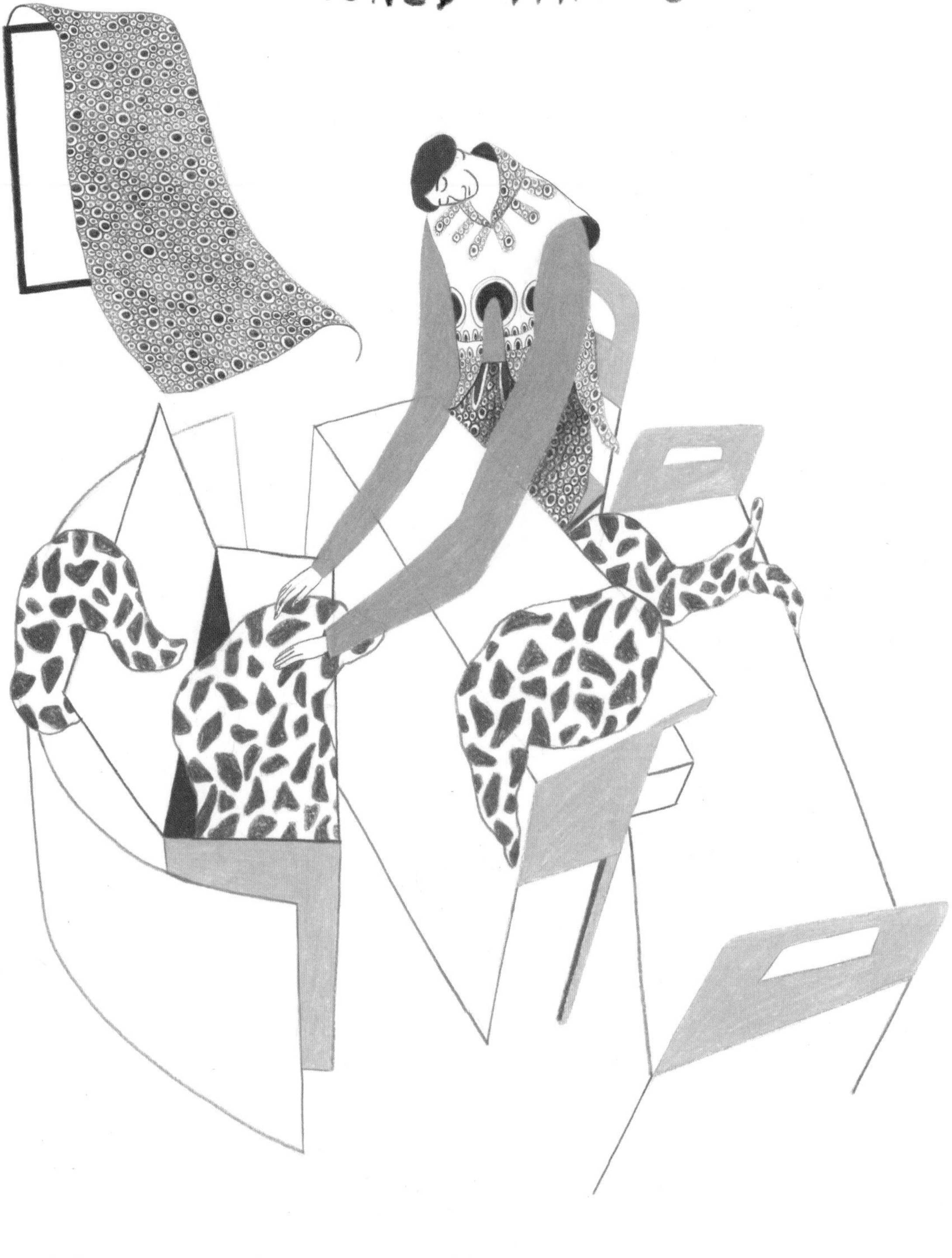

THE WATER HAS STOPPED RUNNING IN THE KITCHEN.

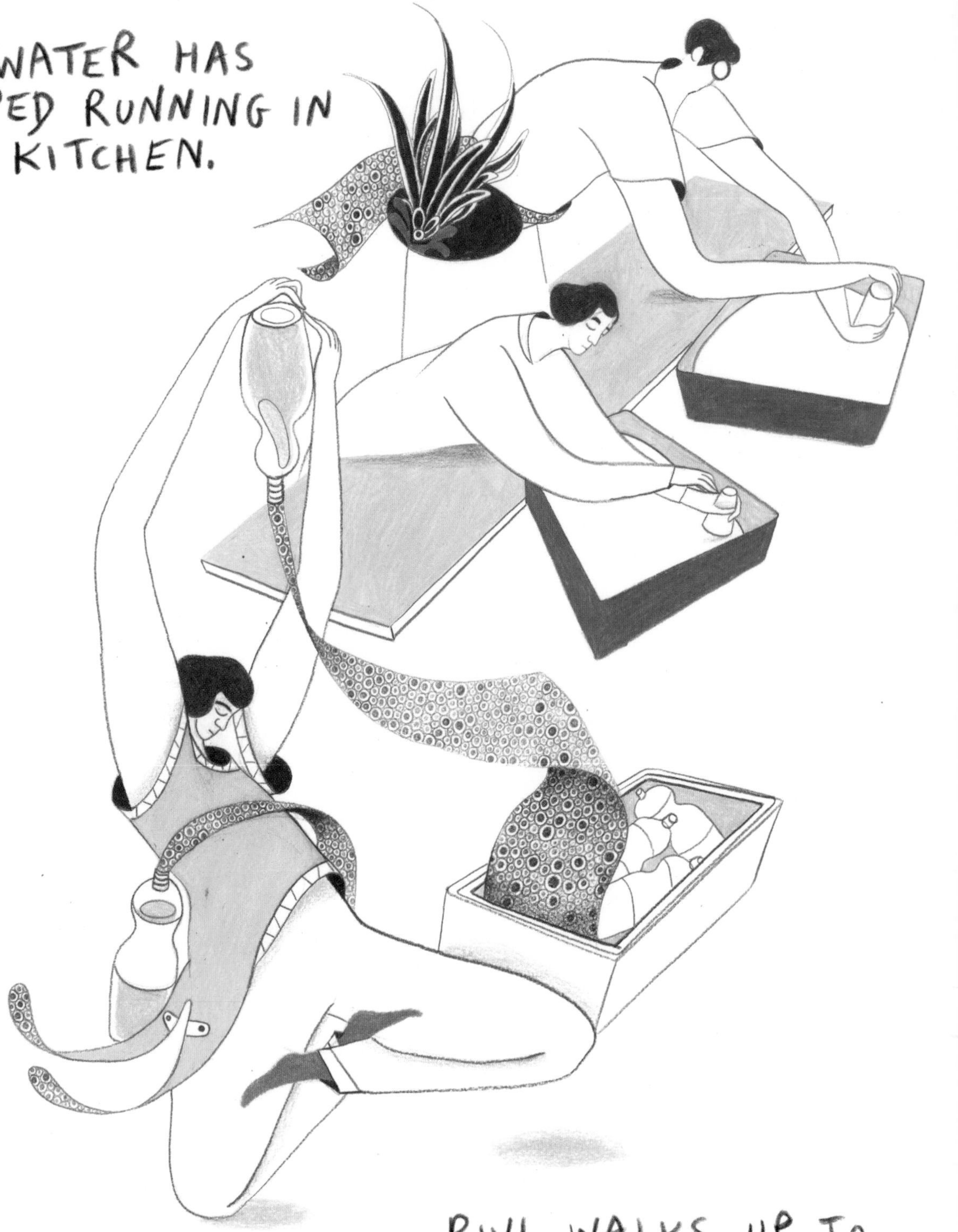

RIVI WALKS UP TO THE FAUCET AND HITS "RECORD."

I have to walk up to the fridge thirty times each day to subdue a haunting sensation with two sips of seltzer.

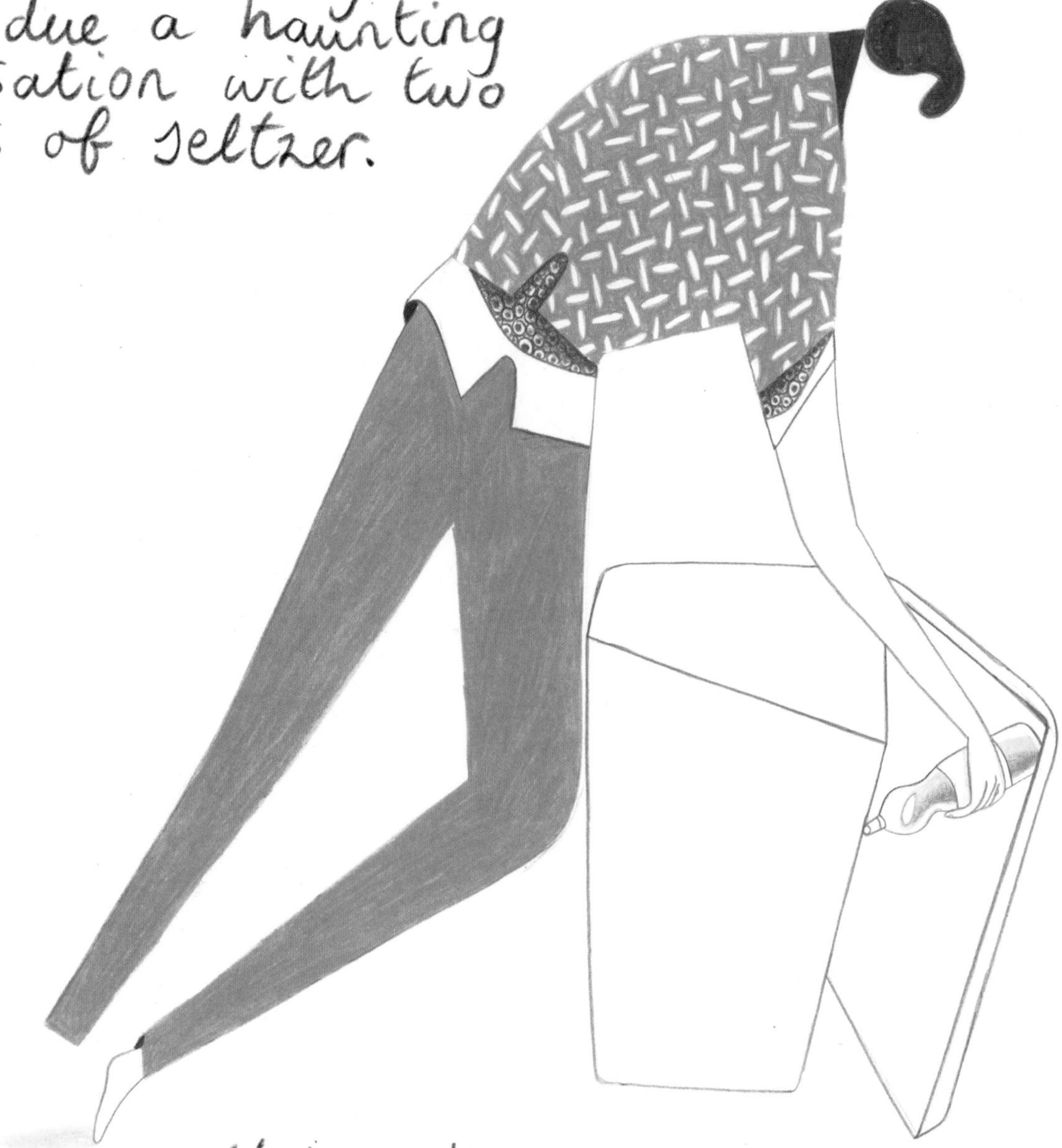

It has been years since I kept anything but seltzer bottles in the fridge.

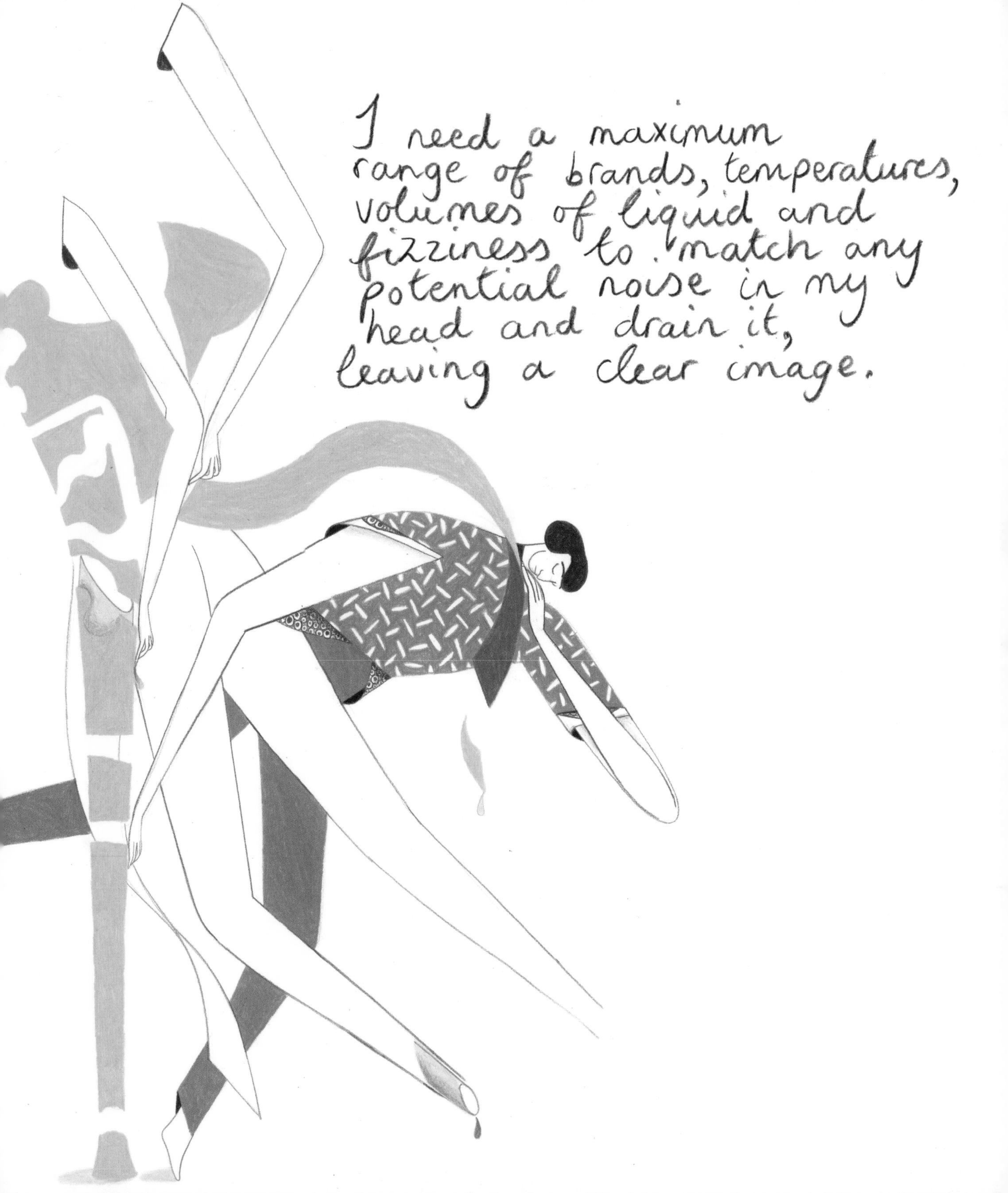
I need a maximum range of brands, temperatures, volumes of liquid and fizziness to match any potential noise in my head and drain it, leaving a clear image.

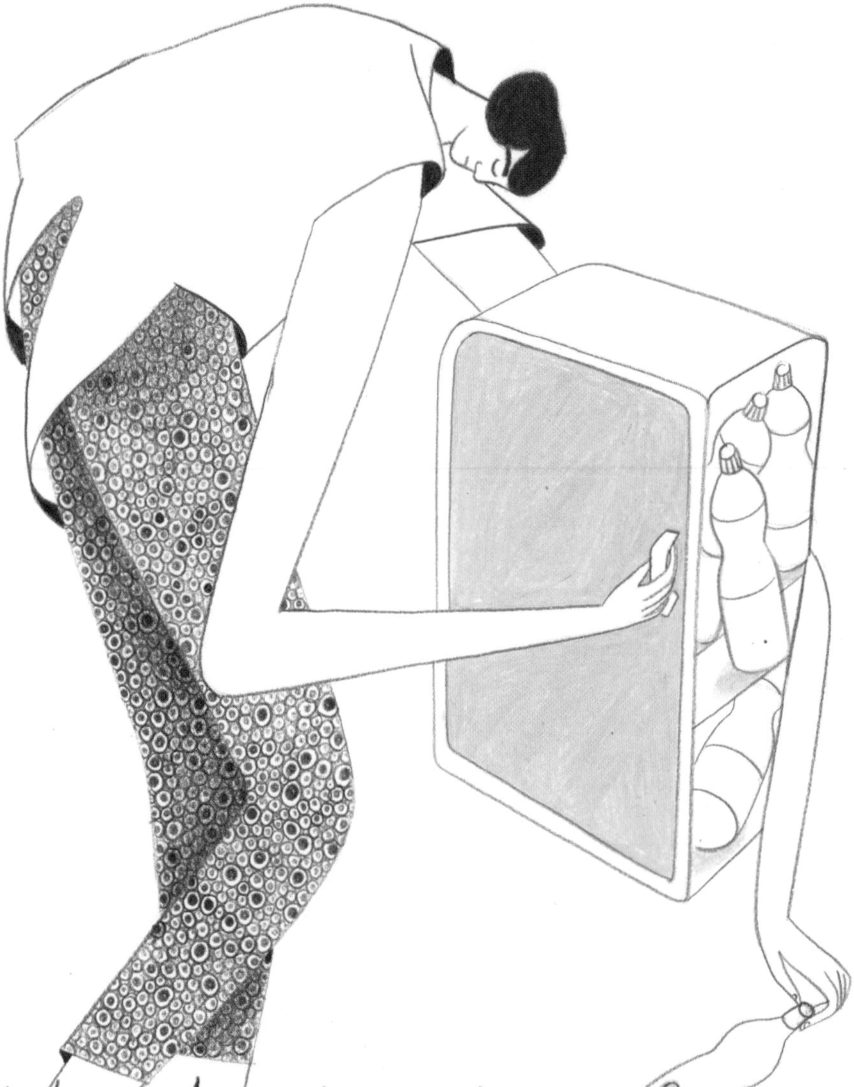

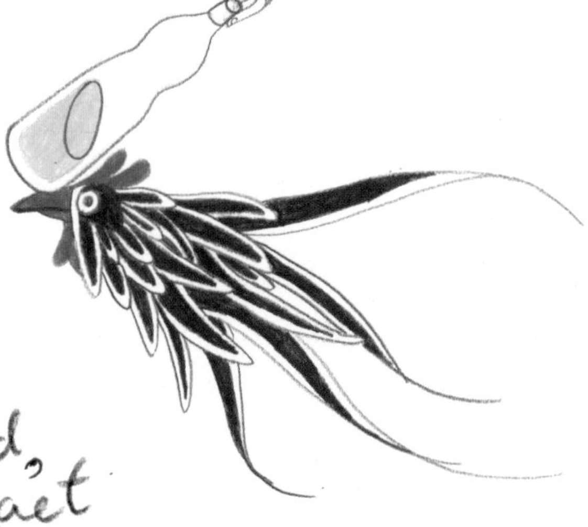

When I next walk up to the fridge, I will be able to feel the time that has passed on my tongue, through the texture of the liquid, returning to that exact memory that would otherwise dissolve and merge into other thoughts.

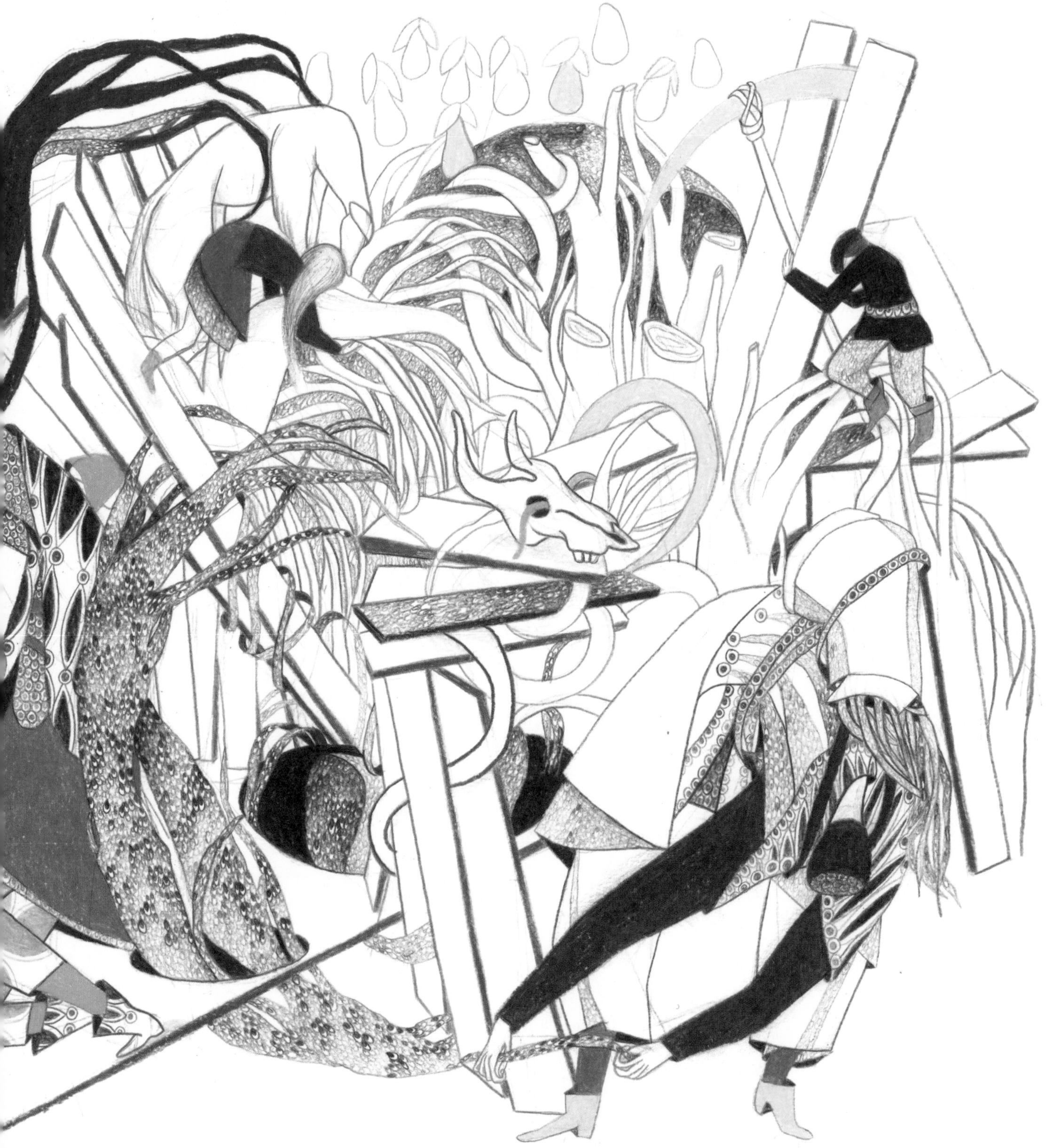

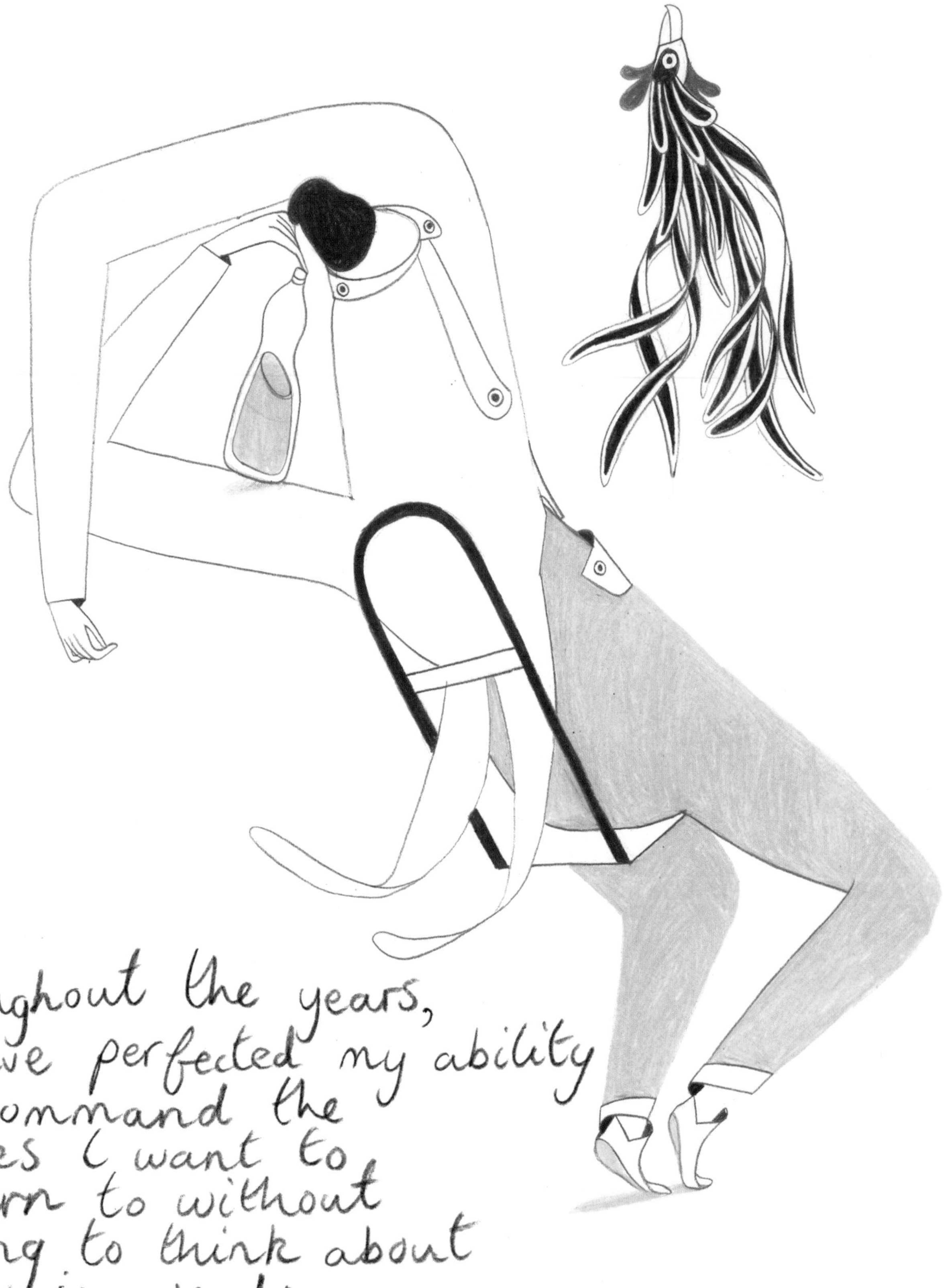

Throughout the years,
I have perfected my ability
to command the
places I want to
return to without
having to think about
them in words.

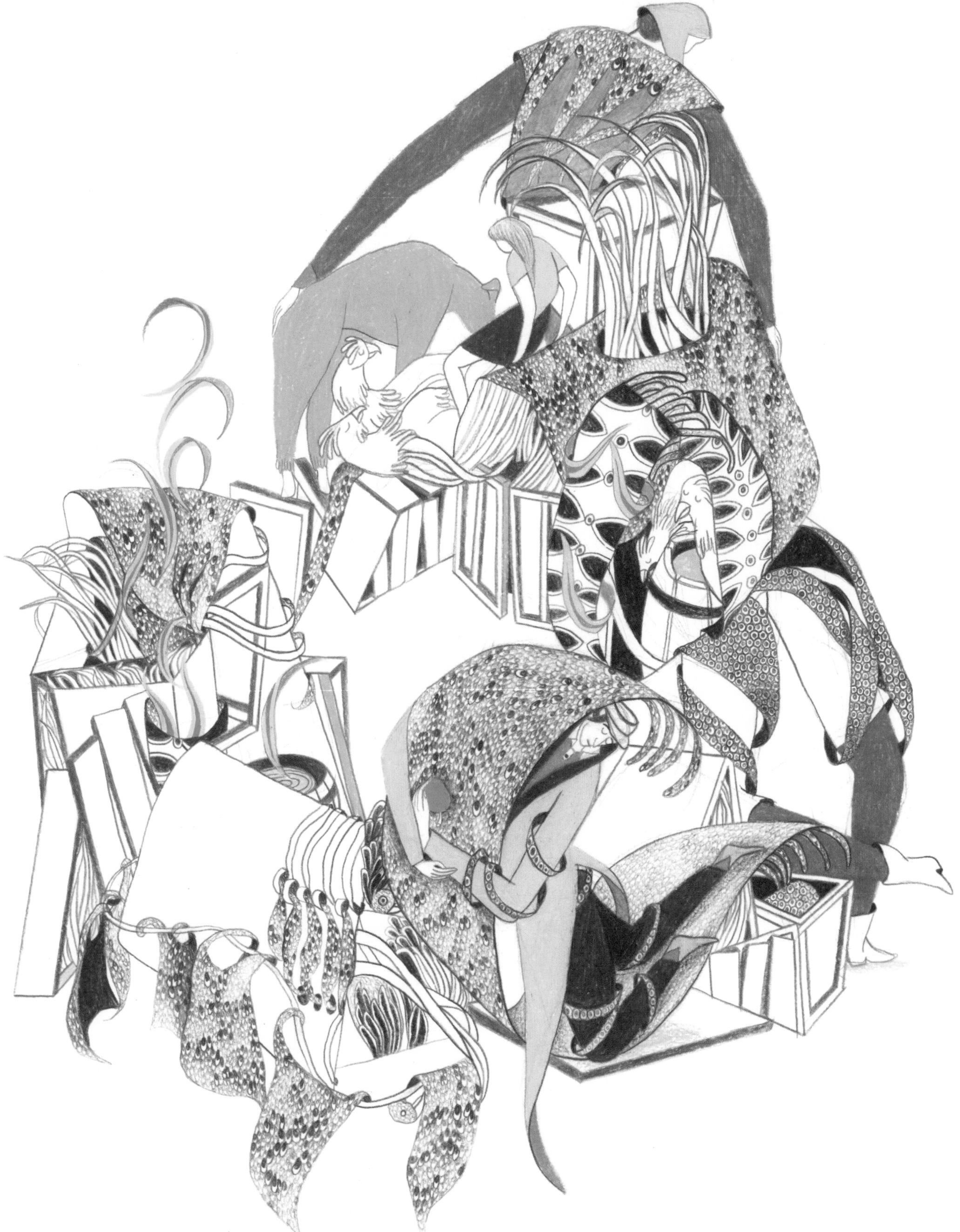

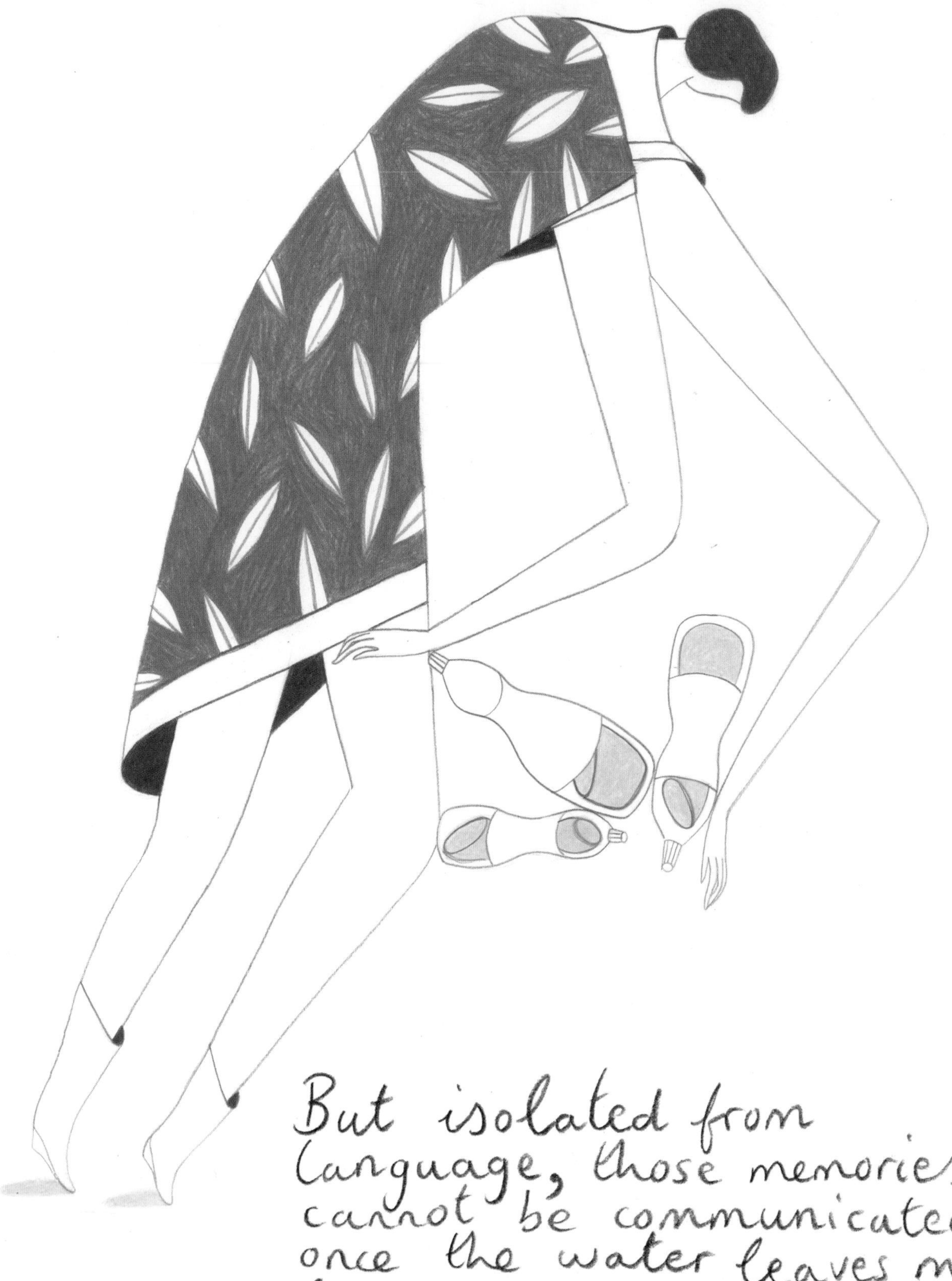

But isolated from language, those memories cannot be communicated once the water leaves my lips.

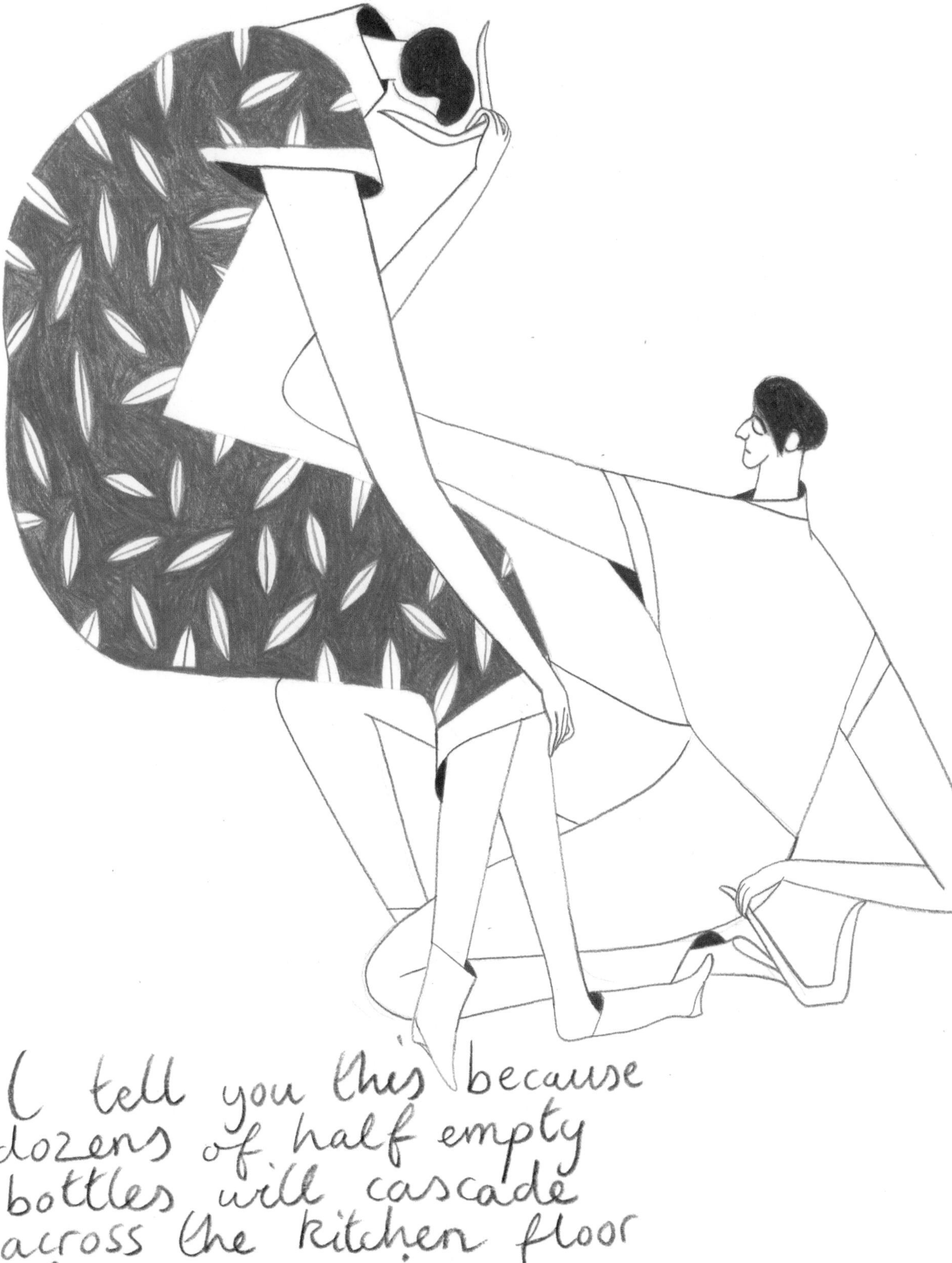

I tell you this because
dozens of half empty
bottles will cascade
across the kitchen floor
if you come in—

– and through my tears and panic, I will have to hastily blurt out an explanation to my disproportionate reaction. Once you hear those words, I won't be able to change the story they belong to.

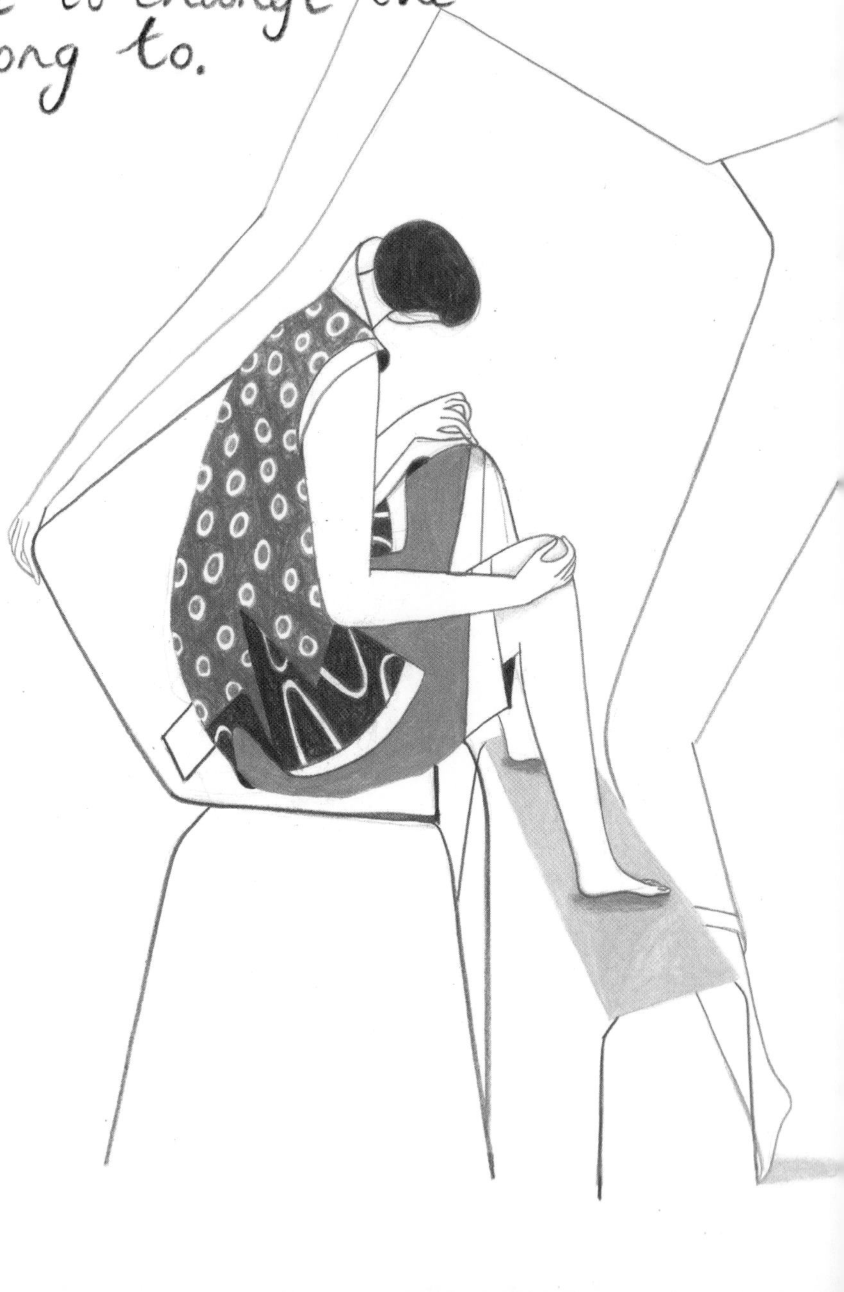

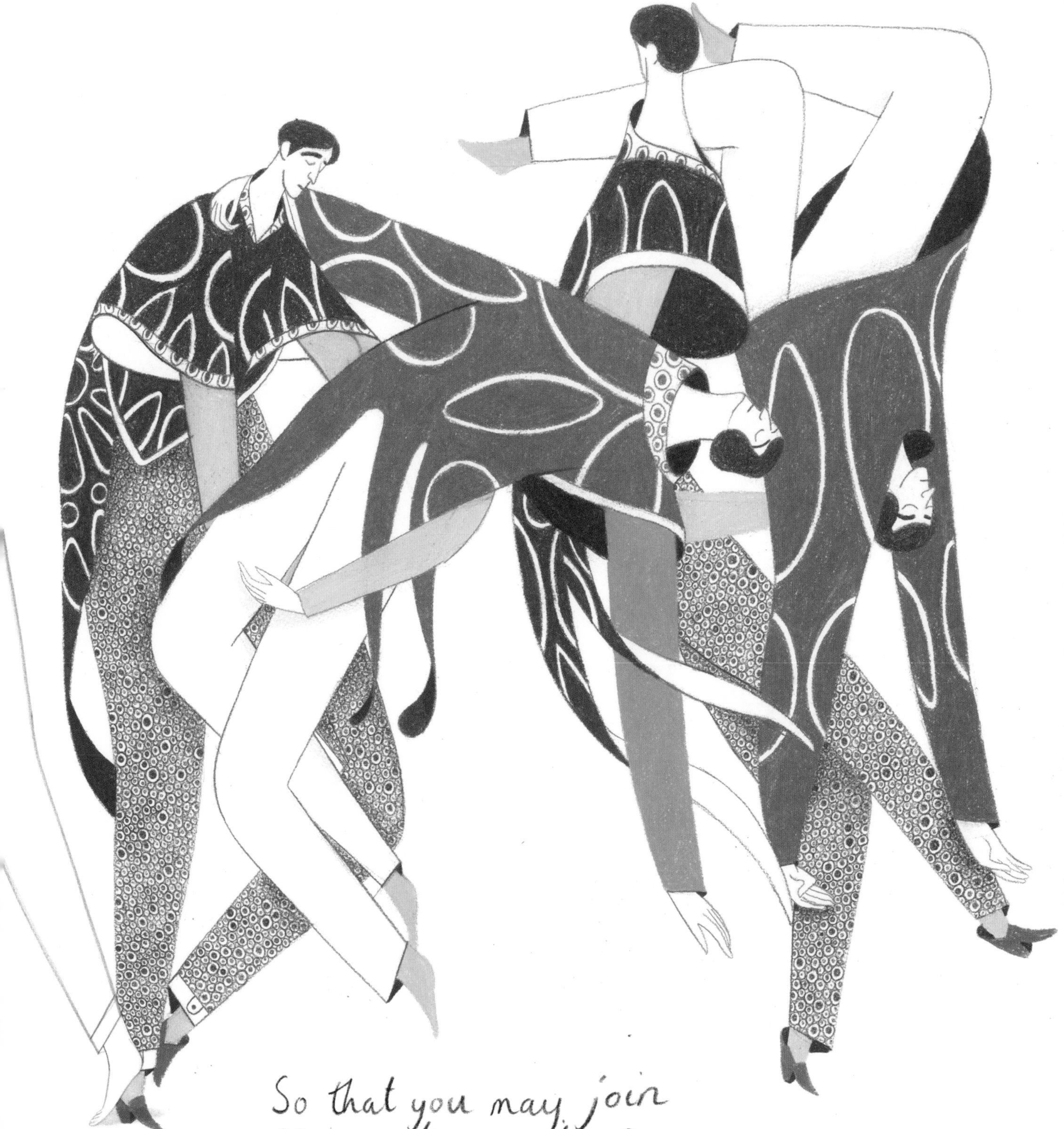

So that you may join
me on stage with a
story that fits you.

The words I
give my behavior
render me invisible -
once I begin to dance
I will be neither one
thing nor the other,
not a bird, nor beast

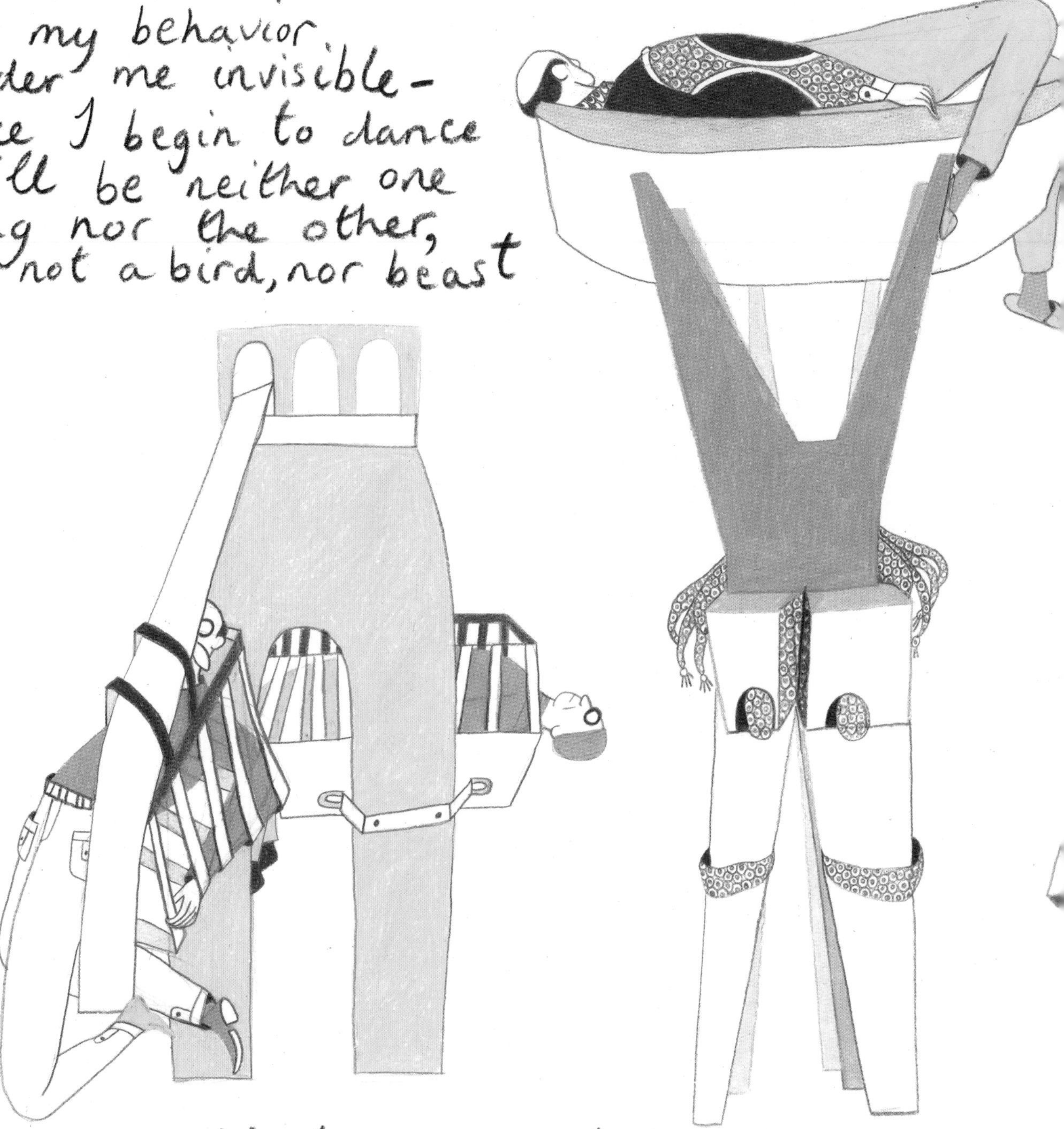

and entirely disconnected
from what I told you.

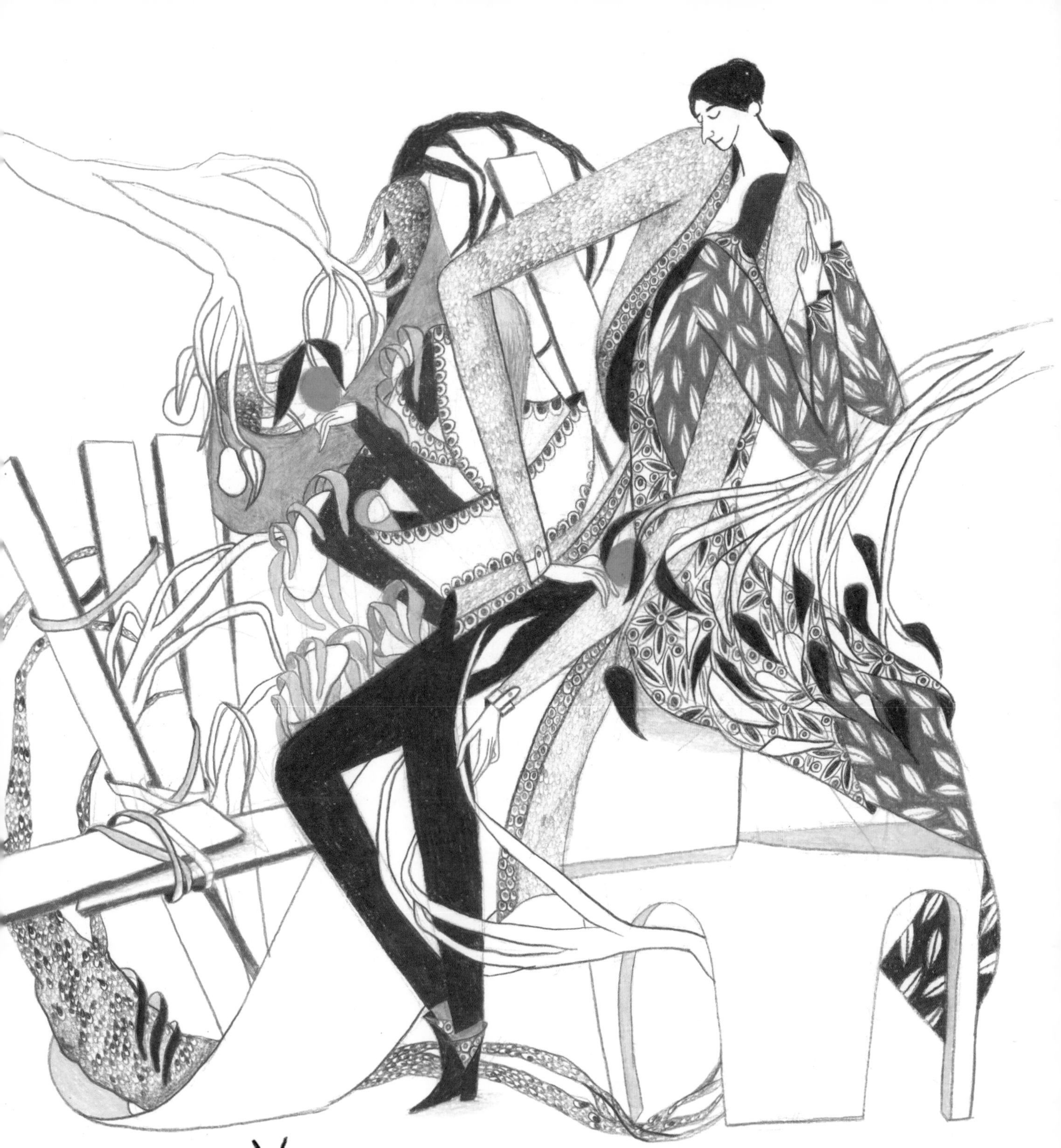

Yakov, are you watching?

EPILOGUE: IMPROVISATION

A DANCER ENTERS AN EMPTY STAGE. THEY BEGIN TO ARTICULATE THEIR LIMBS WITHOUT EXPRESSING ANYTHING BUT THE POSSIBILITIES OF MOVEMENT IN THEIR JOINTS.

LINES ARE DRAWN IN SPACE.

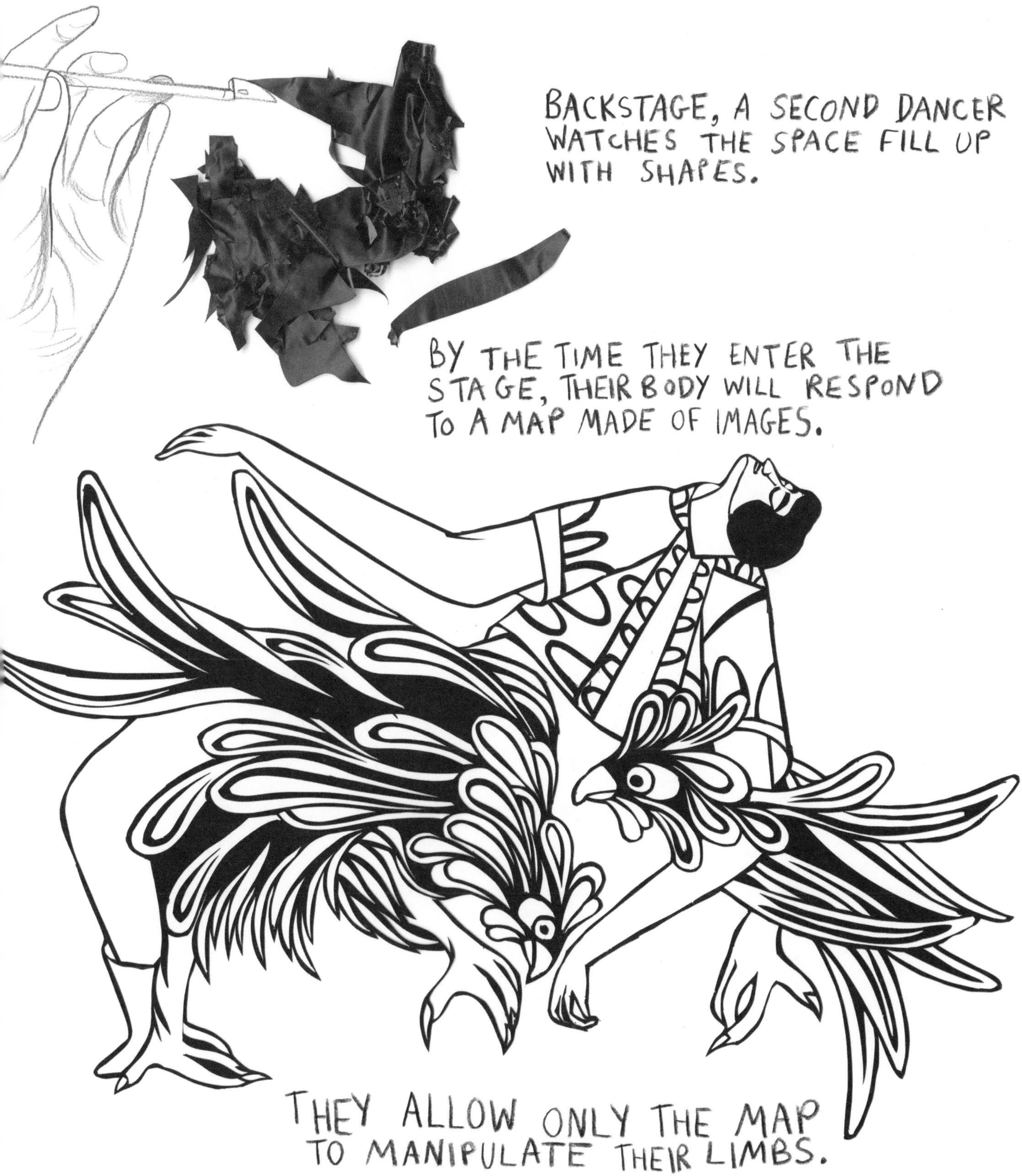
BACKSTAGE, A SECOND DANCER WATCHES THE SPACE FILL UP WITH SHAPES.
BY THE TIME THEY ENTER THE STAGE, THEIR BODY WILL RESPOND TO A MAP MADE OF IMAGES.
THEY ALLOW ONLY THE MAP TO MANIPULATE THEIR LIMBS.

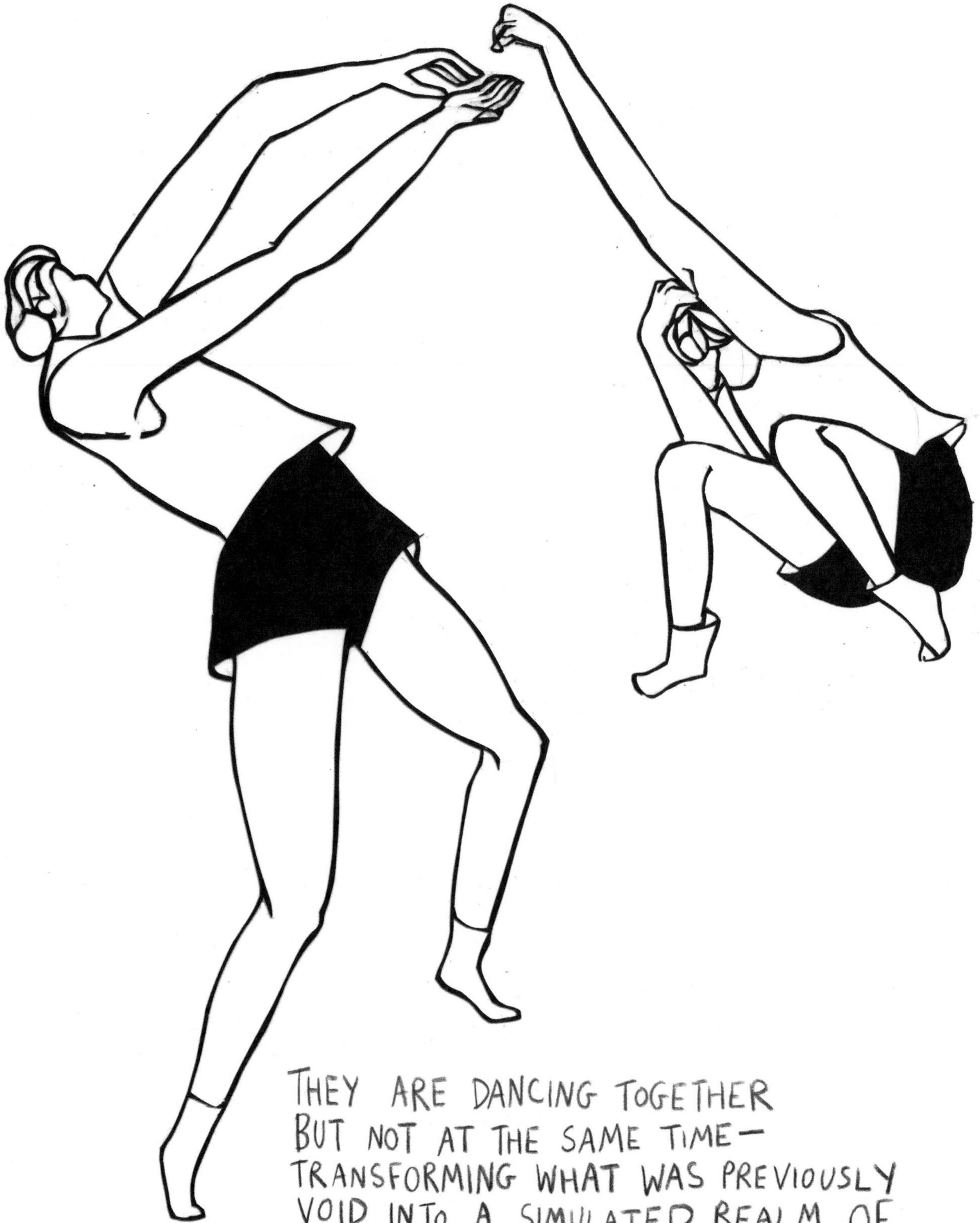

THEY ARE DANCING TOGETHER
BUT NOT AT THE SAME TIME—
TRANSFORMING WHAT WAS PREVIOUSLY
VOID INTO A SIMULATED REALM OF
NOSTALGIA AND LOSS.

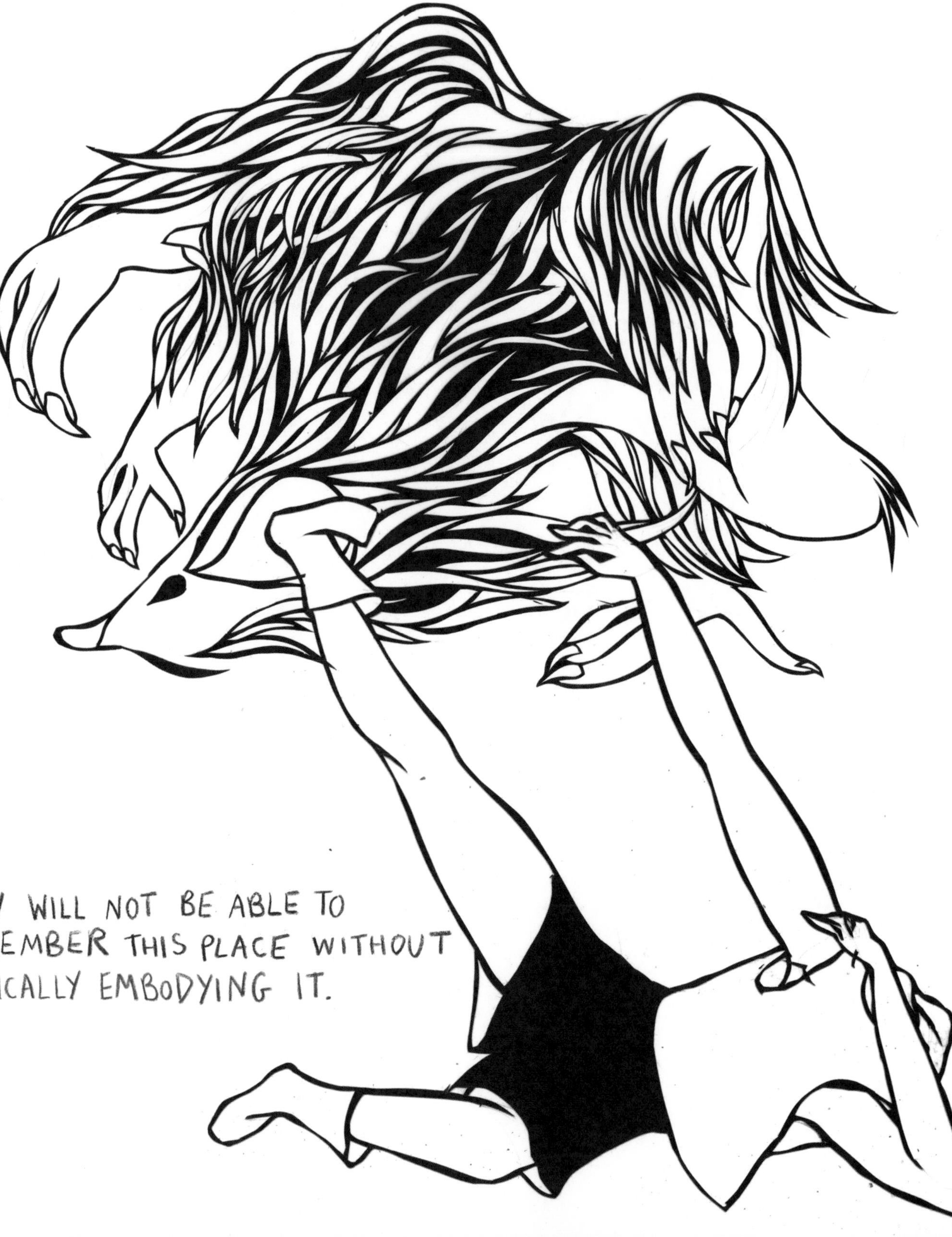
THEY WILL NOT BE ABLE TO REMEMBER THIS PLACE WITHOUT PHYSICALLY EMBODYING IT.

THESE TWO DANCERS
COULD EITHER BE
COMPLETE STRANGERS
TO ONE ANOTHER,

OR A
SINGLE PERSON
REVISITING
THEIR PAST.

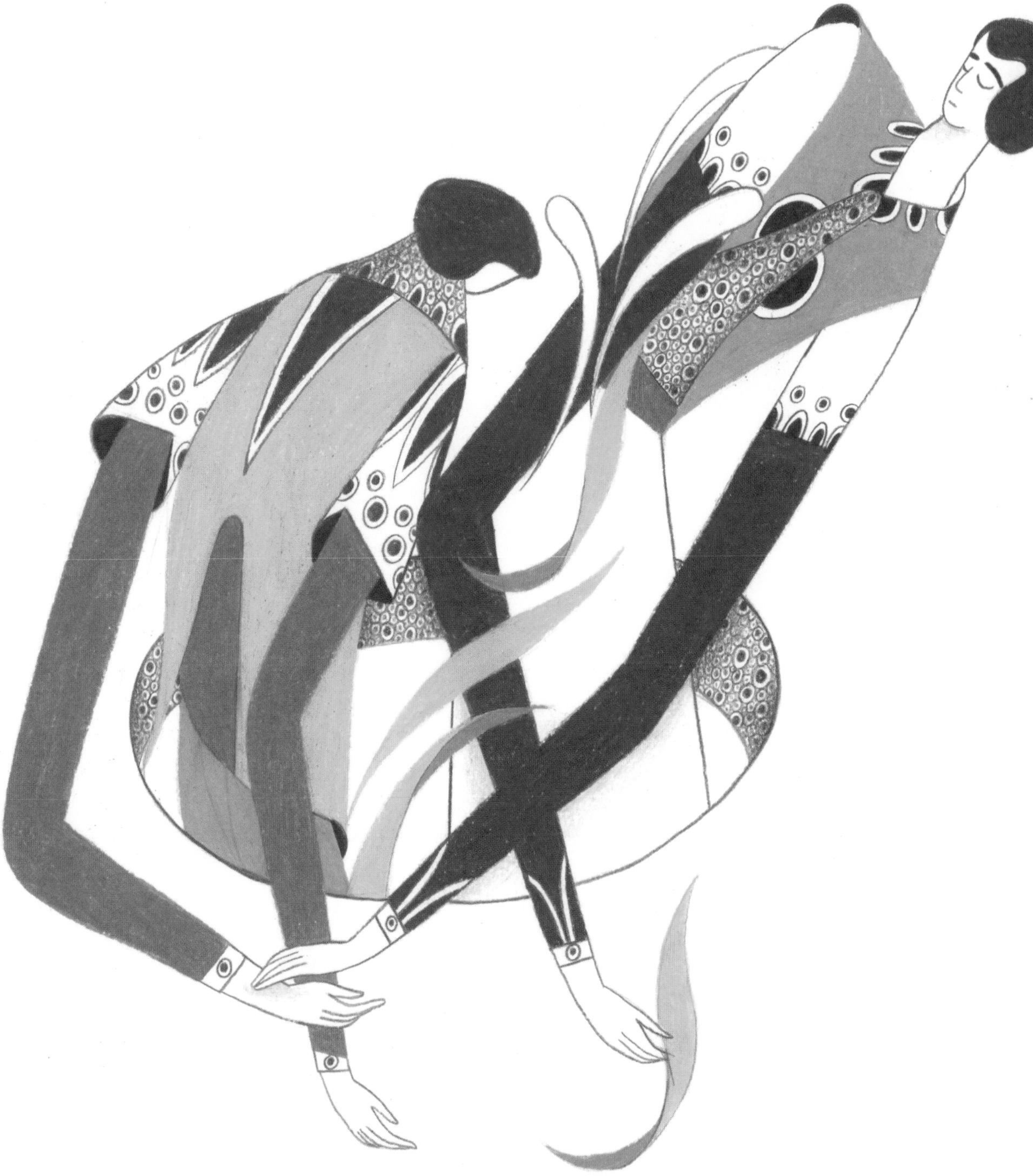

This book was created with
the generous support of:

- The Center for Cartoon Studies
- Cartoon Crossroads Columbus

For my father, for Eran.

For Ella- host of the show:
"Osim Kelim Im Ella Novak"- a live dishwashing webshow, and her cleaning brushes: Zelma Zambac and Wilhelmina.

and for my family and friends who have made my life a wonderful adventure.

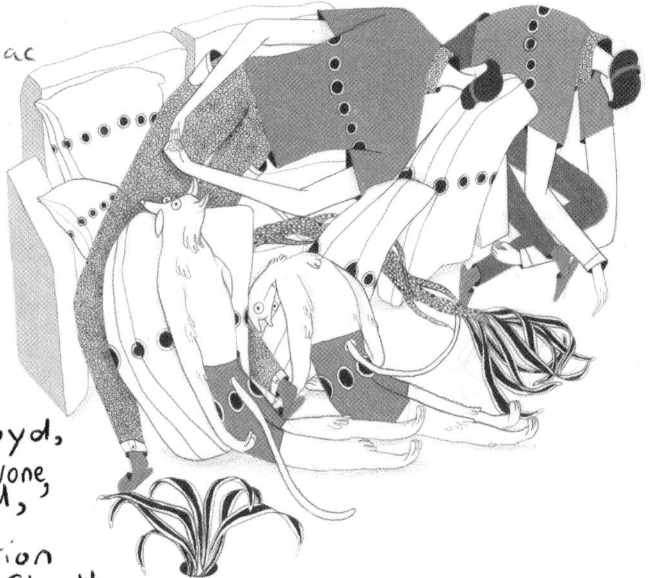

Thank you so so so much Leon, and Barry, and Secret Acres friends, Jeff Smith, Vijaya Iyer, Tom Spurgeon and Lucy Shelton Caswell from CXC.

Thank you to The Center for Cartoon Studies:
To James Sturm, Michelle Ollie, Dave Lloyd, Stephen Bissette, Jason Lutes, Bill Scavone, Jarad Greene, Jon Chad, Luke Howard, Kevin Czap and Sophie Yanow.
To my friends from White River Junction and fellow comics adventurers: Kat Ghastly, Issy, Bailey, Annie, Luna and Kat the Cat of Muff Mansion, TS Moss, Alex, Emily and Kat the Pyromancers from the magic school appreciation society, Kristen, Andres, Jess, Natalie and Dusty, Dan Nott and Daryl Seitchik, Emma, Coco Fox, Hachem and Sage of the Rene Opera House, Tim, leise, Al Nhi, Will, Rainer, Erienne, Ocean, Bread, Amy, Pat, JoJo, Mary, Cuyler, Andi, Jacob, Quinn, Curtis, Kurt, Gaurav, Eddie, Cat the Fairy Warrior, Benjamin, Jillian and Chico and Kori, Paige Kevin, Abby, Eliot the Crow and coin maker.

I'm so grateful to have been part of this community, I have learned so much from you all and owe this book to your inspiration, love and support.

Some drawings in this book have been published, performed or exhibited in variation in:

- Behind The Fence, by C.N Bialik (Hebrew) Yediot Books, edited by Navit Barel.
- Anomaly #27, Camera Obscura, edited by Nick Potter.
- Sipur Pashut Bookstore, TLV 290 Grams Simple Story, inspired by and homage to S.Y Agnon - a performance with Itai Ron Gilboa, TLV Illustration Week.
- Studio Point, 1:50,000, TLV Illustration Week.
- Dead Professors VS. Dead Grandparents - with Shahar Sarig.
- Chamber of Chambers, Pathos Mathos Company, directed by Lilach-Dekel-Avneri
- Hideout, Humdrum Comics Collective.
- Ex Libris, An anthology of magic schools, The Center for Cartoon Studi[es]

Thank you to the Socharim - Alon and Hadar, to Mira Rashty, Yuval Saar, Merav Salomon, Richard McGuire, Andrea Tsurumi, Alexander Rothman, Maëlle Doliveux and Liana Finck, and Ilan Manouach.
Thank you Shahar Sarig for Mintz and his universe of mythologies.
Thank you Alon Go for the mysteries of Mount Scopus.
Thank you David Ford of The Main Street Museum.
Thank you Hila, Omer, Ovadia, Dan, Hadar, Maya and Geffen - the Hideout, Humdrum crew.
Thank you Oren Fischer, Zev Engelmayer, The Red House.
Thank you Daniel Katz, Mom, grandparents.
Thank you Jonathan.
Thank you Tristan for drawing with me.
Thank you to Jay, John, Wendy and The Cover Store. Thank you Eliot for sharing your sculpture world, and treasure box.

THE FIGURINES ON BACK COVER ARE STUDIES OF SCULPTURES BY ELIOT CROW.

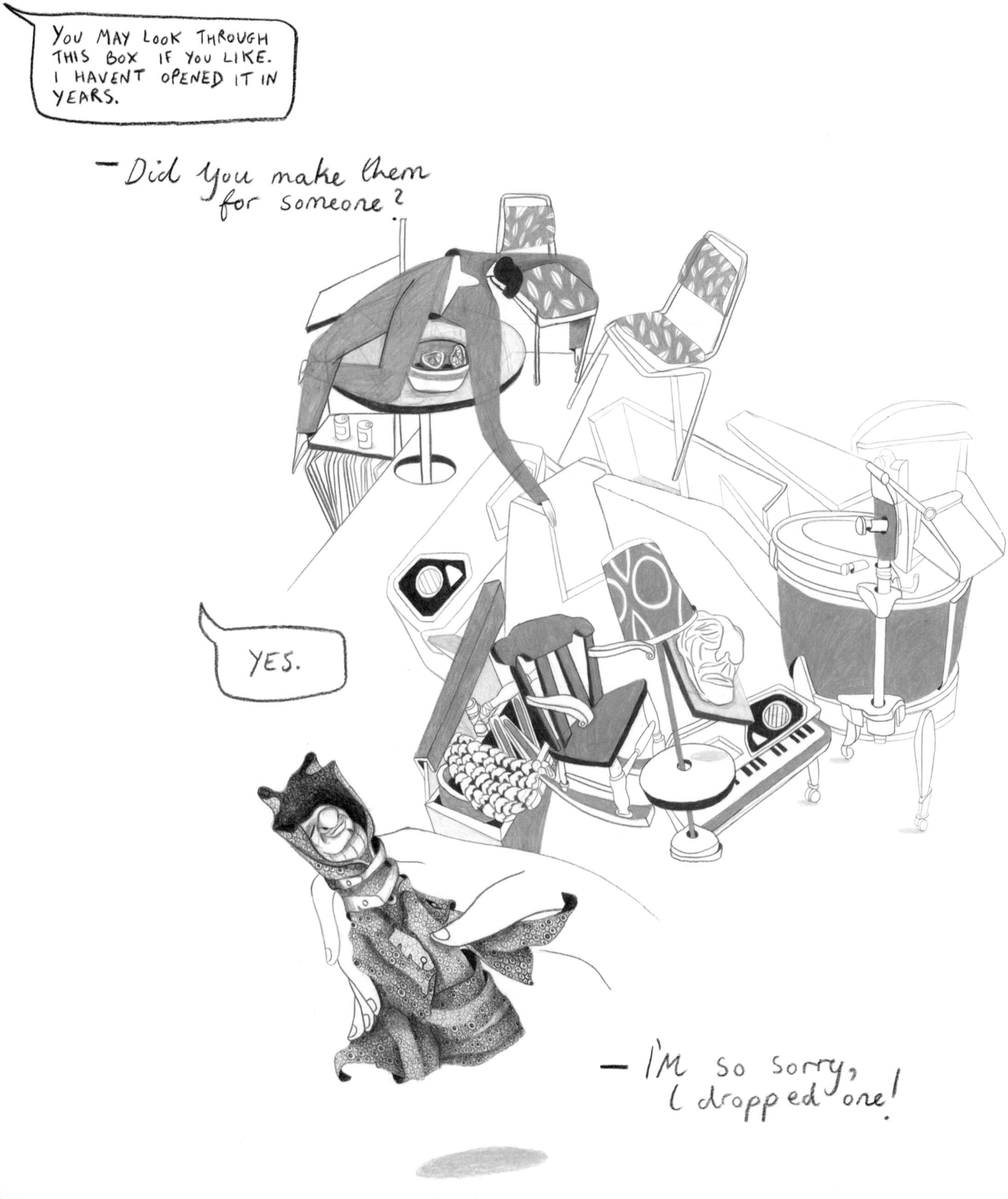
YOU MAY LOOK THROUGH THIS BOX IF YOU LIKE. I HAVENT OPENED IT IN YEARS.
— Did you make them for someone?
YES.
— I'M so sorry, I dropped one!

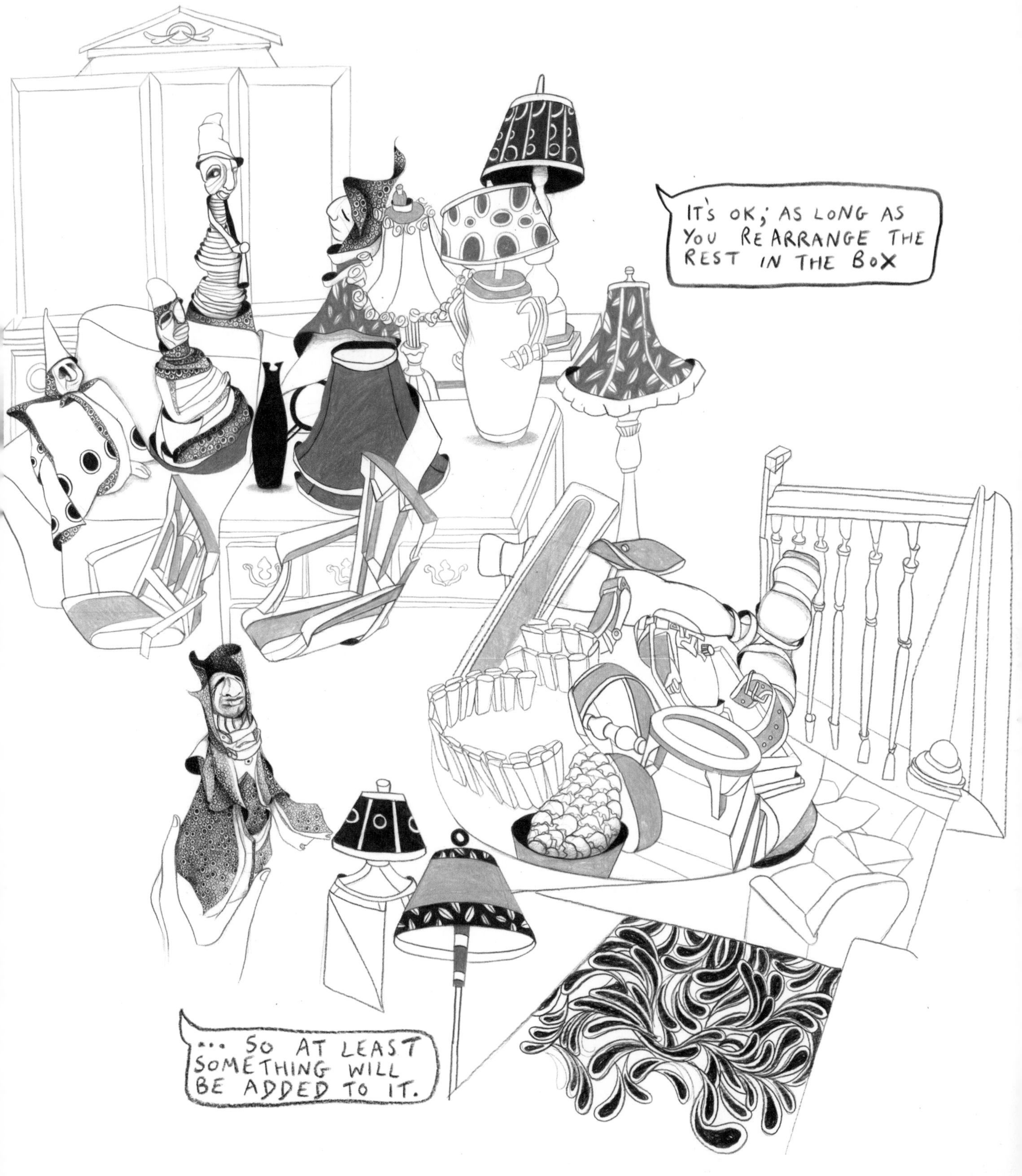
IT'S OK; AS LONG AS YOU REARRANGE THE REST IN THE BOX
... SO AT LEAST SOMETHING WILL BE ADDED TO IT.

KEREN KATZ IS AN ISRAELI-BORN CARTOONIST AND THE NON FICTITIOUS HALF OF THE KATZ SISTERS DUO. SHE IS A GRADUATE OF BEZALEL ACADEMY AND THE SCHOOL OF VISUAL ARTS MFA ILLUSTRATION PROGRAM. SHE IS THE AUTHOR OF "THE ACADEMIC HOUR" (SECRET ACRES), NOMINATED FOR THE SPX IGNATZ AWARD FOR OUTSTANDING ARTIST. HER WORK HAS BEEN PUBLISHED IN ANTHOLOGIES BY SMOKE SIGNAL, LOCUST MOON, RETROFIT COMICS, SEVEN STORIES PRESS, INK BRICK, ROUGH HOUSE, CHIFOUMI, LE MONDE DIPLOMATIQUE, THE BROOKLYN RAIL, AND FANTAGRAPHICS' NOW.

KATZ IS THE CURRENT CENTER FOR CARTOON STUDIES FELLOW AND THE RECIPIENT OF THE SVA ALUMNI SOCIETY 2013 MICRO-GRANT, THE SEQUENTIAL ARTISTS WORKSHOP'S 2014 MICRO GRANT, THE MUSEUM OF COMICS AND CARTOON ART'S 2015 SILVER MEDAL AND AWARD OF EXCELLENCE, THE 2018 SLATE BOOK REVIEW AND THE CENTER FOR CARTOON STUDIES SIXTH ANNUAL CARTOONIST STUDIO PRIZE FOR BEST PRINT COMIC (THE ACADEMIC HOUR) AND THE CARTOON CROSSROADS COLUMBUS EMERGING TALENT PRIZE.

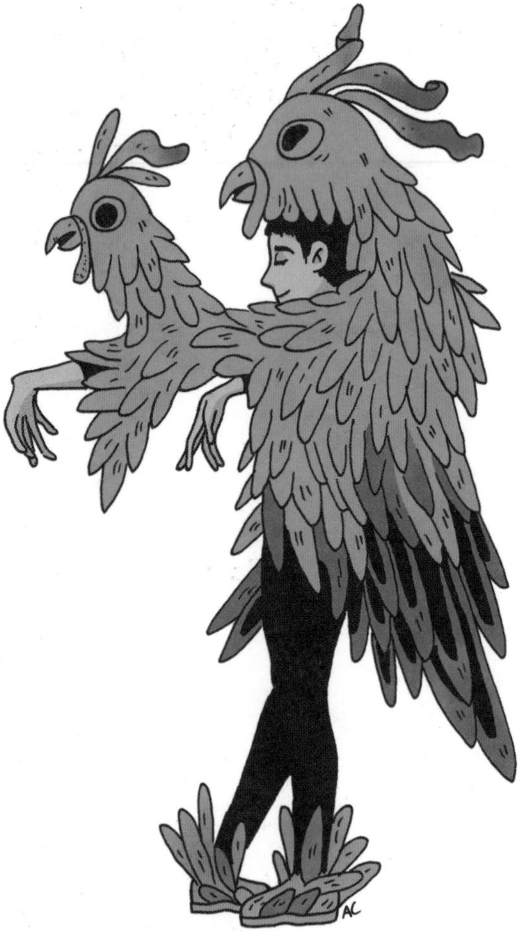
AC

PORTRAIT OF KATZ AS CHICKEN BY ANDRÉS CATTER (CCS 2020)

"WE LIVE IN THE DARKNESS,
DANCE IN THE LIGHT"
– KAT GHASTLY (CCS 2020)